KING NOIR

KING NOIR

The Crime Fiction of Stephen King

Tony Magistrale and
Michael J. Blouin

Featuring Stephen King and Charles Ardai

UNIVERSITY PRESS OF MISSISSIPPI / JACKSON

The University Press of Mississippi is the scholarly publishing agency of the Mississippi Institutions of Higher Learning: Alcorn State University, Delta State University, Jackson State University, Mississippi State University, Mississippi University for Women, Mississippi Valley State University, University of Mississippi, and University of Southern Mississippi.

www.upress.state.ms.us

The University Press of Mississippi is a member of the Association of University Presses.

Copyright © 2025 by University Press of Mississippi
All rights reserved
Manufactured in the United States of America

∞

Publisher: University Press of Mississippi, Jackson, USA
Authorised GPSR Safety Representative: Easy Access System Europe - Mustamäe tee 50, 10621 Tallinn, Estonia, gpsr.requests@easproject.com

Library of Congress Cataloging-in-Publication Data

Names: Magistrale, Tony, author. | Blouin, Michael J., author. | King, Stephen, 1947– contributor. | Ardai, Charles, interviewee.
Title: King noir : the crime fiction of Stephen King / Tony Magistrale, Michael J. Blouin, Stephen King, Charles Ardai.
Description: Jackson : University Press of Mississippi, 2025. | Includes bibliographical references and index.
Identifiers: LCCN 2024055929 (print) | LCCN 2024055930 (ebook) | ISBN 9781496852748 (hardcover) | ISBN 9781496852755 (trade paperback) | ISBN 9781496856425 (epub) | ISBN 9781496856432 (epub) | ISBN 9781496856449 (pdf) | ISBN 9781496856456 (pdf)
Subjects: LCSH: King, Stephen, 1947—Criticism and interpretation. | Detective and mystery stories, American—History and criticism. | Noir fiction, American—History and criticism.
Classification: LCC PS3561.I483 Z7585 2025 (print) | LCC PS3561.I483 (ebook) | DDC 813.54—dc23/eng/20250106
LC record available at https://lccn.loc.gov/2024055929
LC ebook record available at https://lccn.loc.gov/2024055930

British Library Cataloging-in-Publication Data available

Dedication

To the bonds that form between students and their teachers that manage to hold true forever.

CONTENTS

ACKNOWLEDGMENTS IX

INTRODUCTION: Stephen King and the Art of Detection 3

CHAPTER 1
"My Love of Crime Fiction and Its Influence on My Writing" 19
  STEPHEN KING

CHAPTER 2
Passion for the Pulps: A Dialogue with Charles Ardai 22

CHAPTER 3
Edgar Allan Poe, Stephen King, and the American Detective 29

CHAPTER 4
The Multiple Deaths of Richard Bachman 56

CHAPTER 5
The Open-and-Shut Cases of *Mr. Mercedes* and *Holly* 79

CHAPTER 6
Femme Noir: *Misery* and *Dolores Claiborne* 108

CHAPTER 7
The Incestuous *Later* 143

CHAPTER 8
Stephen King at the Brink: The Complicated Influence of
  Raymond Chandler 160

CHAPTER 9
Billy Summers and the Criminal's Redemption 191

CONCLUSIONS: A Need for the Unknown 213

NOTES 225

WORKS CITED 235

INDEX 243

ACKNOWLEDGMENTS

WE COMPOSED THIS BOOK WHILE LIVING MILES APART. THANKFULLY, WE were able to collaborate in Vermont on several occasions due to a Phillips Faculty Development Grant (from Milligan University), a fellowship through the Appalachian Colleges Association, and generous stipends from the University of Vermont English Department. We are forever grateful to these institutions for the opportunity that they provided for us to meet face-to-face and engage in fruitful dialogue. We are also indebted to our respective partners, Jennifer and Kate, and to the support of our children, Christopher and Daniel, Willow and Emerson. Faculty and students at both Milligan and the University of Vermont supplied us with constant feedback about all things King. Most notable in support of the writing of this book, either in reading drafts of chapters or engaged in relevant discussions, were Philip Baruth, Sarah Turner, Sarah Nilsen, Eva Hurt, and Hubert Zapf at the Universitat Augsburg, Germany. Lastly, we are grateful for the tremendous assistance of the University Press of Mississippi in the acceptance and preparation of this manuscript: Pete Halverson for his stunning cover art, freelancer Lynn Page Whittaker for her meticulous, detective-like copyediting, and Mary Heath for her support all through the process of turning this work into a book.

KING NOIR

INTRODUCTION

Stephen King and the Art of Detection

THE ABOVE PHOTOGRAPH FEATURES STEPHEN KING AT REST ON A SOFA INSIDE his winter residence in Florida. On the wall above him is a framed reproduction of Edward Hopper's 1932 painting *Room in New York*.[1] King wrote the story "The Music Room," first published in the November 2016 issue of Playboy magazine, based on this replica painting that he owns. Few people in the writer's enormous fan base realize that King has a keen appreciation for the visual arts; he's an ardent art collector, and art plays an important role in his life. He has admitted on several occasions that many of his stories and novels commence with a single visual image. In multiple email discussions with us, King acknowledged that he is a zealous fan of Edward Hopper's oeuvre. Thus, we begin this book on the connection between King and crime fiction with an unusual reference to Hopper as a painter whose aesthetic has long attracted King; indeed, the urban world of many of his paintings links directly to King's appreciation of crime fiction and the impact the genre has produced on his own art. It is no accident that Hopper's career as a mature painter (1910–67) overlapped the height of the hard-boiled detective genre and film noir (1930–50) as there is a distinct noir-esque quality present in his New York city paintings. At first glance, it may appear that King and Hopper share few correspondences—little appears to be happening in the painter's static urban landscapes, often devoid of characters, a deeply felt feeling of quiet despair featuring buildings with long shadows, as we are made to feel so completely in paintings such as *Early Sunday Morning* (1930) or his many portraits of Manhattan solitude.

King's reproduction of *Room in New York* features an alluring woman in red (a would-be *femme fatale*, perhaps), idly plunking at piano keys, and a man so engrossed in his modern malaise that he might as well be across the ocean. He has business to which he must attend, even if only to read the evening paper, and the glamorous allure of the woman in the room must be kept at bay. The places pictured in Hopper's paintings evoke a sadness that is more expressive than the people who appear infrequently in his work, residing in spaces that feel unoccupied as his men and women are self-absorbed, incommunicative, and lost to each other, buried beneath the weight of a late afternoon's melancholia. What appeals to King in Hopper's world are similar elements to those that have always attracted him to the novels of Raymond Chandler: a lonely atmosphere that becomes a character and tells a story all by itself, where words are unnecessary. In Hopper's best-known painting, *Nighthawks* (1942), a character who might be a hard-boiled private detective, a refugee from a Chandler novel, dons his fedora and waits patiently—his dingy office might be just down the street, in some shadowy corner of the metropolis. He looks poised, if slightly hunched; he remains equal parts weary and watchful. He smokes his requisite cigarette while an attractive woman with red hair and lipstick—a client or maybe his girlfriend, either way a nighthawk herself—sits next to him in silence or, at the most, engages in sparse dialogue. The clean, well-lighted interior of the restaurant contrasts starkly with the darkness that engulfs the world just beyond the seamless wedge of glass; it must be very late at night as even the blackened windows in the building behind the restaurant contribute to the overall noir-like loneliness of the cityscape. King's crime fiction similarly calls our attention to a chivalrous detective as he struggles to stay afloat within an oppressively bleak modernity. This is the Stephen King who grew up as part of a postwar generation awash in crime stories, who has logged more hours reading Ed McBain's novels than Nathaniel Hawthorne's, and who later taught, as one of only two texts in his creative writing course at the University of Maine, James M. Cain's seminal hard-boiled thriller *Double Indemnity*.[2] In sum, the writer's profound affection for Hopper exposes the noir shadings of his fictional universe and opens new ways for King's readers to explore the author's darkest musings.

Yet King's name is synonymous with the horror genre.[3] His readers tend to read his works with a set of crystallized expectations: they look for particular tropes, wait for certain emotional payoffs, and embrace familiar moral lessons. But what if we were to reconsider the author through the lens of the detective tale? King himself admits, in his contribution to our volume, that he has been deeply influenced by the art of detection, in terms of style as well as plot.[4] He laces his prose with jagged similes of the sort cut by Chandler; his characters resonate with the hardened dialogue penned by writers such as McBain. King grew up on a steady diet of hard-boiled fiction as well as film, and its influence on his ideas remains profound. When King talks about his own attitudes toward literature, he overwhelmingly references hard-boiled writers rather than horror writers. One could go so far as to speculate that King became a writer because of his love of pulpy crime fiction, which he continues to hold in high esteem. King scholars have not yet even begun to grasp the scope of that influence. However, once a reader is attuned to its omnipresence, the influence of detective fiction can be found throughout his canon. From *The Dead Zone* to *Mr. Mercedes*, from the crime fiction of his pseudonym Richard Bachman to his most recent novel, *Holly*, King returns obsessively to patterns established by American sleuths of every stripe, paying homage to them at the same time as he innovates on the formulas he has inherited. Indeed, of vital importance, King oriented his storied career around the nucleus of hard-boiled fiction: "I began to entertain," King writes, "the possibility that there might be a bridge whereby the pop fiction of writers like [Ross] Macdonald and Chandler might be joined to literary fiction. [. . .] I even dared hope that I might help build that bridge, then cross it" ("Five" 60; in quotations throughout this book, we put in brackets ellipses indicating text we have omitted to distinguish them from ellipses that appeared in the quoted material). To focus upon a version of Stephen King who is also writer of crime fiction requires us to open exciting new avenues for inquiry into one of America's most enduring storytellers.[5] King admits, "The poster on my side of my freshman dorm room was a large photo of Humphrey Bogart in one of his gangster roles, holding a pair of automatic pistols" ("Five" 32). Just what is it that makes crime fiction so appealing to a writer like King?

To place this question at the center of our inquiry allows us to shed new light on King's prevailing thematic concerns—such as how the writer pits his defiant idealism (and nostalgia) against the omnipresent evils of a corrupt society—as well as his unique style: King's typical sentence structure and diction draw heavily from the hard-boiled tradition. This approach also sheds new light on his well-developed epistemology, that is, his sustained inquiries into *how* we know what we know and the limitations of that knowledge. Finally, reading King in this manner reveals a great deal about the ways in which he positions his critics to be detectives in relationship to his texts, sleuthing through the pages of his prose, which set up multiple traps for overzealous investigators. At times, King closely resembles Henry James, whose short story "The Figure in the Carpet" depicts a critic-detective who spends an inordinate amount of time trying to expose an author's defining "secrets."[6] As such, King's detectives help us to explain the ongoing antagonism between King and literary scholars. To unpack King's extensive reliance on the hard-boiled detective is to provide new insights into the broader meaning of the King multiverse.

First, this book blazes novel trails by examining King's relatively underanalyzed tales of detection. Over the course of the twenty-first century, King has increasingly returned to his roots as a reader of hard-boiled pulps: see, for instance, his three contributions to the Hard Case Crime imprint (*Later, Joyland*, and *The Colorado Kid*), the *Mr. Mercedes* trilogy, and *The Outsider*. In these more recent works, King ruminates on post-9/11 America and the subsequent need for a private investigator, a cunning P.I. who exists at the perimeters of the law as well as public accountability—a moral agent to sniff out and thwart potential terrorists. More generally, King has recycled the American detective to explore how twenty-first-century citizens can (or cannot) make sense of the complex, globalizing, and seemingly chaotic world around them. These texts contain strong elements of nostalgia, but they also play with familiar patterns as King looks to breathe fresh life into well-worn formulas. Secondly, our study extends beyond the confines of King's latest publications and obvious debt to the detective genre, even as these fictions, often overlooked as related to crime fiction by his readership, suggest his long involvement in the genre. The chapters that follow include analyses of plotlines more typically categorized as horror. Once a reader starts to consider King's engagement with ratiocination, she realizes how much it permeates his entire canon. *Dolores Claiborne*, for example, invites its reader to grapple with the issue of murder by assembling clues and exploring complex moral issues. Gordie and his gang perform similar actions in King's *The Body* when they venture into the terrifying as well as titillating realm of the private detective. Elsewhere, in his meticulous search through the history of the Overlook Hotel, Jack Torrance of *The Shining* dons the cap of the would-be detective (although, as we demonstrate, his wife, Wendy, proves to be a better investigator than her power-inebriated spouse).[7] In short, King's major plotlines are intimately tied to questions that have preoccupied his more obvious fellow writers of the American detective story: Can we solve the mysteries of existence? If so, how? Is there a philosophical position that provides insight into how best to handle the meaninglessness of contemporary life? When should the Constant Reader—King's pet name for his imagined audience member—think through problems like a classic detective, and when should he shift gears and become a hard-boiled "man" of action (the gendered qualifier here opens additional routes for consideration)? What, exactly, are the detective's limits? To pursue a hard-boiled Stephen King is to unearth rich veins of interpretive possibility. King may have gained his fame thanks to his ability to employ classic Gothic tropes to contemporary contexts, but he has also proven himself willing, again and again, to hybridize genres—including fantasy, science fiction and dystopian issues, the American western, the prison narrative, the romance novel, and, most especially, crime fiction.

Of course, King has hardly been alone in the blurring of these particular genres over the last fifty years. Thomas Harris is a fine illustration of a King contemporary (and a writer King greatly admires) who is also compelled to merge horror and crime fiction. In Harris's *Red Dragon*, the reader joins Will Graham, the story's forensic FBI figure, in the role of the detective. The novel confronts the techno-bureaucracy of FBI discipline and order juxtaposed against the dark blossoming of the villain Dolarhyde's poisonous flowering. Elsewhere, Joyce Carol Oates blurs these same generic borders in "The Premonition" and "The White Cat"; or consider David Lynch's *Twin Peaks* or David Fincher's *Seven*; one could extend this list to include the booming true crime genre. For reasons intellectual as well as commercial, King cannot help but occasionally swim in the same muddy waters as his contemporaries. Not to mention as well King's own preferred reading material: he once admitted to the *New York Times* that the literary character he might appreciate most as a traveling companion would be Sherlock Holmes. While it is important to acknowledge that some of King's so-called generic innovations remain, in part, derivative of profitable work being done by others, it is also valuable to study how King has meaningfully refracted his brand of Gothicism through a distinctly noir prism.

To begin, let us attempt to define the slippery term "hard-boiled," a term that remains central to understanding the genre's attraction to King. Even though King's canon revels in generic hybridization, if we paint with too broad a brush we risk producing analyses that obscure distinctions among individual genres. King may be drawn to the hard-boiled genre because the genre consistently includes elements of his most recognizable genre: horror. King recalls Edmund Burke's conception of the sublime, insofar as both Burke and King appreciate the way in which it is possible to create amalgamations of pain and danger, control and chaos, violence and beauty. In his *Inquiry*, Burke realized that "terror is a passion that always produces delight"; this claim is at the heart of understanding the lures of both detective fiction and horror art. The detective writer appreciates that, comingled with events that are awful and mysterious, there is a real satisfaction that comes to the reader in solving the origins of that which produces terror. As we will discuss in depth in a later chapter, Edgar Allan Poe, one of the inventors of the ratiocination tale, likewise understood that Burkean sublimity was inseparable from the lure of exercising the power of reason to counterbalance horror in tales such as "The Murders in the Rue Morgue," "The Mystery of Marie Rogêt," "The Purloined Letter," "A Descent into the Maelstrom," and "M.S. Found in a Bottle." To attend to such admixtures moves us to understand part of the appeal of detection, for although Gothic strains of terror can be left to stand alone, detection without a Gothic element has little flavor.[8] There are multiple theories to explain the appeal of this admixture. There is the desire to right awful wrongs; there is the titillation that occurs when we are witness to criminal behavior; there is the confirmation that the detective story's gritty realism mirrors our own partial understanding of the world; there is the quiet satisfaction when order is restored; there is the counterintuitive urge to study humanity's darkest depravities in the hope that, by understanding such crimes, they will be less likely to happen to us. The admixture of horror and ratiocination has long been with us. Its ancestry includes the eighteenth- and nineteenth-century English crime broadsides describing the era's most violent atrocities (although such popular reading was indulged surreptitiously). And yet, despite its incredible appeal, the art of detection—like the art of horror—has routinely been viewed as literature's illegitimate child because it contains allegories of punishment and morality attendant to the grisly voyeurism of throats being sliced open. On the other hand, some of the world's greatest literature—Dostoevsky's *Crime and Punishment*, Hugo's *Les Misérables*, many of Poe's short stories—are essentially tales of crime fiction and detection.

Simply put, since its inception, the line between ratiocinative fiction and horror has never been sharply defined.[9] Film noir—a favorite of King's as he acknowledges in the first chapter written for this book—drew much of its inspiration from horror films. In fact, the term "noir" was originally derived from *roman noir*, a literary Gothic subset. Film noir borrowed its "*mise-en-scène* of repulsion and dread" from works of horror that came before it (Ewing 74).[10] As this book repeatedly demonstrates, King's corpus is replete with references, both subtle and overt, to the dense nexus of horror and crime fiction. Although some of the works discussed in this book do not feature a detective in the strict sense of the term, many of them borrow liberally from the bleak, fatalistic prose of *roman noir* writers like James M. Cain. Andrew Pepper's description of the *roman noir* should resonate with anyone familiar with King's corpus: these works dwell upon "the corrosive effects of money, the meaninglessness and absurdity of existence, anxieties about masculinity and the bureaucratization of public life, a fascination with the grotesque and a flirtation with, and rejection of, Freudian psychoanalysis" (60). King shares these concerns with writers in this tradition.

Because horror and crime fiction bleed into one another in significant ways, we must delineate the hard-boiled King from the horror King, if only to ensure that the subject at hand does not become a turbid composite—or, as James Naremore writes, to ensure that the term "hard-boiled" does not drift "like a fog across the whole of western culture, threatening to dissolve any trace of identity and difference" (31). For a text to be considered hard-boiled, it typically needs to include several stylistic and thematic elements: a chivalrous detective who seems out of place in a deteriorating modern world; witty banter that demonstrates the detective's rhetorical skills; a tension between the art of detection and the brutal violence required to "solve" the case; a grim fatalism at odds with the detective's futile struggle against fate.

John Cawelti's survey of the hard-boiled formula encourages us to recognize how King follows a pattern established by some of his favorite writers. In the hard-boiled universe, "we find empty modernity, corruption, and death. A gleaming and deceptive façade hides a world of exploitation and criminality" (141). In unexpected ways, the Overlook Hotel from *The Shining* nicely conveys King's hard-boiled worldview: it is a glitzy, materialistic setting—a throwback to the golden period of literature and film's private eyes—yet beneath the shiny surface, King's readers discover a world of abject criminality, embodied in the mafia hitman, Vito "the Chopper." Many of King's protagonists respond to an empty modernity by insisting upon an old-fashioned sense of righteousness: "The hard-boiled detective remains unfulfilled until he has taken a personal moral stance" (Cawelti 143).[11] For example, Bill Hodges in the *Mr. Mercedes* trilogy confirms his out-of-favor moral position against the nihilism of his nemesis, Brady Hartsfield. And most of the books published under King's pseudonym Richard Bachman feature world-weary protagonists who must stand up to a vacuous modernity by firming up their antiquated view of good versus evil. The hard-boiled hero that so captivated King in his younger years—"a man of honor in a false society," "a traditional man of virtue"—set the standard for his view of heroism (151–52). King's heroes are always out of step with a corrosive modernity; they do not care about "success" as it has been defined for them, they have been beaten down by an unfair world, and they cling to the less flashy values of their ancestors. Cawelti might as well have been writing about a typical King protagonist when he posits: "His commonness is a mask for uncommon qualities" (145). Many of King's heroes identify with a blue-collar aesthetic even as they read great works of literature, ruminate on deep philosophical thoughts, and possess extraordinary strength and courage. And many of these heroes ultimately must confront the villain in an all-out brawl, since the existential case at hand cannot be "solved" by intellectual posturing, however chivalrous such positioning may be. Cawelti notes, "The hard-boiled detective has learned through long experience that evil is endemic to the social order." King thus shares with his hard-boiled predecessors a "naturalistic view of society," which is to say, his fictional universe remains driven by a pseudo-Darwinian brutalism (Cawelti 149–50). The grizzled newspapermen of *The Colorado Kid* persist despite their acute awareness of cold, inhuman forces that defy easy explanation; likewise, King's local constables, from the novels over which Alan Pangborn presides to *Misery* to *Dolores Claiborne*, continue to hunt for clues despite their acknowledgment that an unyielding environment will always hold sway. To understand the trajectory of King's literary debts, we could do worse than to trace the lineage that connects literary naturalism to pulpy hard-boiled fiction (see chapter 9 on King's recent novel *Billy Summers*).

Most persistently, King's fiction has been influenced by pulpy hard-boiled fiction from mid-century America. Critics might periodize King's work by examining his postwar nostalgia for a more potent "masculinity." The writer's tough guys remain hyper-individualists, sharpened against the stone of the so-called organization man and the military-industrial apparatus that dulled American citizens into rote compliance.[12] The private eye provides for King a good deal of emotional satisfaction in part because this archetype allows him to imagine an alternative timeline for America in which the country never became so institutionalized. On a related note, to recognize King's inheritance of mid-century norms via hard-boiled books is to understand better his self-fashioned identity as a writer who rejects as well as longs for the approval of the intellectual establishment. Sean McCann discusses how hard-boiled writers strove to be "at once anti-elitist and noncommercial," resistant to both "sterile sophistication and commercial vulgarity" (22–23). Echoing the likes of James M. Cain, King oscillates between a populist critique of high society's artifice and an elitist critique of the commercialized rat race in which he and his characters must run. From politics to style, ideology to branding, Stephen King owes much to mid-century detective pulps.

Yet the influence of the hard-boiled tradition on King may not always yield benevolent fruit. Some of his stereotyped depictions of race and ethnicity harken back to a genre that habitually affirmed a toxic white masculinity.[13] The young Black man named Jerome in the *Mr. Mercedes* trilogy both confirms and resists the racialized dynamics of the hard-boiled tradition; although Jerome is destined for the Ivy League and he mocks racist caricatures, he also endows Hodges with a twenty-first-century vitality, and so it can be argued that hard-boiled masculinity continues, in King's works, to borrow "in disavowed ways from the iconography of [B]lack masculinity" (Breu 15). King's crime fiction features a heavy dose of Italian American caricatures as well, including Vito the Chopper in *The Shining*, Sal Magliore in *Roadwork*, Richie "The Hammer" Ginelli in *Thinner*, and Georgio "Georgie Pigs" Piglielli in *Billy Summers* (note this writer's compulsion to belittle these *Tipi duri* with quaint Mafioso sobriquets); these one-dimensional caricatures are invariably vindictive and violent. Along similar lines, King's problematic treatment of women—his presentations of a "disturbingly aggressive and ambiguous feminine sexuality" (155), especially early in his career—borrows from "dick-books," short for popular detective magazines,[14] written almost exclusively by men, in which women exist primarily as sexualized beings: kidnapped and ransomed wives and girlfriends, lurid prostitutes, duplicitous *femme fatales* wearing too much makeup and too few clothes. Isn't the dangerous and unstable Julie Lawry in *The Stand* a version of the *femme fatale*, highly sexually charged at the same time that she is lethal? Or the sexualized bully Chris Hargensen from *Carrie*? Many of King's female characters derive some of their ardor, as well as their corrupting presence, from the archetypes of the hard-boiled genre. As Cawelti argues, "The real hostility of the hard-boiled story is directed toward women" (158). Some of the less desirable aspects of King's prose stem, then, from sins of the hard-boiled tradition.

Still, Ray Browne insists that "American detective fiction" remains "dynamic and developing" (5). King's connection to his hard-boiled lineage is hardly a static one. In truth, the hard-boiled King blurs the line that ostensibly divides criminal from detective (e.g., *Dolores Claiborne, Billy Summers*). The ideal example of King's postmodern spin on the detective tale remains his 1993 novella *Umney's Last Case. Umney* is an homage to King's fascination with detective fiction. Not only does the story begin with a frontispiece from Raymond Chandler's novel *The Little Sister*; it also manages to capture in its pages the atmosphere and playful patter of noir. Here is a good sentence to illustrate how King duplicates the essential tone of the genre: "I was also scared, but that was a feeling you get good at hiding when carrying a heater in a clamshell holster is part of the way you make your living" (28). The edginess of this sentence illustrates that the voice of the detective, following the example of Chandler, represses his feelings, especially his fears, and implies that potential gun violence is omnipresent in the detective's occupation. Set in Los Angeles in the 1930s, the plot moves between two hard-boiled characters, Clyde Umney and Samuel Landry. Landry is the novelist who has invented Umney, a highly lucrative protagonist. The two dialogues throughout the second half of the story as Landry explains why he has decided to assume Umney's place in Landry's fictionalized Los Angeles. As is often the case in the detective tradition, what transpires is a power struggle between the writer and his tough guy *doppelgänger*-protagonist. While the narrative voice and setting certainly show Chandler's influence, the relationship between Umney and Landry also resembles King's own fictional voice from his earlier novel *The Dark Half* (1989), highlighting the conflict between hitman George Stark and his creator, novelist Thad Beaumont. In both *Umney* and *The Dark Half*, the invented literary character functions as a dark but apparently necessary alter ego for the artist, an avenue for venting his most violent and pessimistic inclinations. If, as we argue in chapter 4, Bachman must be read as King's dark twin, their relationship has intriguing parallels to the relationship between Umney and Stark as well as their respective writer-creators. The detective genre therefore bubbles up in surprising places throughout King's canon, frequently functioning as a surreal element connected to the mystery and importance of writing, especially the aesthetics of visceral violence. This dynamic and innovative impulse runs counter to the possible claim that King's detective fiction is merely derivative.

Both Landry and Beaumont have made a living indulging in the milieu of detective fiction through the presence of their respective characters, Umney and Stark. The "crime" in both these texts is found in the uncanny attempt to switch and steal one fictional identity at the expense of another's. In *The Dark Half*, Stark emerges as a secret sharer of Beaumont's most private inclinations. Although the two would appear to be as different as a tweedy professor and an urban street punk (the name "Stark" signals his propensity for raw brutality), Stark wants to take over Beaumont's affluent lifestyle, replete with wife and children, and make it his own. In *Umney*, the plot gets reversed: Landry is running away from his "real-life" version of Los Angeles and into the fictionalized 1930s street life the detective inhabits. Beaumont and Landry have profited financially from the subsequent paperback popularity. The invented hardscrabble environments their fictional characters inhabit fascinate and obsess their creators. They have been constructing Umney's and Stark's fictional worlds for years, taking their writerly imaginations into the uncanny valley, tantalizing them away from the banality of their real-life existences: "It was as if your little part of Sunset Boulevard were the Garden of Eden" (*Umney* 74). An author enchanted by the trappings of the hard-boiled tradition, King here appears to be engaging in a metacommentary upon his own obsessions with that genre.

Ratiocination slips into this mix as we watch Umney and Beaumont work to discover and exploit the liabilities of their respective nemeses. And in these two tales of intersecting multiverses—deeply reminiscent of *The Dark Tower*—the hero turns out to be the detective who assumes control over the narrative itself in order to survive. Like other writers in this vein, King employs an elaborate *mise-en-abyme* (a story within a story) to reflect on detectives who cannot get out of their own way, which is to say, detectives who stick to their own rigid methodology and unexpectedly find themselves chasing their own tails (tales). At its most inventive, King's *mise-en-abyme* exposes a claustrophobic, dead-end formula that swallows whole reader and writer alike.

Umney's Last Case also emphasizes the symbiotic bond that connects detective and criminal, echoing Dupin's relationship with Minister D— in the Poe tale and the relationship between Will Graham and Francis Dolarhyde in Harris's novel *Red Dragon*. This same intimacy mirrors the reflective nature of how a literary character is ultimately an extension of the writer's psyche. As Landry acknowledges to Umney: "I'll tell you one thing about my trade—writing stories in the first person is a funny, tricky business. It's as if everything the writer knows comes from his main character, like a series of letters or dispatches from some far-off battle zone" (74). This bond obviously fascinates King, since he keeps coming back to exploring such psychic correspondences that border, and cross over into, criminality in concrete and believable terms. In these stories, King serves as his own detective as he seeks to probe the degree to which a writer and his characters interface. In fact, a novel such as *The Dark Half* crosses over directly into the world of crime fiction, as Stark and Beaumont engage in physical violence against one another to resolve and recalibrate their inherent dualism. Through these fictional interfaces, King explores the thin line that separates any writer's latent criminal impulses from her desire to exert discipline and control. Far from straightforward or derivative, the hard-boiled King never ceases to employ the genre in unexpected ways.

As much as King at his most postmodern has riffed upon crime fiction, however, King's readers cannot ignore the ways that the author also gestures at his nineteenth-century American predecessors, including Poe as well as Mark Twain. We unpack the connection between Poe's and King's detectives in one of the following chapters; the bond between King's and Twain's detectives warrants a word or two here.[15] Although Twain periodically posed as a cynic, he advocated that his reader should approach his fiction in a state of child-like innocence (this approach to reading provides one reason why *Tom Sawyer* and *Huck Finn* are routinely categorized as young adult fiction). We recall the plain-speaking Finn or the clever Sawyer, boys who are shrewd only in the sense that they can see things directly without the artifice of the adult world. At a deep level, King's detectives more often take their cues from Twain than from the colder, alienating prose of Chandler. King has remarked that he learned to write by copying the style of writers in the noir tradition, but he, like Gordie in *The Body*, eventually had to discover his "own voice"—a voice, we argue, that vibrates at a Twainian frequency.

For example, *The Colorado Kid* closely follows in the footsteps of Twain's well-known short story "The Notorious Jumping Frog of Calaveras County." At one point, King's novel gestures at a "hop-toad" and goads the reader on: "Hop, toad, hop" (62). Although Twain's original story does not feature a detective *per se*, it nonetheless features a cynical audience, and it invites the reader to try, albeit unsuccessfully, to make sense of the tall tales being spun for her. Twain encouraged his readers to read like a detective, only to thwart their attempt. The "good-natured, garrulous old Simon Wheeler" lures his audience within the story—as well as Twain's reader—into making order out of his ridiculous plot, an "infernal reminiscence . . . long and tedious." *The Colorado Kid* likewise includes stories being told within a story, yet another *mise-en-abyme*. This convention again prods readers into thinking critically about the act of *reading like a detective*. Teague and Bowie, as echoes of Wheeler, may be spinning a far-fetched yarn in order to instruct their protégé in some hidden moral lesson. Like Twain's Wheeler, King's storytellers gleefully recount the subplot of a young aspiring detective being manipulated by two aging, cynical detectives. Readers might assume that this subplot reveals the actual intention of the chronicle of the Colorado Kid: to impart a lesson on the impressionable protagonist about the nature of narrative and, more broadly, the art of detection. Twain's "Notorious" underscores Wheeler's values of "simplicity" and "tranquility," while applauding his storyteller's "vein of impressive earnestness and sincerity." King's Teague mirrors Wheeler who is "a man drifting serenely along through such a queer yarn." Anticipating King, Twain divided the head from the heart, and he coded that divide geographically: the head resides in the imagined East; the heart beats in the imagined West. As a result, detectives receive their informal education in the American West, as they shed the inherited skepticism of the elitist East in favor of simplicity, plain-speaking, and a less cynical mode of reading.

Twain occasionally included true blood detectives in his satirical prose. His 1894 novel *Pudd'nhead Wilson* includes modern detective tactics such as fingerprinting, a tool in its infancy at the time of the novel's release; and, in 1896, Twain published a sequel to his iconic novel *Tom Sawyer*, entitled *Tom Sawyer, Detective*. Twain, like King, dallied at length with the tropes of the detective tale, playing with its conventions to ruminate on one of his favorite themes: a worldview based upon honesty at odds with a worldview driven by skeptical investigation. In Twain's 1902 novella *A Double-Barreled Detective Story*, the preeminent cosmopolitan Sherlock Holmes—"stately, imposing, impressive"—visits the American West, only to be defeated at his own game by Archy Stillman, who was endowed at birth with "the gift of the bloodhound" (548, 511). On the one hand, Twain ridiculed the assumed air of authority given to jaded readers like Holmes. Local folks, including the aptly named Ham Sandwich, grovel at the feet of the British sleuth because of his air of respectability; they believe that Holmes is an "Extraordinary Man," perhaps "the greatest man that ever lived" (544). Due in part to the fanfare that accompanies the arrival of Holmes, Twain's locals start to doubt the validity of their own amateur sleuth, Stillman: a man in possession of "a grand animal talent, no more, no less, and prime as far as it goes, but no intellect in it" (542). Twain's divide between sophisticated professional and rustic amateur matches the imagined split between the head and the heart, as Holmes sneers at Stillman's thoroughly unscientific methods. On the other hand, Twain lauded the methods of detection being practiced by the untrained Stillman, whose name emphasizes his tranquility (he is, very much, a Still Man). The busywork of Holmes cannot rival the effortless observation skills of the primitive Stillman: "I will put aside reasonings, guesses, the impressive hitchings of odds and ends of clues together, and the other showy theatricals of the detective trade, and tell you in a plain, straightforward way just how this dismal thing happened" (552). Stillman's instinctual art of detection—stripped of the pretense of intellect, of causal logic—calls to mind King's unorthodox detective Johnny Smith from *The Dead Zone* (see chapter 3). The always-available solution does not linger in a tragic manner, as in film noir; rather, it *comforts* readers. King gestures incessantly at hard-boiled writers like Chandler, but these gestures are at times rather superficial. King is indebted to Twain's intuitive detectives, with their uniquely uncynical outlooks.

In sum, to survey the crime fiction of King is to recognize some of the author's greatest weaknesses as well as greatest strengths. King's optimistic outlook tends to water down plotlines that would otherwise expose audiences to the grit and grime of a heavily commercialized, inherently corrupt, and morally corrosive society (which is why the Bachman books pose such interesting problems in the context of King's larger project). His tendency to shepherd his Constant Reader through a text with reassurances that the protagonist (and the author) always knows what is good, what is *right*, can sometimes clash with the generic demands of crime fiction, a broad genre that defies easy resolutions or puritanical policing. Even when King tarries around the lacunae at the center of anyone's knowledge—that is, the ultimate mystery of the universe—he habitually treats these lacunae as an oddly comforting phenomenon, unlike, say, the gaping abyss that so deeply troubles the fictional world of detective writers like Chandler. At the same time, several of King's noir-tinged stories do glimpse the dark underbelly of American society, especially the plotlines that he penned as Bachman. When he experiments with the blind spots of detectives, he responds in meaningful ways to the various systems that confine the American public, including the patriarchy or the realm of mass-market publishing. He effectively exposes the mysteries that define our relationships with one another and with ourselves. For better and for worse, then, King remains wedded to crime fiction.

The Crime Fiction of Stephen King reexamines the corpus through inclusion of the genres contained under the big umbrella of crime fiction: the hard-boiled pulps, predominantly, but also the classic detective story, the *roman noir*, the mystery tale, and film noir. When he reaches back to the traditional detective, King wants to comment upon his own conflicted relationship to his audience: "With the fair play method the story's battle of wits between detective and criminal became in effect *a battle of wits between reader and author*" (Irwin 172; emphasis added). Yet the "fair play method" of, say, Agatha Christie only appears sporadically in King's body of work; more often, King preferred the pulps, "jettisoning the logic-and-deduction element to allow greater depth of characterization" (183). Moving from King's debt to Poe's more rationally based protagonists to King's metacommentaries on the postmillennial American detective, we ask readers to consider King's oeuvre from a different angle and for several related reasons: to appreciate King's generic mutability beyond the conventional realm of horror; to appreciate the degree to which this writer melds the tropes of horror to those of crime fiction; to consider anew the phenomenal range of fiction that has influenced King, in terms of style as well as content; to obtain more penetrating insights into the variances of King's *Weltanschauung*; and to explore the crux of King's spirit of invention and imagination—namely, the relationship between how an inquisitive person comes to know her world and the inherent limits of that pursuit (in short, the art of detection).

In the chapters that follow, we shift from literary analyses that will surprise no one, such as our treatment of *Mr. Mercedes* and *Joyland* as stories of detection, to texts that King's Constant Readers may never have considered in conversation with the detective narrative, such as *Roadwork, The Dead Zone, The Shining, Dolores Claiborne,* and *Misery*. To bolster our argument, we solicited insights about the art of ratiocination from the publisher of King's three hard-boiled novels, Charles Ardai (Hard Case Crime Books), as well as from King himself. These commentaries, which open the book, shed new light upon the noir-infused King, and we remain eternally grateful to both writers for their willingness to share their keen observations on this underanalyzed subject. To understand why King's canon speaks so eloquently to American audiences living in a nation that has become both the global police and a society thoroughly policed, particularly in the wake of the Vietnam War and the attacks of 9/11, or to understand why King's books continue to resonate so powerfully during a period of extensive anxiety as well as heightened fatalism, we turn our gaze to the author lurking in the shadows: King noir.

Chapter 1

"MY LOVE OF CRIME FICTION AND ITS INFLUENCE ON MY WRITING"

STEPHEN KING

It feels as though we have been writing this book for many years. Perhaps because we have; we have both been reading King, teaching his fiction and film iterations, even writing books about his books without realizing we have also been following unconsciously adaptive versions of crime fiction—the plots, characters, dialogue, even the prose stylistics. As we began to flesh out these connections over time and texts, we thought it might be interesting to supplement our own interpretive gaze with King's take on crime fiction. While he has mentioned detective authors and novels frequently in interviews over the years, even acknowledging his debt to several of them, King has never explored the intertextual relationship in great detail. We supplied Steve with ten questions about the genre, and he sent us this wonderful self-analysis, for which we have provided an apt title; indeed, his commentary provides a background context for many of the assertions we make elsewhere in this book.
—Tony and Michael

January 25, 2023

Dear Tony and Michael,
I can't respond to your questions as written because I'm bad at critical analysis and worse at self-analysis, which always seems like navel-gazing to me. But anything I say here, you are welcome to use in your forthcoming book.

Like most precocious early readers who loved telling and being told stories, I read my way through Nancy Drew and the Hardy Boys. Nancy,

Joe, and Frank were my first detectives. Around the age of eleven, I discovered the 87th Precinct novels of Ed McBain. There's a scene in one of those books that was very important in my development. Carella and Kling are questioning an ill-tempered woman—or trying to. She's wearing a dirty slip. She grasps her breast, squeezes it, and says, "In your eye, cop!" Probably needless to say, but that made an end to Nancy, Joe, and Frank. This was more realistic, and it was exhilarating to me. It felt like a true thing.

Crime fiction (I prefer that name instead of detective fiction) forces the writer to tell a story with a beginning, a middle, and an end. I liked that. I moved on to John D. MacDonald, favoring the stand-alone novels over the Travis McGee ones, because I've never been very interested in detection. *Crime* was what interested me. Oh, I read and enjoyed the Agatha Christie novels, particularly *And Then There Were None* and *The Murder of Roger Ackroyd*, but knew I couldn't do that sort of thing, and decided I wouldn't want to—those books were like crossword puzzles, or jigsaw puzzles. Lots of people want to do those puzzles (me too!), but few have the ability or desire to create them.

I found Patricia Highsmith, particularly the Ripley novels, and understood something that has carried through almost all my fiction (*Joyland* is an exception; that one is more in the Christie mode): let the reader know everything, but let the characters always be a few steps behind. This is particularly true in the forthcoming Holly Gibney novel (*Holly*). She draws a logical conclusion about the man she thinks of as the Red Bank Predator, but she's wrong *and the reader knows it*. It creates a sense of unease. Hitchcock was right about the bomb under the table: if the audience doesn't know it's there, you get five seconds of terror when it goes off. If the audience does know, you get fifteen minutes of excruciating suspense.

I read my way through Ross Macdonald in college. Loved the style, didn't care for the convoluted plots, which usually ended up with Shakespearian stuff like fathers fucking daughters without knowing it. Macdonald led me to Chandler, the truest artist of the bunch. That man knew what he was doing. Hammett, not so much. I got to Elmore Leonard late, but I got there. His style was perfection, but it never overwhelmed the stories. I love the Michael Connolly books and the C. J. Box books. I particularly like the idea that they are all of a piece, with Bosch and Pickett aging and changing from book to book.

You mentioned *Umney's Last Case*. I got the idea for that story because of TV programs like *Mannix* and *Magnum, P.I.* I thought, "Don't these guys ever feel like they are caught in an existential nightmare? Doesn't it ever occur to them that they might be fictional characters? Because after all, how many adventures can one man reasonably have?" That story also gave me a chance to do some hard-boiled, Chandler-esque prose. Loved it.

I have never thought of myself as a horror writer, a supernatural writer, or a crime/suspense writer. I just like to tell stories. But I will admit to a real moment of doubt when I conceived the idea of *Mr. Mercedes*. It felt like a fork in the road. I thought people might not like the abrupt change from books like *Under the Dome* to a straight balls-to-the-wall crime novel, with no fantasy elements. I had real come-to-Jesus conversations with myself on several afternoon walks. What I finally decided was that I needed to stop trying to guess what readers wanted and do what *I* wanted. Because the details kept coming. That story just begged to be written. And really, if readers didn't like it, was my family going to starve? Not a bit.

So I wrote the book. Holly Gibney was supposed to be a walk-on, a sad and mother-ridden woman with a funny name. I never expected she'd be a continuing character. It was she who insisted that there was more to her than that, so I continued to follow her. I don't lead the characters; the characters lead me. That might not be right for everyone, but it's right for me.

The Colorado Kid was another case of the story rather than the author leading. I set up an impossible situation for myself, always thinking that the solution would come clear to me in the end, as it had in stories like *The Green Mile*. It never did, and I decided that was the point. Some mysteries can never be solved, and that inexplicability has its own strange beauty. The book ends with little boys reaching up to an unidentified object in the sky. That was the summation of what I wanted to say. See, we don't live in an Agatha Christie world; there are UFOs in every life. Those Marple and Poirot books endure because when you enter Christie's world, there is always a solution (those books also have an entrancing whiff of *nastiness* about them).

That's about all I can tell you, except that Bill Hodges and Holly Gibney are people trying to do the right thing despite their personal problems. Is it any help?

Steve

Chapter 2

PASSION FOR THE PULPS
A Dialogue with Charles Ardai

When we first reached out to Charles Ardai, the co-founder and editor of Hard Case Crime, which features Stephen King's trio The Colorado Kid, Joyland, *and* Later, *we didn't know what kind of response we would receive. We just knew that we wanted to know more about King's relationship with Ardai and his pulpy book series because these texts remain King's most overt gesture at American crime fiction to date. What we received, however, was a far richer and more insightful response than we ever could have dreamed. Ardai responded to each of our questions with genuine care while demonstrating an abiding love for the genre as well as a deep appreciation for King (as both an author and, more importantly, as a man). Ardai's insights into King's three "hard-boiled" texts deeply enrich our own analysis in later chapters. Enjoy.*

—Tony and Michael

1. How do you define "hard-boiled"? Do you feel the King books in your imprint fit that definition?

Different people propose different definitions, but the best I've found is that "hard-boiled" when used to describe a portion of the crime fiction genre refers to stories that are told in a tough, cynical, world-weary style, akin to the terse, masculine prose popularized in the middle of the last century by Hemingway and his acolytes on the "high" end of the literary spectrum and by authors of less polished prose in the pulp fiction magazines of the same period. The subject matter of a hard-boiled story is usually violent and often sexy, and the cynicism is reflected not only in word choice (use of slang and dialect, for instance, and a more realistic vernacular than one finds in more mannered "Golden Age" or "cozy" detective stories) but also in attitude and plot: public institutions are often corrupt in hard-boiled stories rather than upright; justice is an illusion rather than an end citizens can count on being achieved; the good sometimes suffer and the bad flourish; crime sometimes pays; and if justice ultimately is served, it's more often because of the extralegal acts of a rogue individual than the proper functioning of a well-ordered society. Some of these attributes I'm describing belong more to the subgenre known as "noir" than to "hard-boiled" fiction per se—but the two can overlap. And to the extent they don't overlap perfectly (and they don't), I find "noir" refers more to the cynicism and despair and the inhabiting of a cruel universe that grinds men down despite their best efforts (regardless of the prose style in which the story is told), while "hard-boiled" refers more to the tough prose used to tell a story, which story might sometimes be comedic or jingoistic or institution-affirming—not every hard-boiled story is noir, and not every noir story is hard-boiled.

The books Stephen King has written for Hard Case Crime are not traditionally hard-boiled in the sense of sounding like a pulp crime magazine of the 1940s—no talk of "gats" or "roscoes" when guns come out, and so on. But to the extent the term "hard-boiled" means the use of the vernacular (including slang and dialect) rather than more mannered, artificial styles of writing, King's books very much fit in this tradition (which goes back at least as far as Wordsworth and Coleridge writing in the preface to *Lyrical Ballads* that they wanted to write poetry in the language of "a man speaking to men"—the way real people talk, rather than some stiff and formal language no actual person ever used). The narrators of *The Colorado Kid* speak in the language of a Maine island, and in fact the difficulty an outsider feels in becoming accustomed to those unfamiliar speech patterns is an important part of the opening of the book. The young narrator of *Later* sounds like the child he is, and as he ages, his voice grows up with him—it's a really remarkable piece of writing. And the carny lingo in *Joyland* is a big part of what marks out insiders from outsiders in that world. Language as a tool of identification and community is a big part of what King is interested in, and that's as fundamental to the hard-boiled enterprise as any enumeration of triggers pulled or bodices ripped. And King's prose is hard-boiled in this sense too: it's down-to-earth, working-class, of the streets, of the people. It doesn't put on airs. As Raymond Chandler wrote in "The Simple Art of Murder," "Hammett gave murder back to the kind of people that commit it for reasons, not just to provide a corpse; and with the means at hand, not with hand-wrought dueling pistols, curare, and tropical fish. He put these people down on paper as they are, and he made them talk and think in the language they customarily used for these purposes." King, too, makes people talk and think in the language they customarily use. In this respect, he's as hard-boiled as Hammett.

2. What do you think of King as a detective writer? Who does he remind you of, and how is he unique within the genre?

King isn't generally a detective writer, though he is often a crime writer. The distinction is important. There are some detectives in King's books, but not many, and they are rarely the main characters. But Hard Case Crime doesn't focus primarily on detective fiction—we focus on crime fiction, of which detective fiction is one narrow subset. I guess if you define "detective" broadly to include not just professional investigators (cops and private eyes) but anyone who takes it on himself to investigate a crime (or, more broadly, a mystery), then the two old newspapermen in *The Colorado Kid* are detectives, and so are the college kids looking into the old murders in *Joyland*. But they're not literal detectives, and what's most compelling about those books isn't necessarily the literal mysteries they investigate but rather the lessons they learn about life while going through their investigations. In this respect, King reminds me of detective novelists like Chandler and Ross Macdonald, who did have plots in their books (sometimes very elaborate ones, to the point where the authors themselves lost track of some threads), but where the plots are not the reason you read the books: you read for the heartbreak, as a character you respect and like gets put through the wringer, encountering painful truths and reflecting on them. I don't really care "whodunnit" in a Philip Marlowe novel, but I care a great deal about Marlowe himself and about hearing the melancholy echoes of his voice and getting to inhabit his world. King does something similar: he brings you into an exquisitely rendered world that you feel you really can inhabit, whether that's the seaside island village of *The Colorado Kid* or the 1970s amusement park of *Joyland* or the New York City of *Later*, and as you explore those worlds in the company of a narrator whose fate you care deeply about, your heart breaks or soars. That's so much more satisfying to me than the mechanical working out of train timetables or which suspect was holding what weapon where, à la Agatha Christie or a game of *Clue*.

3. King has written three books for the Hard Case Crime imprint. How did this collaboration begin? How has it evolved? If you had the chance to change or add anything to this collaboration, what would it be?

Max Phillips and I founded Hard Case Crime twenty years ago, with the plan of bringing back into print the undeservedly forgotten work of authors from the paperback era—writers like Day Keene and David Dodge and Peter Rabe and Gil Brewer, who were popular once but whose names essentially no one remembered anymore—and also publishing new books in the same vein by current authors who were not yet well known. And we thought it might help persuade readers passing through a bookstore to pick up one of our books, by an author they didn't recognize, if there were a supportive quote on the cover from an author they did recognize. So, I reached out to Stephen King and asked if he would be willing to write a blurb of that sort—one sentence that we could quote on our books and that might help entice readers to give them a try. I chose Stephen King because I knew from things he had written that he shared our passion for these old crime novels of decades past. But I knew that reaching him wouldn't be easy and that he very well might never respond—you can imagine how many requests he must get every day from people hoping he might endorse one project or another.

A few months later, I heard from his agent, who said, "Steve does not want to write you a blurb . . . because he would like to write you a book instead." That book was *The Colorado Kid*, and his allowing us to publish it in Hard Case Crime was an act of incredible and unasked-for generosity. Hard Case Crime would not still be here twenty years later if not for that book and that act. It put our little labor-of-love line on the map and sold well enough to keep the lights on here while we published a hundred books by authors no one had ever heard of. When, eight years later, Steve reached out to us again to say he'd written another book we might like to take a look at (that was *Joyland*), it took an already incomprehensible act of generosity and multiplied it exponentially. And then eight years later he did it again, offering us the chance to publish *Later*. Stephen King is not just a deeply gifted novelist; he is a mensch: a deeply good human being, who wants to do what he can to help support the things he cares about. And I am profoundly grateful that our peculiar little publishing line is one of the things he cares about.

I wouldn't change a thing. Each of his contributions to our line has been a wonderful surprise, from the mere fact of its existence to the story told on its pages. It's a cliché to compare something to opening a package on Christmas morning, but that's what it's been like each time a manuscript from Stephen King has arrived. My face beams. Would I love the chance to work with him a fourth time? Of course. But as my people say: *dayenu*. If he had only written the one book for us: it would have been enough. Had he stopped at two: it would have been enough. At three? *Dayenu*: it would have been enough. I am not such a churl as to ask for more.

4. Do you have a personal favorite of King's three books for the imprint? Why?

As a longtime fan of carny novels, it would be hard for me not to pick *Joyland* as my favorite, and not only for that reason either. It's just such a perfect evocation of a time and place, such tender and painful meditations on aging and loss and sadness, and that ending—as I said when we published it, it would take a reader far more hard-boiled than me not to cry at the end of *Joyland*. All three of Steve's books for us are dear to me and I love them all, but *Joyland* is special.

5. King's contributions to the imprint have been relatively unorthodox, especially *Later* and *Colorado Kid*. How have readers responded to these unusual detective stories? Do you think King challenged readers to do something new—and, if so, to what end?

When we initially published *The Colorado Kid*, opinion was divided and heated—as Steve predicted in his afterword to the book, some people loved it and some really hated it. That was because it set up a mystery and then refused to provide a solution, which was a violation of the fundamental pact between a mystery writer and his reader. But it was an intentional one, since the story is all about the nature of unsolved mysteries and unanswerable questions, and I find that now that the book is *known* to end in this way, readers' response to it has become almost uniformly positive. Those who felt betrayed back in 2005 when it was brand new and they had no idea how it might end have come around to seeing how good a story it is now that they no longer expect it to be something it isn't.

Later doesn't contain any such provocative violation, but it does have a strong supernatural element, which is something you don't generally find in conventional mystery novels (or in most other Hard Case Crime novels, for that matter), and telling a strong, legitimate mystery story in such an unfamiliar universe, with new rules you have to learn (for instance, that ghosts cannot lie), isn't easy. But King pulls it off beautifully and in so doing challenges readers to think beyond the narrow boundaries they might have in their heads for what a mystery story can be allowed to contain.

Later also contains a revelation about the main character, unveiled at the very end, that some readers have found shocking and disturbing, and

I love it. That so many decades into his career, and working in a genre that too often treads only well-worn paths and delivers only familiar pleasures rather than genuine surprises, Stephen King is still able to deliver a shock that genuinely shocks is a testament to the man's skill—and his delicious audacity.

6. What do you think future readers will find most surprising/rewarding about this trio?

I think what's most beautiful about these three books is their focus in each case on an outsider being accepted into a community in which she or he genuinely belongs and finds fulfillment: the out-of-town journalism intern finding her place in Maine in *The Colorado Kid*; the heartbroken college kid finding a home among the carnies in *Joyland*; and the little boy in *Later* finding a way to feel at home and at peace in the strange world he rather unwillingly occupies, populated by phantoms only he can see. It's subtle, but the three books also each contain a time jump of astonishing emotional impact, a moment when we race ahead from the time of the main action to a time years later, a rueful moment in the future from which the narrator can look back on the passage of a life and offer the perspective of one nearing or confronting death. In the end, the subject of these books is mortality, and the loss it brings. As the light wanes toward the end, we treasure its earlier brightness all the more. Each of these books is a bright light that flickers for a moment and is gone. As are we all.

7. What was the purpose behind the distinctive cover designs for each of these novels? Did King have any input?

All Hard Case Crime books share a common cover design, which is intended to evoke the look of the old paperback crime novels of the 1940s and '50s. Hand-painted cover art, lush and fleshy, often suggestive or (as they would have said back in the day) "spicy," with no great connection between the zaftig and underdressed heroines featured in the art and the actual story featured between the covers. This is the pulp tradition we created our line to celebrate and revive, and it's the style we used for all three of Stephen King's books for us. I believe our cover art style is a big part of the reason he wanted to work with us in the first place, and though he did have input on what image we put on each cover, there was never any discussion of the cover style itself, since that was the foundational premise of working with us. If you write a book for Hard Case Crime, you get a Hard Case Crime cover. That's who we are and what we do.

8. How well do you feel King fits in with the other titles published under the Hard Case Crime imprint? What makes his inclusion on your publishing list unique?

He is of course by far the best-known author we have ever published (though our list does contain other well-known authors, ranging from Mickey Spillane and Gore Vidal to Michael Crichton and Ray Bradbury), and in that sense he stands out. His books are also unique in containing elements of fantasy and the supernatural, which most crime novels do not. But his books also fit in with our other books in the senses I described earlier: they tell gripping stories written in the language of "a man speaking to men," they draw you in and create a world you are eager to explore and inhabit, and they focus on mortality, cruelty, justice, despair. And of course, they all have mysteries at their core.

9. Do you have any interesting stories about the production/reception of these three books?

The three books Stephen King has written for us have all become bestsellers, as all his books do; they are also our only bestsellers. Which isn't to say that our other books haven't done well—some have—but it's a different level entirely. So, working with Stephen King has given us a taste of a different level or category of publishing. Normally, when we publish a book, even a truly exceptional one, one that deserves and winds up winning awards, it's a struggle to get anyone to pay attention to it. When we publish a book by Stephen King, we instantly have three television networks competing to be the one to run coverage of it on their highest-rated program, not to mention ten major newspapers and a hundred websites. Everyone wants to interview him, everyone wants to run a review—it's heady and gratifying and I'm thankful for it and take all the pleasure in the world from this frothy experience. But I do wish, dearly, that other authors of other excellent books could enjoy even just a small fraction of the attention Steve's books so deservingly receive. Still: I'm grateful we get to touch these ambrosial, Olympian heights at least once in a long while. It's like Willy Wonka's golden ticket, and I'm poor Charlie Bucket, holding on for dear life.

10. Was it difficult to market these novels, given King's popularity as a horror writer?

In a word: no. It was not difficult. That's like asking Christie's whether it was difficult to auction Leonardo da Vinci's *Salvator Mundi* in 2017, given Leonardo's popularity as the painter of the *Mona Lisa*. The only thing less difficult I have ever done is breathing.

Chapter 3

EDGAR ALLAN POE, STEPHEN KING, AND THE AMERICAN DETECTIVE

SEVERAL CRITICS INTERPRETING STEPHEN KING'S FICTION APPRECIATED early in his writing career the debt that King owed to Edgar Allan Poe. King acknowledged to Tony Magistrale in an interview in 2002 that "Poe influenced me plenty" (*Hollywood's* 11). In his survey of King's first decade of publishing, Joseph Reino traces echoes of "The Fall of the House of Usher" in the conclusion of the 1983 novel, *Christine* (91–92); elsewhere, Leonard Mustazza's essay "The Red Death's Sway: Setting and Character in Poe's 'The Masque of the Red Death' and King's *The Shining*" posits how the short story and novel shared structural parallels due to their mutual reliance on Gothic architecture, "the bizarre opulence to be found in Poe's setting," as well as the specific reliance on the importance of a clock as a central operating image in both texts (108). This intertextual connection is given greater elaboration and substance in *Poe, "The House of Usher," and the American Gothic*, where in their penultimate chapter Dennis Perry and Carl Sederholm explored the various ways in which *The Shining* and in particular its main character, Jack Torrance, are the literary descendants to Poe's arguably most famous Gothic tale: "King's descriptions of Jack's behavior point to a rationale similar to Poe's concerning a primitive desire to act contrary to one's best self" (156). "In *The Shining*," they note, "King's House of Usher is reimagined to symbolize the decaying sense of American culture in the late twentieth century" (160). And in *On Writing*, King recalls that between 1958 and 1966 his favorite movies were "the string of American-International films, most directed by Roger Corman, with titles cribbed from Edgar Allan Poe. [. . .] Of all the Poe pictures, the one that affected Chris [Chesley, King's closest adolescent friend] and me the most deeply was *The Pit and the Pendulum*. *Pit* took a bunch of standard gothic ingredients and turned them into something special" (47).

The connections between King's work and Poe's have thus been amply documented and have been discussed in more sources than those we cite here. However, what is interesting in both King's own recognized appreciation for Poe and in the scholarship that has brought the two writers together is the fact that their relationship is always analyzed in terms of a specific genre: most critics assume that it is exclusively Gothic-supernatural elements that King inherited from Poe's work. Most frequently referenced are the Poe chestnuts: "The Pit and the Pendulum," "The Masque of the Red Death," "The Fall of the House of Usher," and of course "The Raven." However, neither King himself nor any critic discussing King's fiction in this context has ever mentioned—much less deconstructed in detail—Poe's importance to, and influence on, King's detective fiction. By revisiting Poe's influence on King not simply through Poe's more obvious contributions to the American Gothic, but through the complexity of his ratiocination tales, we propose a paradigm shift in King scholarship. Like Poe, King remains obsessed with detectives, not just in his more recent crime fiction but throughout his career.

In the decade of the 1840s, in tales such as "The Murders in the Rue Morgue," "The Purloined Letter," and "The Mystery of Marie Rogêt," Poe gave the literary world its first literary detective in C. Auguste Dupin. John Gruesser opines that "scholars have lauded Poe for establishing key conventions of modern detection, including the presentation of clues, the use of ratiocination, the rivalry between an amateur sleuth and the police force, and the detective's explanation of the solution to the mystery" (660). Other Poe stories that do not include directly the famous sleuth and his narrator-associate indicate that Poe, like King a hundred and fifty years later, possessed a constant fascination throughout his writing career with solving mysteries and exploring criminal behavior. We would go so far as to argue that just as Poe's detective tales contained an element of horror (often in the grisly murder of a young female), his horror stories were equally as reliant on elements more typically linked to the detective genre. In narratives as diverse as "The Gold-Bug" and "A Descent into the Maelstrom," Poe's characters employ varying elements of ratiocination: enough observational skill and rational self-control to triumph over the terrors they face, be those terrors an Arctic whirlpool or a descending razor-edged scimitar. Consider, for example, the case of "The Fall of the House of Usher," a story regularly cited as epitomizing the use of Poe's predilection for and reliance on Gothic and horror tropes. It certainly exploits them effectively—from a decaying mansion set in a noxious environment to a brother-sister relationship riddled with a secret family legacy that keeps them trapped inside to its strongly theatrical, specifically melodramatic, terror. However, the story also manages to cross genres through the inclusion of an outside narrator who functions, albeit unknowingly, as a detective seeking answers to the many mysteries he uncovers in both the house and within its inhabitants. What went wrong with the relationship between these two siblings so that they fail to communicate with one another except on a spectral plane? Why is Madeline apparently unable or unwilling to speak? What is there about the history of the Usher family legacy that underscores their current status? What made Roderick so intellectually and emotionally disabled? Like the reader of the tale, the narrator must use the evidence he witnesses to gain sufficient insight that leads to a degree of understanding. He avoids the fate that dooms brother and sister because his observational skills warn him of impending danger, and he maintains enough level-headedness to abandon the Ushers before their Gothic mansion comes tumbling down. In other words, while the narrator is technically unable to influence the circumstances that unfold during his visit, he nevertheless understands them sufficiently to know when it is time to get out. His deductive logic preserves his life.

This is a plot pattern that occurs throughout Poe's fiction: surviving horror is predicated on employing the same set of rational skills embodied in the detective. In *The Reason for the Darkness of the Night: Edgar Allan Poe and the Forging of American Science*, historian John Tresch reminds us that Poe was a complicated thinker who used at least part of his prodigious brain and literary output to speak as a scientist engaged in rational theories and speculation. While working as an editor for *Burton's Gentleman's Magazine* (1839–40), Poe forged a persona as America's first scientific reporter, speculating on atmospheric pressure, anticipating Einstein in his belief that time and space are one, and establishing a theory that the universe started out from a handful of matter, exploded outward to form stars and planets, and would eventually collapse in on itself—Poe labelled the latter attraction and repulsion (Brown). For Poe, the schism between poetry and scientific discourse was artificially imposed, an imposition most dramatically explored in *Eureka*, his last and posthumously published work that brought together Poe's theories on the structure of the universe. Poe insisted that *Eureka* should be read as a "poem" that explored scientific theory and intuition, essentially welding together art and science while also providing a roadmap for understanding many of the landmarks in Poe's fiction. This generic hybridity, as we shall see, likewise informs much of King's writing, especially his detectives.

Eureka poses the existence of a universe lying on its side, constantly changing and evolving, expanding and contracting as it rotates in a galactical vortex. The use of the whirlpool as a spiraling metaphor for the universe and the intersection with a cosmic oneness emerges in several Poe stories, often employed in a similar manner to what we find in *Eureka*: as a vehicle for synthesizing the powers of the individual imagination and relating them to the context of a larger, comprehensive whole. In bringing together the separate genres with which he is typically associated, not only did Poe amplify the possibilities for exploring the individualized realms of horror, science fiction, comic grotesquerie, philosophy, parody, hoaxes, poetry, speculative science, and, most importantly for our purposes, detection—he also marked them ultimately not as oppositional, but complementary. That is, Poe typically blurred the perimeters defining each of these genre categories just as he did the expanding and contracting of an embracive universe, to the point where it becomes impossible to distill transformed amalgamations back to their original, elemental parts.

In his first detective story, "The Murders in the Rue Morgue," Poe focuses attention on the ratiocinative details of the murder and the chain of events that leads to the revelation of a broken window nail as the key element to solving the locked room mystery. Dupin begins his analysis not with an examination of the battered bodies of the victims, but with an exploration of the environment in and around the scene of the crime; it is as if the detective does not want to be distracted by the "'extraordinary murders'" (405) that occurred inside the L'Espanaye apartment itself, recognizing the potential danger that might "'impair his vision by holding the object too close'" (412). The detective's eventual realization that the crime occurred by access through one of the chamber windows is made possible because of his extensive observations of the building itself and eventually drawing his attention to the lightning rod and shutter near the roof and window: "Before going in we walked up the street, turned down an alley, and then, again turning, passed the rear of the building—Dupin, meanwhile, examining the whole neighborhood, as well as the house, with a minuteness of attention" (413). Similarly, Poe recognizes in *Eureka* that establishing "the extent and diversity of [a] scene" provides Dupin with a god-like perspective that differentiates him from the police: "Only by a rapid whirling on his heel could he hope to comprehend the panorama in the sublimity of its oneness" (1261). The gained knowledge of the murderer's entry and exit is counterpointed by the horrific details of the murders themselves—one body stuffed up the chimney with such force that it takes several men to free it, a second with its throat so severely slashed that the head falls off when the body is lifted—which bring the focus back to the story as a presentation of horror. The victims are both women whose helplessness is not respected, and whose victimization, as in many Gothic tales, makes their fate much more shocking: "'A ferocity brutal, a butchery without motive, a *grotesquerie* in horror absolutely alien from humanity'" (423). The horror details of "Rue Morgue" are thus balanced by Dupin whose distinctive faculties permit him to stay in absolute control of himself, to avoid being overwhelmed by the bloody carnage that has recently transpired to the two vulnerable women within the apartment and to retain a focus on how their violation actually occurred. Dupin solves the crime by moving backwards through time, starting with the bodies of the women and tracing events up to and including the escape of the "Ourang-Outang" from the hotel closet of a French sailor on leave from a Maltese vessel.

It is important, then, to remind ourselves that Gothicism cannot be easily delineated from patterns of ratiocination. The use of mystery, so frequently aligned with the detective genre, also pervades the Gothic genre as its fictions, originating in eighteenth-century novels such as Horace Walpole's *The Castle of Otranto* (1764) and Ann Radcliffe's *The Mysteries of Udolpho* (1794), are permeated with enigmas that its skeptical protagonists are always seeking to explain via rational explanations. Just as Poe sutured together elements of horror and detection not only in his detective tales, but also in those stories not typically categorized as tales of ratiocination, Stephen King has created multiple occasions where horror and detection form an uneven admixture. King's literary universe is no more exclusively contained within the horror genre than is Poe's. King has likewise overlapped and amalgamated genres in his explorations into science fiction (*The Mist*), the prison narrative (*Rita Hayworth and Shawshank Redemption* and *The Green Mile*), the American western (*The Dark Tower*), the political thriller (*The Dead Zone*), the romance tradition (*Misery*), the naturalist novel (the Bachman books), feminist fiction (*Dolores Claiborne* and *Gerald's Game*), various versions of the *bildungsroman* (*The Body, IT*), and the hard-boiled detective novel (*Mr. Mercedes* and the Bill Hodges trilogy). It is the impact of the detective genre that we wish to focus on here, as King scholars have largely ignored its impact not only in King's explicit explorations into the genre, but likewise in those novels where his characters often find themselves unwittingly propelled into roles that come to resemble those of the detective. Many King protagonists are forced to rely on the specialized skills of the detective—close analysis, investigative curiosity, rational self-control, and the synthesizing of disparate facts to attain a eureka-like unity—in order to solve whatever mysteries confront them, and just as often, to save their lives and the lives of others. This chapter focuses on three specific attributes of King's detectives: the balance of Gothicism and ratiocination (Wendy in *The Shining*), the emphasis on intuition over deduction (Johnny Smith in *The Dead Zone*), and the fraught relationship between author and critic that parallels the link between criminal and detective (Edgar Freemantle in *Duma Key*). Poe's tales serve as a vital prototype for this sort of work.

USHERING IN A NEW READING OF THE DETECTIVE

Points of Poe-King connection tend to be most often referenced in relation to *The Shining*, probably because the novel conjures Poe himself during Jack Torrance's perusal of the seemingly random scrapbook he discovers in the basement of the Overlook Hotel early in chapter 18. Jack Torrance is quick to dismiss Poe's intrusion: "What left field had that come out of? This shining, glowing Overlook on the invitation he held in his hands was the farthest cry from E.A. Poe imaginable" (156). But in the chapter's direct allusions to "The Masque of the Red Death" and Jack's subliminal allusion to "Poe, the Great American Hack," the reader is less apt to overlook the connection as well as its origins: is the Poe inclusion inspired by Jack because he is a writer and one-time teacher of American literature envisioning the masked ball that took place at the grand opening of the Overlook in 1945? Or is the reference courtesy of the hotel itself, a shameless metatextual implant imposed on Jack's writerly imagination and meant to highlight its arrogant similarities to Poe's tale? After all, Poe's Prospero exhibits an intrinsic selfishness that is epitomized in his willingness to sequester himself and his friends safely in his sealed castle, "the external world could take care of itself" (Poe, *Poetry and Tales* 485), while the plague ravaged the rest of his countrymen. In a similar act of callousness, the Overlook feted its decadent debut in a masquerade ball held in the immediate aftermath of World War II—indeed, at the very moment that Europe was starving and Hiroshima and Nagasaki were still smoldering ruins. Yet another way to draw a meaningful line between Poe and King's *The Shining*, however, is to dwell upon Jack's *failures* as a detective—although he hunts down numerous clues to the Overlook's sanguinary past, and he comes terribly close to "solving" the case, he ultimately becomes too engrossed in its shadowy business to serve as a chivalrous corrective. With a name that means "tool," Jack is a pale substitute for Poe's Dupin. However, an unexpected character does emerge in King's novel to don the mantle of Dupin: Wendy Torrance.

Wendy's initial introduction to the Overlook Hotel takes place literally at a scenic turnout somewhere high in the Rocky Mountains. Looking out over the vast expanse of a "whole valley floor spread out below them," Wendy and her family peer out across "at an even taller mountain reared into the sky, its jagged tip only a silhouette that was now nimbused by the sun." The pine trees and other mountain tops surrounding her "give way to a wide square of green lawn and standing in the middle of it, overlooking all this, the hotel. The Overlook." Wendy's first impression "was discovering truth in a cliché: her breath was taken away. For a moment she was unable to breathe at all; the view had knocked the wind from her" (64). The reader shares Wendy's perspective; his first view of the place comes exclusively through her eyes. However, while she is nearly bowled over by the aesthetics of the vista in front of her, she also intuits that such magisterial beauty has a flip side to it: "To look down there for too long would bring on nausea and eventually vomiting." The view of the hotel and its place in the mountains inspires awe at the same time as it creates a counter-intuitive response "beyond the rein of reason, and to look was to helplessly see one's self plunging down and down and down, sky and slopes changing places in slow cartwheels, the scream drifting from your mouth like a lazy balloon as your hair and your dress billowed out" (64). We must remember that it is also Wendy, and not Jack, who maintains—at least in the back of her mind—the foreboding awareness that "they were beautiful mountains but they were hard. She did not think they would forgive many mistakes" (63).

The Burkean split that characterizes her first view of the Overlook, actualizing the awe and terror blend that Edmund Burke describes in his observations on Vastness and Verticality, and its place at the edge of the world actually typifies Wendy's dualistic response through the rest of the novel in dealing with both Jack and the hotel that eventually imposes its will. She is, in other words, capable of maintaining a balanced, albeit multifaceted reaction to her husband and the Overlook. While she seeks to keep her marriage and family together, she also gains enough insight into the ghosts and Jack himself to realize that she and her son are being overpowered by the supernatural forces pitted against them. Like the narrator in Poe's "Usher," there comes a point where Wendy deduces that it is time for her to take her son and get out, that the Overlook, like the Usher mansion, means to do her harm. The hotel gradually, albeit steadily, sets up its own relationship with Jack and, on a wholly different level, with Danny as well. The ghouls that are permanent guests on the hotel registry enter into conversations with, and manifest physical form for, the Torrance males exclusively. Wendy is essentially shut out from all such ghostly interactions—at least, she remains isolated until she starts to piece together for herself the reality of the situation that is being secreted from her. This insight begins with the physical evidence of a hotel party that she finds in chapter 36, "The Elevator." While Jack continues to deceive Wendy about the presence of spirits at work in the hotel, referring to the spontaneous operation of the Overlook's elevator as "an electrical hiccup," "a short circuit," by this point in the novel Wendy is not so easily manipulated. She refuses to accept her husband's explanation of events, discovering the physical evidence of confetti, a party streamer, and "a black silk cat's-eye mask, dusted with sequins at the temples" when she checks the inside of the elevator for herself (302–3). It is the first moment in the book when Wendy is forced to confront the fact that her husband is a liar and, worse, that he is in league with the hotel against her. Moreover, it is the first time when she is forced to accept that her definition of reality no longer jibes with either her husband's or the hotel's.

In her analysis of maternal figures in the horror film, Sarah Arnold groups Wendy (Shelley Duvall) from the Stanley Kubrick film adaptation of King's novel with "The Good Mother" archetype of film heroines "devoted to her children, but her acquiescence to the Law of the Father and her acceptance of a subordinate, passive role in decision-making and action-taking place her and her children at increased risk" (46). Most critics of *The Shining*, be it King's novel or Kubrick's film, underscore the same core liabilities Arnold finds in Wendy's character. While we would not disagree with this overall assessment, it necessitates qualification, primarily because Wendy emerges as more than a figure of "maternal devotion and self-sacrifice aligned with utter passivity" (46). When she is forced into a position where information is deliberately withheld from her by both Jack and the operative forces at work in the hotel, it becomes her job to figure out the meaning behind the supernatural events that threaten the welfare of her family, to realize that the hotel ghosts are real and malevolent, and to comprehend the changes that are happening psychologically to both her son and husband. In the course of the narrative, Wendy finds herself in a position where she cannot afford to operate "beyond the rein of reason," but must, instead, maintain her wits to protect at least herself and her son from the supernatural collusion plotting against them: "*There are certain realities, as lunatic as this situation may seem. One of them is that you may be the only responsible person left in this grotesque pile*" (*Shining* 370; emphasis in the original). While Danny suffers from bouts of catatonic withdrawal and Jack eventually bonds with the supernatural agents of the hotel against his son and wife, Wendy is left as the only member of the Torrance family capable of understanding what is going on around her and performing rational acts that lead to survival. As her knowledge base deepens and her family becomes more dysfunctional, King challenges Wendy's self-assessment that "She was soft. When trouble came, she slept." The "overly weak and passive" Good Mother, as termed by Arnold (49), ought ultimately to capitulate to the patriarchal forces at work in the Overlook. Instead, as King reminds his reader in this same paragraph, "the trial was upon her, not fire but ice, and she would not be allowed to sleep through this" (369). Like a proactive detective, Wendy reacts to the situation that presents itself to her. She may not resort to Jack's potentially lethal level of overt violence, employing the butcher knife against Jack (also a bat in the Kubrick film and a Roque ball in the miniseries) when she has the opportunity, which certainly sustains the ongoing ordeal at the Overlook; but the point is that she does fight back against her husband, thwarting his will and incapacitating him to the point where she believes he is safely contained inside the kitchen pantry.[1] On this front, she anticipates the hard-boiled detective, who must turn to violence in the final confrontation with personified evil. By the time she escapes the Overlook, Wendy possesses a complete understanding of what is going on inside the hotel and, unlike Jack, she makes a deliberate decision to choose life over death.

The orthodox Gothic tale, a staple of Poe's day, describes a dissolving world in which horror comes close to triumph; in contrast, the classic detective tale takes charge of a world where rationality contains and manages the horror. The reader of a classic detective tale operates under the assurance that he or she is consciously reading a fiction *as a fiction*, one that will end, if not happily, then at least with the mystery solved, a situation acknowledged by reader and author alike. As Poe reminds audiences in "Rue Morgue," the analyst "glories" in "that moral activity which *disentangles*" (397; emphasis in the original). The more straightforward horror story, on the other hand, contains energies that are dangerous and disruptive, venturing into a landscape where evil is not always comprehensible, much less contained. This type of horror story unleashes Dionysian energies that threaten to overwhelm the world; meanwhile, the classic detective tale confronts these energies and seeks (not always successfully) to return the world to an Apollonian status quo. Unlike the classic detective story, Poe's horror narratives seldom end with a clear resolution. Readers are left wondering, for example, what happened to Lady Rowena's corpse in the reanimation of Lady Ligeia? How will the amalgamation of Ligeia-Rowena eventually respond to her husband? What produced the collapse of the Usher mansion into the tarn? How did the Red Death contagion manage to enter the sealed quarters of Prince Prospero's castle at the end of the tale? Compare these unanswerable speculations to the manner in which the murders in Rue Morgue are comprehensively explained and resolved.

Their generic differences notwithstanding, horror and detection habitually merge, and the reader is asked to recognize points of identification that pervade both genres: the bond that exists in detection between the detective and the criminal, as in "The Purloined Letter," and the repulsion and attraction that attend the reader's response to the monster's Otherness in the horror tale, as the reader is fascinated by and simultaneously rejects the monstrous behavior manifested by Jack in *The Shining*.

When we reread *The Shining* with an admixture of these two genres foremost in mind, novel interpretations start to emerge. In the first half of the book, Jack serves as a kind of detective. Detached and desexed, he pieces together rationally the history of the Overlook thanks to the infamous scrapbook of chapter 18. In the second half of the novel, though, Jack drops his analytical persona, plunges into party revelry, and transforms into a Gothic villain who stalks his tortured maiden, like some twentieth-century Manfred, through the macabre corridors of the grand estate. For Wendy, King reverses this trajectory. In the first half of the novel, Wendy is an innocent maiden torn from the pages of the Gothic, still positively affiliated with her husband and led rather passively like a lamb to the slaughter. *The Shining* is a reminder of the close affinity that exists between the Gothic horror tale and acts of ratiocination. One of the great examples of this connection is also Poe's tale "The Pit and the Pendulum," which fluctuates between the personal horror of entrapment and torture and the rational mind's effort to establish some semblance of control (e.g., despite being drugged, the clever employment of rats to help free the narrator from the wrath of the descending pendulum blade) over an unstable environment designed to push the protagonist steadily closer toward insanity's edge. A similar process occurs in *The Shining*, as Wendy, in reaction to her confrontation with terror and the unknown, chooses to embrace the role of detective. Increasingly desexed, which is to say, removed from the intense sexual attractions that drive so much of what happens in the Overlook (consider the *femme fatale* in the bathtub of Room 217), due to her repulsion at the sight of "deviant" sexual acts in shady corners of the Overlook, she sharpens her rational mind as she uncovers clues and pieces together the story of the haunted hotel, thus completing the task that Jack-as-detective never could because he is ultimately overwhelmed by the personal temptations promised by the Overlook. In contrast, like the conventional hard-boiled detective, Wendy steels herself against modern temptation by erecting psychic barriers that protect her against the surreal world her husband and the ghosts unleash.

In other words, when we reframe *The Shining* as a generic hybrid, shaped in the eddies of Poe's Janus-faced legacy, the entangled fates of Jack and Wendy take on an entirely new valence. In the first half of the novel, we find Jack awake from his drunken stupor and ready to don the role of detective, while Wendy moves as if walking through a suburban dream, only tangentially aware of the menace at the margins. By novel's end, Jack descends into the dreamscape of a Freudian *Alptraum*—merging with the destructive domestic Saturn-father, lost in the unconsciousness of his id via alcohol, violence, the repetition of his past, and self-indulgence—at which point Wendy comes fully awake, suddenly alert to the criminal potential that surrounds her and threatens to consume her and her son. The ghosts at the hotel recognize the awakening that takes place in Wendy as "'she appears to be somewhat stronger than we had imagined. Somewhat more resourceful . . . Perhaps we should have been dealing with her all along'" (386). In sum, Jack dies a monster's death while Wendy is reborn as an action-oriented detective. The father-husband perishes in the hotel boiler's conflagration or, in Kubrick's film, freezes solid in the convoluted maze of his own psyche. Just as Poe's protagonist in "The Pit and the Pendulum" buys time by refusing to succumb to the terrors that reside inside his prison cell, Wendy fights—literally and psychologically—against the madness that threatens to engulf her at the Overlook. Wendy, similarly, buys enough time and psychic space to enable the salvation of herself and her son and to reconstitute a new family in the absence of the lost father.

In an interesting juxtaposition, Dick Hallorann's arrival with a snowcat parallels General LaSalle's *deus ex machina* rescue of the besieged narrator in Poe's tale. Both Wendy and Poe's narrator inhabit elaborately contrived prisons that are designed not merely to kill, but primarily to induce madness in their respective prisoners; and the drive toward madness in both texts requires the rational resistance of a detective. Following Poe's lead, King blends the terms and conditions of detective fiction and the American Gothic to complicate our understanding of both. It is to this internal complexity that the remainder of the chapter attends.

PSYCHIC DETECTIVES

The core argument in Maurizio Ascari's *A Counter-History of Crime Fiction* is that the evolution of detective fiction in the nineteenth and twentieth centuries needs to be viewed in light of the hybridization and cross-fertilization of multiple literary categories and genres. For Ascari, crime fiction shares a cross-pollination with the Gothic ghost story, sensation fiction, and discourses in parody and multiple pseudo-sciences (xii). As a result, Ascari's reading of the crime genre challenges the early twentieth-century prescriptive view implying that rationality was the guiding light of the genre, arguing instead that the evolution of the detective relies increasingly on his ability to juxtapose rationality with explorations into supernaturalism and the occult. Accordingly, crime fiction includes the conventional reading of the detective as a paragon of rationality but likewise shaped by antirational motivations and influences. Thus, as we will witness in applying this construction to the goal of our current book, just as Poe's Dupin emerges as a complex blend of reason and speculative imagination, King's Sheriff Alan Pangborn sutures the existence of the supernatural to his rational faith in police science (see the conclusion).

Along similar lines, in his invention of the detective genre, Poe concurrently invents the anti-detective story—that is, he enfolds within his ratiocination tales an element that undermines the detective as a pure, unadulterated embodiment of reason.[2] Poe's ratiocination tales invite his reader to invest in the hyperrationality of detectives like Dupin only to reveal that reason is never quite sufficient to solving crimes and mysteries. Nearly two hundred years later, King too employs the figure of the detective not as a ceaseless celebration of rational thought but as a reminder that trying to be "too clever" may prove to be as destructive an impulse as failing to adjust to "what has occurred that has never occurred before" (Poe, "Murders" 414).

Undoubtedly, the two authors write in different cultural contexts, and we should not ignore these important distinctions: Poe's detectives respond in part to what they perceive to be the inflated idealism of the Transcendentalists, while his singular sleuths also push back against excessive confidence in Jacksonian reforms; King's detectives, on the other hand, remain a byproduct of King's neoliberal moment insofar as they reflect the plotting of agents ensnared within the social fabric of a complex military-industrial apparatus. Said another way, King's detectives respond to short-sighted prefects by learning to mimic the random, unplanned, and spontaneous mindset concurrently being preached in the high temples of Wall Street.[3] Yet Poe and King share a common thesis: reason reveals itself to be as much a fantasy as unreason. In turn, their chastened detectives must confront the Gothic lineage that defines their pursuit.

Poe's critics comment extensively upon the uniquely irrational roots of his ratiocination stories. These stories, J. Gerald Kennedy argues, "return continually to the process of reason—the way in which the mind orders and interprets its perceptions" (185). Kennedy was one of the first critics to demonstrate that Poe complicates the delusion of abstract reason rather than singularly singing its praises. Kennedy insists that Poe mocks "the inclination to play detective" and ultimately expresses dissatisfaction with the overly mechanical genre that he formulates (191). Importantly, Kennedy establishes his case by repositioning Poe's ratiocination tales within the larger trajectory of Poe's career, by placing his prototypical detective story "The Man of the Crowd" (1840) at the intersection of Poe's Gothic output from the 1830s and his subsequently more explicit examples of ratiocination, published between 1841 and 1844. Kennedy's attention to chronology suggests that the detective genre is not a clean-cut *departure* for Poe, but a *transitional* moment, one in which his Gothic sensibilities can be seen to "evolve," to grow increasingly complex, as they merge into his ratiocinative tales. The detective genre demonstrates how Poe gradually complicated his thinking on what distinguishes horror from reason, and so it would be a mistake to read his deduction tales as a "break" from what came before them. After all, the concept of mystery pervades both the Gothic and the detective tale, even as the latter seeks rational explanations for apparently inexplicable events that characterize the former. Both genres remain "poised between rationality and irrationality"—the known and the unknown; answers and questions; the supernatural and the empirical (190). Poe's work thus embodies many of the rational principles associated with eighteenth-century neoclassicism mixed with the passionate intuition of nineteenth-century Romanticism. While Poe's poetry, for example, relies heavily on the traditional poetics that epitomized the Augustan ideal of order, unity, and form—for example, meter, rhyme, conventional lyrical forms—at the same time it blurs and eventually erases the barriers separating dream from reality, the indulgence of remembrance and mourning in highly emotive responses to the past, the promulgation of worlds that do not and will never exist, and a celebration of exaggeration and excess, all elements that depict the late stages of the Gothic as it was assimilated into nineteenth-century Romanticism.

A glance at Poe's publications from the 1840s illustrates his reliance on multiple versions of this hybridization. For example, in "The Gold-Bug" (1843), a lesser-known blueprint for the detective story, Poe presents the remarkable unraveling of a mystery, performed by the shrewd William Legrand. Against all odds, Legrand locates a priceless treasure by deciphering a pirate map. His ability to decode the locations of the map/text strikes the reader, at first, as incredibly improbable and impressive. Yet in the final section of the story, in which the proto-detective describes his process of deduction, Poe unveils the truth behind the pomp associated with Legrand's design: the solution to the riddle unfolds as the result of a "series of accidents and coincidences" (585). Although there is technically no crime to be solved, the story involves many of the same qualities and attitudes to be found in Poe's detective stories. Like Dupin, Legrand's eccentric mode of detection enables him to crack the puzzle of the Gold-Bug. These superior intellects surmount the "temporary paralysis" that impairs lesser minds who cannot synthesize reason and imagination. Beneath the story's outward expression of deductive rationality, then, we discover a supernatural presence of being—a mysterious noumenon that ostensibly directs the phenomenal realm.

Similarly, in the much more famous "The Murders in the Rue Morgue," Dupin solves a case that the police fail to crack by exposing assumptions held by seemingly reasonable individuals. Witnesses of the crime, for example, assume that the murderer is a foreigner, despite the fact that they do not themselves speak any foreign languages. Dupin departs from this blind egoism by allowing himself to go on "wild whims" (401), that is, to set aside formulaic methods derived from a proclivity for ratiocination and subsequently embrace the inexplicable: "[Dupin's] results, brought about by the very soul and essence of method, have, in truth, the whole air of intuition" (397). At the very center of Poe's detective tales, there exists a gaping hole—the unknown—the *absence* of reason, accompanied by a reliance on intuition. Dupin's intuitive impulse runs counter to the rigorous methods that the prefect and the police employ in both "Masque" and "The Purloined Letter." Just as the sublimity of the Gothic castle or its landscape vistas thwart easy efforts at description or understanding, Poe's nascent detectives succeed once they have tapped into the irrational, what Poe might have called the poetic, parts of themselves—the parts that leave plenty of room for accident as well as coincidence, which is also a major explanation for why Poe labelled *Eureka* a poem instead of a scientific treatise. *Eureka* posits the existence of an oppositional universe that manages, ironically, to find unity in its oppositions. As such, it provides the operative paradigm for reading Poe's earliest efforts at genre subversion and blending. The universe of *Eureka* is in constant tension—attraction versus repulsion—and this tension between opposing principles underscores the same oppositional energies that connect Poe's Gothic tales to detection and eighteenth-century science to nineteenth-century poetry: "'Attraction' and 'Repulsion.' The former is the body; the latter the soul: the one is the material; the other the spiritual, principles of the Universe. *No other principles exist*" (1282; emphasis in the original).

By the end of the nineteenth century, the popular novel and "pulp fictions," including the detective story, were elements of the terrain onto which the Gothic novel had migrated (Matheson 44). Claustrophobic urban space opened to include the alienated wandering of the Gothic villain (e.g., Dracula, Mr. Hyde, Dorian Gray) and the figure of the detective as he was first envisioned by Poe and distilled later by others (e.g., Arthur Conan Doyle). In "The Murders in the Rue Morgue," Dupin and his narrator friend stroll the streets of Paris "roaming far and wide until a late hour, seeking, amid the wild lights and shadows of the populous city, that infinity of mental excitement" (401). In a little over one hundred years, the indulgent urbane lifestyle of Dupin and his associate, literary prototypes for Baudelaire's flâneur in the 1870s, would transition into the nocturnal chronicles of Anne Rice's vampires Louis, Claudia, and Lestat. The city, whether London or Paris or New York, emerged in the late nineteenth century as a place of violence and anomie that fed the plotlines for both the detective genre and the modern Gothic tale. The great railway stations in the earliest decades of modernism—Victoria, King's Cross, Grand Central Station—contained racks of illustrated periodicals and detective novels that not only created a particular sensation unique to their environment and changing times, but went on to suggest, like the literal railway lines crossing and intersecting in an underground tableau, the mixing and morphing of genres. Beneath the modern avenues of bourgeois shops and electric lights, there existed a dark, criminal underworld of secret cellars, tunnels, and sewers running for miles, places where real-life Jack the Rippers (1888) flourished as inspirations for fictional recreation as the intimate connection between Gothicism and detection grew ever more explicit.[4]

Like many of the contemporary writers who inherited nearly two centuries of this cross-pollination, much of King's fiction bears the hybrid shape of detection as it has emerged out of the Gothic. He similarly complicates his own Gothic output by enfolding within his macabre prose everyman/woman detectives that are put into situations where they must solve crimes. We have already investigated *The Shining* on these terms; in what remains of this chapter, we revisit *The Dead Zone* (1979) as well as *Duma Key* (2008), as novels that similarly becloud the lines that supposedly demarcate the American Gothic from detective fiction. *The Dead Zone* tracks Johnny Smith, a supremely ordinary young man who suddenly gains the extraordinary psychic ability to see the future of individuals with whom he comes into contact. As a result, Smith eventually undermines the campaign of an aspiring fascist. Smith demonstrates sleuth-like qualities by harnessing his newfound powers to discover an impending apocalypse. King provides dramatic evidence of this connection when the sheriff of Castle Rock invites Smith to join his investigation into the "Castle Rock Strangler." Chapter 16 unfolds in a manner that resembles a miniature crime novel: Smith arrives on the scene, examines clues, outwits the criminal, and ultimately solves the mystery. Like Dupin, he delivers to the sheriff a litany of facts so surprisingly accurate that the sheriff initially believes Smith has supernatural abilities—which, of course, he does. Although Smith, unlike Dupin, does have psychic capacities, so his powers of deduction cannot be deemed solely "natural," King goes to great lengths to underscore Smith's genuine skill as a would-be detective. Because of his "sharp, honest curiosity," the sheriff assesses that Smith has "got a head for this work" (293, 297).

Following in Poe's footsteps, King appears unwilling to relinquish all traces of his story's neoclassical roots. Echoing Poe's "The Purloined Letter" (1844), chapter 16 of *The Dead Zone* concerns itself with how everyday individuals tend to see what they want to see. In "Purloined," the police look for clues only in the manner in which they have been trained, so they miss the evidence right in front of their noses; similarly, there is evidence in *The Dead Zone* that the police look for clues only in the places where they have been conditioned to look, so they miss the fact that the killer is, like the Queen's letter in "Purloined," right under their noses. The culprit is actually one of their own, a fellow police officer. Despite any formal training in the field of investigation, Smith proves to be a detective with considerable dexterity. Unlike the police in "Purloined" as well as Castle Rock, Smith harbors no preconceived prejudices to inhibit him from remaining open to the notion that criminal activity can originate from unanticipated sources.

Nevertheless, by presenting his detective as an actual psychic, King complicates a clear distinction between unreason and reason, forcing his reader to contemplate an alternative *modus operandi* for the conventional detective (not Poe's detectives, who are no less complicated than King's, but many of the derivative variants that emerged in Poe's wake). In effect, *The Dead Zone* cautions against the dangers of ratiocination run amuck, since excessive knowledge leads to excessive power. The rising fascist of the novel, Greg Stillson, a consummate politician, plans everything out with meticulous attention to detail, and he very nearly succeeds in destroying the nation. In contrast, Smith—with his symbolically chosen common name—longs to lead a "normal life," so he shuns the trappings of fame (276). During his impressive streak as a detective in Castle Rock, Smith confesses: "'What I don't know about you would fill about five books . . . the knowing is sometimes a pretty limited thing. Because of the dead zone'" (295). Indeed, the very title of King's text stresses its central message: the dead zones in Smith's memory, the blind spots that he cannot fill, define him and, in turn, define King's Poe-like vision of the detective. In our everyday deductions, we should admit what we do not know and thus submit ourselves to the random whims of a world of accidents and coincidences. Of course, Smith eventually does act because he cannot retreat to the sidelines and let his powers atrophy; he does not entirely relinquish the social function of the sleuth. Still, King strongly advocates for the value of intuition over excessively disciplined calculation. On this front, he does not so much depart from Poe's seminal works as build upon their foundational premise: namely, that reason and imagination have an intimate bond, and we can rarely tell where one begins and the other ends.

What, exactly, is a *psychic detective*? The confluence of the two professions remains tense as well as effortless. On the one hand, a detective is definitively not a psychic, in that he ostensibly utilizes logic, while the psychic indulges in precognition; on the other hand, the two figures are eerily similar, as they are seemingly capable of pulling answers out of the ether, where no common person could ever hope to find them. In King's hands, the concept of the psychic detective reveals something crucial about the fantastic roots of the detective genre itself. Consider how the scene of the original crime functions in the detective story. The scene of the crime is a preternatural remainder that intrudes, like a nightmare or a phantasm, into the normal order of things. In turn, the criminal act amplifies the detective story's fantastic dimensions as it returns from oppression as a "perverse epiphany," one endlessly teased to the surface. On the subject of Poe's ratiocination tales, Geoffrey Hartman writes, "Crime induces a perverse kind of epiphany: it marks the spot, or curses it, or invests it with enough meaning to separate it from the ordinary space-time continuum" (165). Even as the detective uses reason to repress the horrors of the crime, in true Gothic fashion, the initial crime returns repeatedly. In fact, the generic structure demands it: as in the Gothic, the detective tale obsesses over the unnerving infraction at its core. In "The Murders in the Rue Morgue," Dupin's invasion of privacy—into the lives of the other apartment dwellers as well as the L'Espanaye women—mirrors the initial invasion of the violent "Ourang-Outang." Likewise, the detective tale "masochistically" forces its reader to feel "shock and disorientation" by carefully recreating the horror of the original crime (Thoms 25). What could be more Gothic?

Hartman goes a step further: tantalizingly incalculable crimes serve a fantastic purpose by allowing the detective as well as the reader to penetrate the mind of the villain or the victim. The concept of crime magically transports the reader from one consciousness to another, like a superpower that enables the subversion of time and space. The detective has no trouble accessing the innermost secrets of the vulnerable individuals that surround him. *The Dead Zone* capitalizes upon this "perverse epiphany": each person that Smith touches enables him to leap psychically from one horror to another. In chapter 16, King unveils how the crime scene structures the entire work of detective fiction, as unreason intrudes like a flash of lightning into terrain previously patrolled by agents of reason. The crime scene remains suspended, out of time and out of space; only the fantastical detective can access it. At every level, then, the detective genre depends upon darker, supernatural fantasies—a connection fostered by Poe and amplified by King when he endows his psychic detectives with unprecedented potency.[5]

THE CRITIC AS DETECTIVE

Another common thread that links Poe and King is their mutual distaste for academic analysis, which is to say, for critics that probe too deeply into their fiction in the name of being "cleverer than thou." Pete Thoms notes how in Poe's prose "the reader becomes a detective and the detective a reader" (1). Because the puzzle-maker Poe famously antagonizes readers who pride themselves on their own wit (see, for instance, his cryptograms), the germination of the genre doubles as an attempt by Poe to outmaneuver his critics.[6] Also writing in a heightened era of American anti-intellectualism, and often confronting his own hang-ups regarding the literary canon and his perceived omission from it, King dismisses literary critics as "little elites," "avatars of high culture," and "the 'enlightened' cognoscenti" (Underwood and Miller 52–53). The pages of his fiction are riddled with not-so-subtle jabs at intellectuals—in particular, literature professors. Brian Kent argues that "King often sells himself short when he shrugs off his own literary significance and takes broad swipes at the more high-mended arbiters"; "there's a hollowness, a falseness, to it that contrasts with the general honesty and integrity of his work" (55). On one level at least, both Poe and King utilize ratiocination tales to chastise the probing critic and to reinforce the way they want their works to be read. In this section, we place Poe's best-known detective story, "The Purloined Letter," into conversation with King's lesser-known novel *Duma Key* to illustrate how each writer employs the detective in an effort to challenge the critic's relationship to works of art.

While a word or two may suffice to remind the reader of the overall plot behind "Purloined," fewer readers will be familiar with King's underanalyzed novel. In "Purloined," the dastardly Minister D— blackmails the Queen by stealing a scandalous correspondence and leaving in its place an insubstantial letter. In a series of canny moves, Dupin does the same thing to the Minister that the Minister does to the Queen: he locates the letter (which D— has copied from the original) and then steals it, leaving in its place a missive of his own design, written as both an acknowledgment and payback to D— for "an evil turn" he did to Dupin once in Vienna (698). While the hapless prefect probes into every nook and cranny of the Minister's hotel room, Dupin demonstrates that *sometimes the answer is right out in the open*—a lesson, one might surmise, for critics that delude themselves in trying to read between the author's lines and therefore "outmaneuver" him by unraveling his puzzle. Nearly two centuries removed from "Purloined," King's *Duma Key* initially appears to be a very different kind of story: it follows the injured Edgar Freemantle as he retreats to Florida and realizes that art may be a means with which to rehabilitate himself. Suddenly infused with the mysterious gift of being able to paint gorgeous works of art, Edgar channels the haunted energies of Duma Key onto his canvas, and as the novel unfolds, he slowly pieces together the island's unnerving history through images that he psychically transposes with his brush. King acknowledges the novel's connection to Poe, especially with its references to "The Fall of the House of Usher," a story to which he alludes frequently when describing the house on Duma Key—a metaphorical structure under constant threat by psychic and physical erosion (49). Written just after his own horrific hit-and-run incident in 1999 and his subsequent rehabilitation, the novel is a metatext wherein King reflects upon his own healing process. In the novel's more nuanced moments, King has a good deal to say about art, intuition, and the art of detection (a set of concerns that tie him directly back to Poe). King's Edgar Freemantle, following Poe's archetypal sleuths, acts like a detective by exploiting his sudden artistic inspiration to hunt down clues and "make sense" of the recondite Duma Key and the brutal murder of an enslaved person that happened on its shores. Like Smith in King's *The Dead Zone*, Edgar feels compelled to take advantage of his newfound psychic skills to solve a local murder, and King once again quilts his private investigator into a larger supernatural tapestry by inserting into his novel a detective story in miniature. Although readers may initially view these works as quite distinctive, "Purloined" and *Duma Key* share a central thesis: the poetic detective must transcend quotidian approaches to the interpretation of art as well as criminal behavior.

To frame this conversation, let us first consider Jacques Derrida's commentary upon Poe's story. In his (in)famous analysis, Derrida helps us to delineate many of the major points that "Purloined" and *Duma Key* share, and, more important still, he articulates why such a comparison matters. Derrida argues that Poe's famous ratiocination tale puts the reader in the position of the prefect by encouraging the reader to bypass, too hastily, the "structure of the text" in her heated pursuit of uncovering its truth (180). Critics and readers alike yearn to uncover the secret of the text—to penetrate into the most private recesses and expose the hidden contents of "letters" composed by the Queen (as well as Poe). But of course, the hidden contents of the letter do not actually matter. What truly matters in Poe's narrative is the possession of the letter, which is to say, the opportunity to hold the coveted text and lord that fact over others. As such, Derrida *avec* Poe contends that language always functions as a sleight-of-hand trick that confounds guileless prefects. Ever slippery, Poe fools the naïve reader into believing in the capacity of language to elicit the thing-in-itself when it only ever offers a substitute (to use Derrida's terminology, the signifier instead of the signified). Like a detective story, language always promises resolution, but it only delivers more mystery. "Purloined" is not about putting the letter back into its "proper place," then, or finding the ever-elusive point of origin; in fact, Poe's story is only superficially concerned with answering its primary riddle. To understand the futility inherent at the heart of the detective genre is to understand *the beguiling nature of language itself*. Poe's secret can never be solved. It exists—like any text—to be (re)circulated. We write and we read in an endless parry with one another, promising finality where none could ever be achieved: clever detective and evasive criminal, all at once. Derrida's analysis of "Purloined" therefore demonstrates how literary criticism and the art of detection inform one another at the most intimate level.

To prove his case, Derrida proposes several key interventions, each of which allows us to expand the dialogue between "Purloined" and *Duma Key*. First and foremost, Poe's story launches from a circulation library in which texts live in conversation with one another. The site of the circulation library reminds readers that the social exercise of art is not based upon some substratum of universal truth, but upon a free-floating state of drift. Instead of a rock-solid truth, Derrida *avec* Poe gestures at an unwieldy circulation that undergirds the aesthetic enterprise. Like a text that goes from pen to print, or from first edition to second, Derrida *avec* Poe privileges replicas that no longer depend upon an "original source." At the start of the narrative, Poe's narrator meets Dupin by accident, not design. Similarly, the plot of "Purloined" is driven by misreadings as well as miscues, accompanied by a seemingly redemptive impulse to confuse counterfeit texts with so-called primary sources.

Duma Key reiterates the circulatory logic developed by Derrida *avec* Poe in its commentary regarding the slipperiness of art. King's novel undercuts the naïve belief that neoclassical reason, when applied to a given mystery, inevitably results in linear, straightforward conclusions. *Duma Key* remains replete with intertextual references that muddy the proverbial waters: one character compares the protagonist, detective-artist Edgar Freemantle, whose first name already suggests a latent debt to Poe, to the character of Robinson Crusoe. King also references Shakespeare several times, including a reference to Prospero from *The Tempest* when Edgar is said to manage his own "island kingdom" (200). And the narrative even gestures at other staples from the King canon: the surname "Freemantle," which is shared with Mother Abigail in *The Stand*, or the wasps that show up alongside the book's biggest revelation and conjure an unnerving metaphor from *The Shining*. King's *incessant intertextuality* goes beyond the author's typical gestures at his own personal library: at an existential level, Edgar experiences a phenomenon that he describes as "cross-patching," in which he cannot recall names and so he must use different signifiers to map meanings for himself. Every text proves to be a reference to another text. For example, Edgar psychically channels the work previously done by a series of artists that precede him on Duma Key, and because his *sui generis* paintings, which appear to be so distinctive, are actually only reproductions of other artists, every "authentic" expression reveals itself to be a recreation of a preexisting work of art. By making the fatal error of selling off his cursed artworks, Edgar accidentally spreads the evil of the island into the wider world. The curse that serves as the locus of King's text is an infernal impulse to circulate.

In turn, much like Poe's "Purloined," *Duma Key* presents aesthetic criticism as a form of detection. Derrida highlights that the final letter from Dupin to D— closes not with a traditional signature, but with a citation. Derrida then asks, "What is a signature between quotation marks?" (206). *Duma Key* offers another signature of this variety—Edgar's highly personal confession—between quotation marks, as King unveils Edgar's entire missive to be a purloined copy of another artist's experiences. What are we as critic-detectives meant to learn from Edgar's futile pursuit of the autochthonous crime? In their hunt for deeper meaning, Poe's readers wind up lost in intertextual mazes, chasing the impossible objects of their desire. King's *Duma Key* forces its audience to follow a similarly elusive design.

In "Purloined" as well as *Duma Key*, the critic-detective ostensibly pursues his own tail in perpetuity. Derrida notes that the name of Poe's story mirrors the ever-slippery object at its center. Because the title of the tale parallels the purloined letter that proves so cagey, no line demarcates the inside of the text from its outside. To further illuminate this circularity, both Poe and King populate their prose with doubles. In "Purloined," the detective and the arch-villain manifest as carbon copies. Readers can readily surmise that the obscure name "D—" signals an intimate relationship to Dupin. Perhaps evidence of a biological kinship between Dupin and D—, and certainly proof of at least a metaphorical twinning, the closing citation of "Purloined" gestures at a sibling rivalry between Atreus and Thyestes. *Duma Key* is equally overflowing with doubles. "I felt doubled," Edgar laments. "Like a man watching a man" (622). King twins Edgar with another E name, Elizabeth, an artist on Duma Key whose life closely parallels his own. To go one step further: if the name Edgar alludes to Poe—a reasonable deduction, given the many signs of influence—the name Elizabeth could be a gesture at Poe's poem "Elizabeth," which dwells upon the topic of how an artist becomes an artist (the central plot of *Duma Key* as well). Poe's "Elizabeth" chastises a poet who pursues truth without recognizing the part that he or she plays in shaping it. The poem calls to task the narrow-minded empiricist who gets caught up in logistics when, in fact, as Poe posits in both "Elizabeth" and the essay "The Poetic Principle," poetry is about the soul. Like Derrida, then, Poe dismisses the reader who mistakes the word for the thing-in-itself: "Called anything, its meaning is the same" (61). Or maybe by linking Edgar to Elizabeth, King gestures at an even closer relation: Poe's mother Elizabeth (or "Eliza"), a primary figure whose absence haunts so much of Poe's work. What does Poe the existential detective pursue if not a glimpse of his mislaid mother? In short, King's novel contains layers of connection to Poe.

In *Duma Key*, King doubles Edgar with the character of Elizabeth, just as Poe uses the name Elizabeth to project a double that shares his poetic aspirations. Convoluted mirror images abound. Even more visibly, Edgar interacts with the character of Wireman, another symbolic twin who lives nearby. As King's *Duma Key* progresses, Edgar begins to utter Wireman's strange colloquialisms, before acknowledging that Wireman is "my fate," which makes sense because a "Wire man" is just another term for an electrician and, as Edgar openly admits, his own "wiring" is very much out of whack (146). Frequently denounced as a "cannibal," that is, a person who consumes his own likeness, Edgar appears to be stranded on a Cartesian island, condemned to confront various aspects of himself: "Talking to myself and answering myself back" as "in some kind of crazed loop" (60, 38). King's subtext becomes text when the novel finally admits: "All my voices were speaking clearly and coherently to one another" (143). But what do King's many doubles have to tell us about the detective? Derrida elucidates that Poe's doubles invoke a "crazed loop" in which the critic-detective suddenly realizes that he has been pursuing not the criminal Other, but himself—or, more accurately, he suddenly comprehends that the criminal Other is already part of himself. In yet another intertextual reference, Poe as well as King summons that ancient detective Oedipus who, in his eager pursuit of the culprit, accidentally uncovers his own guilt. Dupin *is* D—; Edgar *is* Elizabeth (as well as Wireman and a host of other characters). The clues lead the critic-detective back to himself. Consequently, the detective never resolves the case at hand. She merely repeats it.

Just as Edgar repeats, rather than resolves, the criminal past of Duma Key, Poe's "Thou Art the Man" (another title that doubles as the central conceit within the story itself and another title posited within quotation marks) stresses the utter circularity of the interpretive act. In this early ratiocination tale, Poe's narrator compels his reader to trust the wrong person and, as a result, to repeat the grave error of the townspeople. Everyone, including Poe's reader, ends up trusting a criminal. As we have already seen, the detective genre relies upon a thorough rehashing in which the reader is ushered into recomposing the events that precede the story at hand. The plot is always doubled: there is the plot that readers must move through alongside the detective, and there is the plot of the original crime that is being reconstructed for them. In this way, seminal detective tales double as a metacommentary on art and its critique. The title of the narrative "Thou Art the Man" offers a neat pun: in addition to restating a constitutional refrain from the formula, in which the detective deduces the solution and points to the culprit, Poe employs old-fashioned language to evoke a secondary meaning: "art" doubles as "are" and so, according to Poe's title, art also means "to exist." Art *is* the man; the man *is* art. Like the gullible townspeople, Poe reveals how readers—especially his most vehement critics—are effortlessly fooled by art. He dupes his critics into thinking that they, as would-be detectives, can somehow stand outside of his text and deal with it in a detached, hyperrational manner. In truth, they remain engrossed within the work of art, unconsciously driven to repeat the miscalculations of the story's characters by assuming that they are the critic-detective when, in fact, they are the ones "being read" by an ever-more cunning Poe. To "resolve" these dilemmas posed by relentless intertextuality, endless doubling, and "crazed loops," Poe posits himself as a transcendent, nearly godlike figure who orchestrates the entire illusion from on high. Dupin declares himself to be a poet, not a mathematician, and it is his whimsical, intuitive, poetical nature that allows him to outwit his opponents. It is always better to be a poet than a prefect.

In the final tally, Poe and King rely upon the trappings of the detective to advocate for a different approach to the interpretation of art. While art may ostensibly push us to feel *whole*—King's Edgar yearns to heal himself through painting—in truth, art is about *holes*: traumatic voids that can never be filled. The work of art is not about what is present, but what must remain absent. The orthodox detective would never admit such a thing, but Edgar has many questions that remain "beyond [his] ability to answer"—a reality that he slowly comes to accept as the story of *Duma Key* progresses (167). Even as Edgar attempts to organize his paintings in chronological order, and by so doing expresses a longing "to believe things happened a certain way," the reality of *Duma Key* is that art is a coping mechanism, a compensation for the randomness of the universe (a randomness on full display when Wireman recalls how the main trauma of his life—the death of his daughter—occurred when she swallowed a marble). Sometimes the culprit is just an impulsive Ourang-Outang. In neoclassical fashion, art provides what the detective frequently provides for readers of Poe's and King's fiction: an illusion of rationality to cover up the "gulf of mystery" (465). Edgar initially mistakes drawing something for knowing it. By the close of the novel, though, he realizes that art is often the opposite of knowledge, so art school proves to be "a bunch of bullshit" (417). Rather than put the pieces of the puzzle back together, like Jack Torrance with his scrapbook in *The Shining*, Edgar realizes that to forget is often the best available solution to our most pressing problems.

Poe and King both wonder if the detective-critic could ever approach the text without an obsessive need to create order out of chaos. Edgar decides to try painting without intellectualizing the pursuit, relying instead upon his intuition as well as his muscle memory. He stops trying to fill in the blanks of the canvas and embraces willful ignorance: "We don't *know* what we need to know" (632; emphasis in the original). Rejecting the detective's impetus to know the future by knowing the past, Edgar opts to relish the unknowns, or the dead zones. The implication for literary critique is fairly straightforward: first, the critic-detective must recognize that the proverbial case can never be closed, since the work of art (the object as well as the labor) can never be "completely done," and there is always "room for one more" (437). Language defers meaning; it does not solidify it. Second, the critic-detective must recognize that art exists to be appreciated, intuited, and consumed without excessive ratiocination: as Edgar puts it, instead of painting to impose a sense of order and meaning, he should have been listening. Poe's Dupin likewise outwits his opponents by recognizing the patterns that they follow, not by mastering their innermost secrets. He will not violate the Queen in the manner of the police; he believes it better to examine crime "in the dark" (*Poetry and Tales* 680). Like Edgar, he advances a brand of anti-intellectualism—a posture that may strike readers as rather odd given the presumed air of reason that has been guiding the detective all along: "By undue profundity we perplex and enfeeble thought" through "a scrutiny too sustained, too concentrated, or too direct" (Poe, "Murders" 412). As Richard Hull notes, Poe's late prose shifts from plots of epistemic closure to ancient forms of cyclical storytelling, and hence his detective tales end "not with knowledge, but with repetition," a paradigmatic shift that speaks volumes (209). *Duma Key* likewise ends with a plea for repetition rather than revelation as well as a renewed zeal for poetic gaps that cannot be filled. For Poe as well as King, wisdom comes not from a rush to resolution but from sublime silences.

Beyond complicating a relatively facile understanding of the detective genre by opening novel readings of King's corpus, our analysis of King's indebtedness to Poe's ratiocination tales reveals something critical regarding King's perceived estrangement from the literary canon (although his concern with that oversight appears less valid with each new literary award that he garners). Certainly financially rewarded as a writer from his very earliest publications, King felt something of the same lack of respect from American cultural arbitrators, such as Harold Bloom, who continually disparaged his talent.[7] King still maintains a kind of professional bitterness not dissimilar to the acidity underlying Jack Torrance's "Great American Hack" reference to Poe (*Shining* 157) and the latter's perceived slight by the nineteenth-century American East coast literary establishment that rewarded arguably less talented writers, such as Henry Wadsworth Longfellow, while leaving Poe in penury. Both Poe and King utilize detectives to highlight what they perceive to be the gross offenses of the fools that maintain the literary establishment. By ostensibly outwitting their critics, these two writers proclaim their own creations to be too ingenious to be fully appreciated by upholders of the so-called literati. Like Poe, King's writerly persona retreats from the idea of literature as a form of social engagement and treats it as a solitary activity, mostly divorced from the input of other human beings. King's persona thus doubles with the personas of his nomadic protagonists, decoupled as they are from the pressures of the outside world.[8] This realization is relevant not because it reflects potential personality flaws in Poe and King, but because it helps to explain the enduring significance of the detective genre for these two writers as well as their readers.

At the sociopolitical level, this tendency to isolate themselves reveals how each author ultimately positions himself as an uber-detective who stands apart from "the rabble"—a kingly position. "Poe's detective arrives at his solution in the isolation of his mind and does so before the story proper has gotten under way," Larzer Ziff comments. Therefore, "[Poe's] world is a closed system" (81). And even though King, unlike Poe, outwardly fashions himself as a "man of the people," fine-tuning a so-called blue-collar sensibility, his Constant Reader might wonder if the influence of Poe's ratiocination tales tacitly undercuts the egalitarian ethos that King outwardly promotes. Despite his outward affection for unpredictability, King—like Poe—orchestrates a relatively closed authorial system. Dead zones are already anticipated; detectives are only ever psychics in disguise. As such, readers ought to inquire into whether the mutual dependence upon a certain type of detective for these two extraordinarily influential writers has contributed to the shrinking ability of American consumers to read, and thus to think, democratically. If so, King's reliance upon Poe's American detectives may prove to be of dire consequence.

Chapter 4

THE MULTIPLE DEATHS OF RICHARD BACHMAN

STEPHEN KING'S NOTORIOUS TENDENCY TO PRODUCE "HAPPY ENDINGS" would appear to confirm the author's fundamental belief that while we inhabit a fatalistic universe of macabre disruptions in the form of a father's insanity or a bomb-toting domestic terrorist, these forces are contravened by righteous heroes and heroines pursuing just ends. For example, *The Dark Tower* series requires seven volumes for its hero, Roland the gunslinger, to obtain painful insight into why the Beams and the Tower they support are worth saving. Roland's descent into the wastelands that permeate locales such as Calla Bryn Sturgis and Lud—places that threaten to disturb the medieval quaintness of Mid-World itself—locates the King hero in an environment in which there are few human beings worth saving, and many of those who are, such as Susan Delgato or Father Callahan, die by the very forces that Roland must thwart. By the time he reaches the end of his quest, the gunslinger has been tainted by his contact with evil; Roland has wandered a long way from any unequivocal definition of goodness or purpose. Nevertheless, *The Dark Tower* ends in a final restoration of an Apollonian norm: the Tower and its Beams remain intact. While *The Dark Tower* series is replete with cross-genre texts, establishing aspects that connect them to thriller, horror, mystery, and especially western and epic-fantasy, these seven novels can also be read as sharing something with the detective tale, most particularly in terms that ultimately speak to Roland's discovering the reason for the quest itself. Accordingly, as we will trace in this chapter, the noir fictions of Richard Bachman (Stephen King's now-deceased pseudonym from the 1980s) serve as a kind of bridge between the twin impulses of fatalism and blind optimism—a bridge that speaks volumes to King's development as a writer as well as to his complicated generic profile. In revealing ways, the personal split between King and Bachman mirrors the generic bond between horror and crime fiction.[1]

Crime fiction borrows from the Gothic in its reliance on violence, mystery, and disruption. A missing link in this lineage is the *roman noir*: bleak, even dystopian fantasies that may or may not feature a detective (of note, Bachman's texts never feature a full-fledged private eye). While the Gothic tends to focus its primary energies on the release of Dionysian forces—the source of both genres' core emotive impulses—the classic detective more often looks to find solutions to counter this release in restitution of some semblance of order and control. The Gothic tale describes a dissolving world swaying toward the dystopic in which horror comes close to triumph; the detective tale takes charge of a world whose rationality strives to contain the horror. The Gothic presents readers with energies that are so evocative precisely because they are dangerous and disruptive, exploring a realm without limits, a world of extravagance. Classic modes of ratiocination (problem-solving through rationality), on the other hand, represent a domain of perimeters suggested by the death or capture of the criminal-monster. This fantasy is underscored by the assurance that each reader of classic detective fiction possesses knowledge that she is consciously reading a work of fiction as a fiction—one that will end if not happily, then at least with the problem resolved. King's career demonstrates that he has similarly been drawn by a compulsion that takes him in the opposite direction, away from the "happy endings" that characterize the majority of his work and toward submergence into the nihilism that characterizes so much of the Gothic as separate from the solution-oriented goal found in tales of detection. For example, as *The Dark Tower* winds down, the reliance on escalating violence and the philosophy of the end justifying the means employed by Roland suggest the difficulty King experienced in distinguishing his hero from his nemesis, the Crimson King. Clearly, the dialectical "split" between the forces of societal and personal coherence and Gothic dystopia is also traceable elsewhere in King's work, as is the mutual propensity to resolve this conflict through the death of the criminal-monster. While the conservative nature of the classic detective tale thus runs counter to the general spirit of anarchy that underscores many Gothic narratives, affirmation more or less trumping negation, in tracing King's general commitment to happy resolutions in a fictional canon that now stretches over half a century and includes better than fifty novels, we find plenty of evidence to suggest that the hero sometimes transforms into the antihero, that the social community is not always worthy of salvation, and that penetration into the realm of noir is not always mitigated by positive outcomes.

Without question, King has generally defined himself as an "optimistic" individual, and over the years, given his emergent status and responsibilities as a serious literary artist and attractive Hollywood wellspring, he tends to produce fiction that his Constant Readers *want* to read. And King is highly motivated to please that loyal readership: to present them with a vision of hell from Shawshank Prison that is eventually displaced by hope and friendship as shining alternatives. A quick review of the titles in the King corpus reveals a preponderance of books that mirror the uplifting conclusion of *Rita Hayworth and Shawshank Redemption*. But this in turn leaves us with the very real problem represented by the Bachman books: a series of early novels that King deliberately chose to publish under a *nom de plume*.[2]

The bridge between Gothicism and detection extends into the realm of hard-boiled fiction and its spiritual twin, film noir. King has professed his love of noir, perhaps nowhere more emphatically than in the first chapter of this volume. According to Paul Schrader, "noir is not a genre—it is a tone, a feeling, a sensibility" (581); "to be considered noir, a work must be 'sardonic,' 'fatalistic,' or 'hopeless'" (533). Jean Pierre Chartier describes American noir as "dispassionate accounts of monsters, criminals whose evils nothing can excuse" (qtd. in Naremore 4). American noir frequently features a disenfranchised detective who clings to his own sense of morality against his sinful environment. Texts of this sort cater to quasi-Freudian notions of guilt and punishment and forbidden desire. Don Leifert posits that "the undeniable influences shared by film noir and horror" materialize in a number of themes and tropes (57). Importantly, King's alter ego Bachman was born in the 1970s, during a neo-noir boom in Hollywood that included films such as Robert Altman's *The Long Goodbye* and Roman Polanski's *Chinatown*. Bachman borrows heavily from the syntax as well as the semantics of this tradition, and in doing so he joins a chorus of creators tarrying at the nexus of horror and the hard-boiled.

Indeed, the protagonists in the Bachman novels confront many of the same problems that confound other writers' characters with noir sensitivities, such as characters found in the work of John D. MacDonald, Raymond Chandler, and Thomas Harris. It was as Bachman that King most consistently sounded like Chandler: "Mr. Chandler is interested in writing, not detective stories, but serious studies of a criminal milieu, the Great Wrong Place, and his powerful but extremely depressing books [are to be considered] works of art" (Auden). Lost in a milieu that is at best indifferent, and likely hostile to their fate, Bachman's characters haunt the periphery of society. Either the consequence of personal illness (mental and/or physical), societal alienation, or some combination of the two, Bachman's antiheroes are devoid of positive constructions of reality in their recognition of life's absurdity. It is no coincidence that Bachman's *The Long Walk* so closely mirrors Horace McCoy's seminal noir *They Shoot Horses, Don't They?*, in that both texts track disenchanted, fatalistic characters as they drag themselves through a game rigged against them. Suffering from psychic imbalances leading to self-hatred, aggression, and sociopathology, the Bachman male finds himself pretty much alone in a world bereft of faith in family, community, sexuality, friendship, religion, government, and the assorted virtues. In his isolation, he is left to rely on himself alone, but even his best qualities are taxed to the extreme—both physically and psychologically. These characters are part of an existential universe offering no assurances before or beyond the grave; their lives are shadowed in the truth of Kurt Vonnegut's "contemptibility of man in the vastness of the universe" (167). Trapped by biology as much as by economics, these hardened males have only the code of the lonely individual on which to rely in a world where love and religion are defunct, where the proofs of personhood are challenged daily, and where every protagonist must learn to define his own moral conditions and strive to live up to them.

After the realization that life is unfair and that the odds are stacked against the individual, the question becomes what should be done with what few last choices are available. The protagonist of the *roman noir* and the Bachman antihero must learn to live without illusions and abstract ideals, such as can be found in religion or political ideology. Although tempted to wallow, the hard-boiled hero must avoid self-pity because self-pity leads to intellectual overthinking and passivity as a substitute for action, however limited in scope. Many artists in this vein are concerned with the sapping of an otherwise virile masculinity. Although women are often present in these narratives, they occupy severely curtailed roles, even more restricted than typically found elsewhere in the King canon. To make the point even more emphatically: a stereotyped feminine posture to life—via manipulation or passivity—is an anathema to be avoided because the feminine principle is identified with nature and thus emblematic of man's biological predicament. Instead, the noir male and Bachman antihero assume roles similar to how the existentialist Albert Camus interpreted the Greek mythic figure Sisyphus, who finds whatever self-respect and purpose left to him in defying the curse Zeus has assigned him, retaining the initiative to stand up against both bureaucratic and biological forces that threaten his dignity, against the unknown, against overwhelming odds, and the certitude of death. (Camus famously paid homage to James M. Cain's *roman noir*, *The Postman Always Rings Twice*, in his novel *The Stranger*.) As seen with the adolescent in the earlier Bachman book *Rage*, the rejection of socially acceptable roles and codes of behavior forces Bachman's protagonists to envision a wholly new construction of reality.

While it would be accurate to argue that King's canon has always maintained a certain fascination with the dangers that threaten American civil liberties, the fiction associated with Richard Bachman is unequivocal in its production of men and women who are victims of both a remorseless governmental bureaucracy and the cruelty of fate—twin pillars that also prop up the fictional universes of the *roman noir* and film noir. With Bachman, King infuses the pattern of the *roman noir* with the same bitterness and pent-up aggression that transitioned America from the stagnant 1970s to the anti-government bravado of Ronald Reagan. Sometimes Bachman's treatment of a grim fate takes the form of bad fortune, as when characters contract cancer or lose their jobs, but all of his characters find the odds stacked against their survival. King has acknowledged the influence of literary naturalism, particularly the novels of Thomas Hardy and Frank Norris, on his own writing,[3] and there exists no better example of their shaping presence than in the Bachman books (we will discuss the connecting line from naturalism to noir in even greater detail in our discussion of *Billy Summers*). Like Hardy's protagonists in his later fiction (*Tess of the D'Urbervilles* and *Jude the Obscure*) and Norris's *McTeague*, the Bachman protagonists are distinguished by their loss of agency and sense of entrapment. In the naturalist tract, there exists no positive figure from the detective genre to explain the mysteries of a Gothic universe that is remorseless in its oppressiveness, much less to correct the enormous wrongs of poverty and class injustice; there is only the individual, stranded to face the consequences of overwhelming forces that threaten his very existence.

The Bachman world is devoid of governmental and institutional action designed to ameliorate the suffering of besieged individuals; it operates under the spirit of Darwinian capitalism without conscience. In fact, the American government itself forms a collusion with biological determinism to thwart the survival efforts of selected representatives of the underclass. No matter how they struggle, even the survivors in these tales are overwhelmed by inevitable powers—the force of biological nature in *The Long Walk* and *Thinner*; the force of inflexible authority figures in *Rage* and *The Running Man*; futuristic televised "sporting contests" that are sanctioned by a totalitarian regime to enflame the bloodlust of its oppressed denizens while at the same enforcing the need for conformity and obedience in *The Long Walk* and *The Running Man*; and bureaucratic "progress" and zoning laws that serve to displace the sanctity of private property and individual human rights in *Roadwork*. Michael Collings summarizes the naturalistic qualities that give shape to the environments of the Bachman texts: "Isolation in turn suggests helplessness, a final motif that unifies the Bachman novels and makes them an inherent part of King's imagined universe. In spite of everything—pain, suffering, death—no one can finally do anything. Characters become enmeshed in social pressure, politics, the external environment; they can no longer control themselves, their actions, or the actions of others" (17–18). Bachman's men are handicapped by a variety of limitations, but the biggest one that they share is a sensitivity to humankind's predicament on the planet, their mutual feeling of spiritual exile. This midcentury malaise found its initial expression in the hard-boiled pulps that King read with such avidity as a young man.

In the 1985 essay "Why I Was Bachman," King explains that his decision to publish under a pseudonym was motivated primarily out of perverse curiosity. Like a child in possession of a wounded bird he had nursed back to health, King wished to see if his fiction could fly without the aid of his brand-name: "Of course we'll never know now, will we? Bachman died with that question—is it work that takes you to the top or is it all just a lottery?—still unanswered" (ix). More revealing, however, is King's ambiguous statement in the same essay where he justifies turning to writing under the Bachman pseudonym, "when I had to have relief" (vii). The thoughtful reader might well ask in response: relief from what? King fails to address this question directly in the essay, so we will attempt to do so now.

THE DARK HALF

Bachman constructed a world torn from the pages of crime fiction that allowed King to indulge his darkest impulses toward violence and despair. Bachman's was an early, visceral voice that allowed King to find his way to the more mature work to come. Taken together, the Bachman books contain little of the general optimism available elsewhere in the King canon, and, coincidentally, that exist in the usual conclusions found in the classical detective genre. They are King's *Chinatown*: dystopic milieus wherein the protagonist is overwhelmed by dark forces beyond his ability to understand, much less to control. They call to mind the closing line of *Sadie When She Died*, an utterly bleak and brutal detective story by one of King's favorite writers, Ed McBain: "Sometimes, none of it made any goddamn sense at all" (180). This degree of fatalism is perhaps the real reason King felt it necessary to hide the corruption and pessimism of these narratives under the cover of a pseudonym, especially when he was simultaneously publishing bestselling fiction under his own name. It is helpful to recall that most of the Bachman fiction was written when King was neither wealthy nor famous, including periods when he was in high school and college. The Bachman voice is thus influenced by some of King's anxieties as an English major trying to figure out what to do with his degree, a young father, a fledgling writer whose work had been universally savaged by the national press, an unassuming man from Maine struggling to cope with an abrupt and unexpected international celebrity while battling alcoholism and addictions to a variety of other drugs, and, finally, a disillusioned product of the 1960s still plagued by the aftereffects of Vietnam and Watergate.[4]

From their unbridled anger to the genuine outrage of their social commentary to their bleak perspective on the future, Bachman's books may be more representative of their particular moment in American history than anything else King has written. Politically speaking, some of the Bachman books were written (and all of them were published) during the Reagan era; taken collectively, they reflect the spirit during a time when America had become a cultural wasteland. These novels are consistent reminders of American vulnerability at that unique historical moment: the energy crisis of the 1970s that incapacitated the nation's lifestyle, America's increasing fascination with violent sport that appealed to increasing national levels of crime violence and proliferation of automatic weaponry, the defeat in Vietnam (frequently referenced throughout King's oeuvre), and the callous multinational corporate takeovers without concern for loyalties or ethics. The frustration that points the way to the violent conclusions in these novels centers on the characters' impotence in attempting to influence the new realities shaping American society. These were the pressures from which King sought "relief" in assuming the Bachman persona; they point the way to the nagging consistency of King's darkest prognostications even as he was emerging as a best-selling author. The Bachman books are only equaled in darkness in *Pet Sematary, Apt Pupil,* and *Cujo*; most of King's fiction offers at least some redemptive possibility, one that effectively counterbalances whatever limits—personal as well as societal—are imposed upon the protagonists.

The novel *The Dark Half* provides us with a parallel to the Bachman-King relationship by featuring two very different genres of art: Bachman-like texts in the *roman noir* mold from "not a very nice guy" George Stark and King-like authored narratives of a "very nice guy," novelist Thad Beaumont, "hailed as America's most promising novelist" and National Book Award nominee (22). With the name of his protagonist, King-Bachman likely gestured at the anti-hero of Dashiell Hammett's hard-boiled novel *The Glass Key*: Hammett's Ned Beaumont is torn between his dark side as a political thug and racketeer and his "nice guy" role as a pseudo-detective trying to solve a murder. As seen in the resonant name of Beaumont, Bachman's *The Dark Half* shares the deep ambivalence of Hammett's seminal text. Stark and Beaumont compete against one another for control over their shared pencils and typewriter in a way that poses uncanny parallels to the relationship that formed between Bachman and King. The details defining the relationship between Stark and Beaumont are rendered explicitly in the novel; they clearly reflect King's consciousness of his relationship with the *nom de plume* Bachman. Even information regarding the particular incidents associated with the unearthing of the secret pseudonym corresponds perfectly between the fictional *Dark Half* and King's own reality. But unlike events in the novel, Bachman was never really King's antagonist. He was, rather, a vehicle necessary for exploring the dark half of King's psyche, a means for releasing the noir side of King's artistic vision. In *Dark Half*, Beaumont acknowledges self-consciously that "'The idea of a pseudonym had this funny draw for me. It felt *free*, somehow—like a secret escape hatch, if you see what I mean. . . . Thinking about writing under a pseudonym was like thinking about being invisible'" (23; emphasis in the original). We contend that this "invisibility," while maybe not exactly "an escape hatch," is nevertheless precisely what King discovered in writing as Bachman: a degree of freedom that allowed him to express and perhaps even to purge his gloomiest fictional inclinations toward both American society and humanity in general.

Subsequently, King has been sheepish—one might even risk calling his response that of mortification—in his attitude toward the Bachman collection, finding ways to explain away and dismiss the quality of the books (he even demanded, for several reasons, that *Rage* be yanked from circulation). When King was an undergraduate, he wrote a series of commentaries during his junior and senior years under the title "King's Garbage Truck" for his college newspaper *The Maine Campus*, ostensibly because you never know what you might find in a garbage truck. Accordingly, this column contained a variety of musings on current cinema, campus activities, the police, and the politics of the late 1960s. Several years ago, King's alma mater, the University of Maine, Orono, considered publishing a collection of these entries, thinking that they would be of immediate interest to the writer's enormous fanbase. The university was planning on publishing it without the courtesy of telling King, who, when he found out about it, was adamant about not wishing to see these columns again in print, arguing that these essays represented unpolished early work, juvenilia, and were no longer relevant to the present (Beahm 81). He ultimately decided that he would not provide the school with his permission to publish. King has often relied on some of this same protective rhetoric regarding his Bachman fiction, as we have noted, most of it written, like the entries in "King's Garbage Truck," by a neophyte writer. The seedy and sordid aspects of King noir have been swept aside; the stench has been fastidiously suppressed in the name of mass-market appeal.

Bachman's reservations are those that King had as a young man; indeed, most of these novels were written approximately before, during, or just after the time that he was enrolled at the university. The majority of these novels were composed when King had not yet gained international fame and assumed the mantle of "America's Storyteller"; consequently, he was freer to express his reservations about the future. Bachman represented a side of King before his economic status was radically transfigured, before his name brand transitioned from an ever-encroaching disillusionment to child-like wonder and the power of hope, which is to say before King transitioned from his hard-boiled persona to a more pastoral sort of prose. Since Bachman died, King has transformed himself into a public celebrity: his fiction fills four complete shelves at the local Barnes & Noble; he has been awarded the National Medal of the Arts, the highest national tribute a civilian can receive; he has become a respected Man of Letters; his stories are now published in major American magazines, such as the *New Yorker, Atlantic,* and *Esquire.* King's opinion matters. The fatalistic orientation of young Bachman is no longer shared by the mature author whose name is familiar even to people who do not read novels. From another perspective, Bachman may now embarrass King because the latter's work has become more nuanced and sophisticated, and the maturation of King as a writer has transported him (especially in his own self-identity as a writer) beyond the rawness of Bachman's pessimistic vision. (Of course, as this book demonstrates, King never fully sheds his appreciation for, and indebtedness to, a darker world shaped by crime fiction.) Fame and the accumulation of extraordinary wealth have certainly been factors contributing to this algebraic equation. Since the writing of the Bachman novels, King has self-transcended from someone aligned unwittingly with the Bachman protagonists, struggling barely to survive in a hostile world, to a modern-day Horatio Alger—nothing less than a spectacular American success story. During the years when King wrote the Bachman's novels, he had no inkling that his art would turn out to be so appreciated or so lucrative.[5] The fictional universe of Richard Bachman was a dystopic prognostication, perhaps even a paranoid projection, of King's own future. Bachman thus served as a figurative bridge between King's initial mimicry of his hard-boiled predecessors and his eventual status as America's preeminent *horrormeister*. King buried Bachman for multiple reasons, including the public discovery of his pseudonym before his experiment was concluded, but the noir nightmares he conjured in these novels continue to plague America's uneven slumber.

Still, the question persists: why did King don the guise of Bachman? Because the Bachman novels are so relentless in their pessimism and despair, this chapter contends that King wanted to do much more than simply run an experiment to see how well his books would sell without the help of his bestseller name, and he certainly did not publish them for the money. As King writes in the first chapter of this volume, on the subject of a later book in this vein, *Mr. Mercedes*, "If readers didn't like it, was my family going to starve? Not a bit." We read Bachman's output primarily, then, as an experiment in genre writing.

THE GENRE EXPERIMENT

In King's two attempts to explain why he first generated the Bachman persona, one thing becomes crystal clear: Bachman was for King an exercise in genre writing. There are subtle clues to Bachman's placement within the larger detective/mystery lineage, as when King uses the analogy of Sherlock Holmes and the episode at Reichenbach Falls to examine his return to Bachman; and there are less subtle clues, as when King evokes the hard-boiled hero by describing Bachman as a "rainy-day sort of guy," living in a state of "simmering despair" (King, "Importance"). When we contend that Bachman serves as a noir version of King, then, we are not stretching the case because, in King's estimation, Bachman remains quite literally ensconced in the language and legacy of crime fiction. Further proof of this focus on genre distinctions is that, when King began to unpack his need for Bachman, he immediately felt compelled to point out that only one of the Bachman books (*Thinner*) could be classified as straightforward horror. King celebrated how, when he donned the Bachman guise, he could compose "just plain books"—that is, the sort of paperback fare peddled in airport terminals and supermarkets (King, "Why" ix). Yet when King substitutes the word "earnest" for "Bachman" in the title to his second explanatory essay ("The Importance of Being Bachman"), he reveals a more explicit motive: that Bachman could presumably speak more plainly—and more honestly—than he could when writing under the name Stephen King. Bachman, unlike King, could converse in the language of gritty realism. The Bachman books created a seamless connection to the intense violence and rhetorical strategies borrowed from crime fiction, including film noir and the hard-boiled detective story.

It is no coincidence, we would argue, that King sets up his Bachman persona by citing three examples of popular writers who have also adopted pseudonyms with the explicit purpose of producing work in subgenres associated with crime fiction: Donald Westlake becomes Tucker Coe as well as Richard Stark (the surname King borrowed in *The Dark Half*); Evan Hunter assumes the name Ed McBain; and Gore Vidal chooses Edgar Box. In other words, King justifies his Bachman moment by referencing popular writers who published under an assumed name *for the very deliberate purpose of delving into the genre of crime fiction*. The Vidal example remains especially instructive insofar as Vidal, unlike King, did not become Edgar Box to explore his darker side, nor to excavate what is too repugnant for his mainstream persona—indeed, Vidal published far more graphic material in his non-pulpy prose, like *Myra Breckenridge*. Similar to Vidal, King sought an excuse to shift gears into an alternative genre. In addition to elements of stylistic flare, King wanted to explore a defining characteristic of noir: namely, its emphasis on the question of tragic fate in a modern context. While many narratives written under King's name have tried "to make sense" of various issues—for example, the impact of history on the present (*Apt Pupil* and *Pet Sematary*), the struggle associated with ordinary men who are called upon to perform in extraordinary circumstances (*Shawshank* and *The Dead Zone*), or the dangers of overzealous governmental agencies (*The Stand* and *The Mist*)—the noir face of Bachman afforded King an unusual opportunity to speculate alongside other authors within an established tradition. He was able to test the degree to which his success as a writer was based more on popularity or talent, whether "it's all a lottery," even at the expense of straying into a fictional register that might prove too *bleak* for his Constant Readers, one that suggests, on a noir register, that life is "all—or even mostly—an accident" ("Why" viii).

King was one of countless disaffected youths who experienced the shift from the heady days of the 1960s to the stagnant melancholy of the 1970s, and Bachman was one of the vessels through which King opted to channel his own acute disaffection. Although Bachman also drew on the iconography of the horror novel, King's readers might wonder why Bachman didn't primarily write in the horror tradition, King's unquestionable bread and butter. In generic terms, the subject material that Bachman wrote about may have included an existential abyss (Gothic), yet these novels simultaneously interrogate the ways in which dissatisfied individuals come to terms with their own disaffection. The genre that better suited Bachman's purposes was crime fiction. In American crime fiction, especially the *roman noir* and film noir, a frustrated protagonist must confront a widespread evil or corruption before recognizing that his polluted society is never going to change—and, consequently, he must be the one to change. Whereas King's later heroes tend to emerge triumphant, Bachman's hard-boiled antiheroes eventually resign themselves to an unspectacular death in an imperfect world. In the Bachman books, unlike so much of King's non-Bachman fare published in the 1980s and '90s, the struggle never truly resolves itself.

Bachman's hard-boiled protagonists are flawed, like the gangster or the world-weary private investigator, and certainly one way of identifying their flaw is that they, like the George Stark pseudonym and his Alexis Machine main character in *The Dark Half*, all maintain one foot in the realm of criminality. Bachman's protagonists are exceedingly witty, without a doubt, but unlike most of King's fictional characters, there is a dark cynicism to their sense of humor that is a consequence of their awareness of the absurd. A Bachman character's wit is not an effortless substitution for wisdom—in fact, these fast-talking fellows follow in the footsteps of the hard-boiled gumshoe by using their wit to help them get by. Many of King's post-Bachman heroes begin their novels already fully formed; they change very little over the course of their narrative journeys (think, for example, of Stu Redman, Dolores Claiborne, or Roland Deschain). Bachman's antiheroes, however, cannot avoid confronting their own deficiencies; indeed, their deficiencies become the defining hallmarks of their personalities. Because of the generic terms and conditions of crime fiction, they must come to terms with the utter dissatisfaction at the core of their constitution.

Of all the Bachman novels, *Roadwork* is the most representative, in terms of style as well as substance, of the American crime novel. *Roadwork* recounts the misadventures of Barton Dawes, a long-time company man who becomes, following the death of his only son, deeply alienated as the city plans to demolish his house to erect an unnecessary extension for the highway. Dawes closely resembles Walter Huff, the creation of James M. Cain: an insurance claims investigator driven to extremes by the inhumane logic of modernity. "You spend fifteen years in the business I'm in," Huff tells the reader, "Maybe you'll go nuts yourself" (*Double* 124). Bachman's Dawes lives on Crestallen Street—one letter away from "crestfallen"—and he spends most of the novel struggling mightily to defend his modest home with its myriad personal memories of a happier time with his now-deceased son. He loses his job, his wife leaves him, and he begins to waver at the imaginary border between correct conduct and criminality. By the end of the book, Dawes has blown up his abode, though not before leaving an important message to the world: modernity is corrosive, he tells a local newsman, and while the fight may be in vain, a man must push back wherever and whenever he can. Raymond Chandler famously writes of the hard-boiled hero: "Down these mean streets a man must go who is not himself mean, who is neither tarnished nor afraid. The detective in this kind of story must be such a man. He is the hero; he is everything. He must be a complete man and a common man and yet an unusual man. He must be, to use a rather weathered phrase, a man of honor" (*Simple* 18). Dawes utters a bitter cry against the onrush of progress at any cost. It is a melancholy lament for a version of the past that once existed—if not in reality, then at least in Dawes's imagination. He yearns for the receding world of familial permanence, secure suburban neighborhoods, American nobility abroad, and complacent bourgeois values and loyalties. It would not be too far a stretch to read Dawes's subjective nostalgia as a desire to return to a sentimentalized version of the American 1950s, the era of King's own childhood—a decade that stands in contrast to the version of America in deep transition that followed King to college in the mid-1960s. The 1950s was an era before the fall of the American empire, a time that paralleled Dawes's own idealized past when he possessed a greater level of civic and personal coherence than he does now. It is worth noting that King routinely sets his fiction—*The Body, IT, Christine, 11/22/63*, for example—in the 1950s to highlight these exact contrasts. Just as most American crime fiction pines for a premodern America, King employs Bachman as a tool to lament the loss of an immutable past, at the same time as he permits himself a corresponding opportunity to strike out violently against the various symbols that dominate a dismal present. Like the hard-boiled detective, Bachman screams for things irrevocably lost. When he eventually abandons the Bachman game, King may not have silenced his own screams, but they certainly became less primal. They would never again strike the same resonant chord of despair.

Although Dawes is not a detective, and the events of *Roadwork* are not identical to the events of a typical hard-boiled tale, some significant similarities warrant investigation. Bachman's fictional universe offers a noir-infused journey into King's multiverse. Since noir is more of a style than a proper genre, our analysis ought to begin with a survey of the stylistic trappings on display in *Roadwork*. Dawes's dialogue snaps and crackles with the rhetorical flourishes of the quick-witted hard-boiled detective; his effortless patter echoes the sort of gamesmanship exchanged by formulaic mainstay Humphrey Bogart and his brethren, at the same time romantic and resistant. In Part One, Dawes comes armed with street slang and clever quips whenever he banters with the young rube, Vinnie. Later, Dawes's boss informs him, "'You're going to have to do some fast talking if you want to save your job'" (99); Dawes readily obliges, entering a flow of improvisational deception that marks him as a master rhetorician, perhaps the most important skill required of any hard-boiled hero. Like his generic ancestors, Dawes dives into the thrusts and parries of verbal jousting matches, even when he doesn't "know what his idea was" (159). In his noir world, every man must be a salesman, capable of wheeling and dealing to gain the upper hand. "I could con you for the next ten years," Dawes thinks to himself at one point (50). If the slipperiness of language is a defining trait of hard-boiled fiction, *Roadwork* exemplifies this type of rhetorical flourish.

And it isn't just the characters who enter curt dialogue with each other: Bachman's third-person omniscient narrative voice mirrors Dawes's verbal strategies. This stylistic profile extends beyond the Bachman books: once readers recognize Bachman as a bridge between crime fiction and King's larger oeuvre, Bachman's grimy fingerprints become noticeable throughout King's canon. A glaring example of their stylistic overlap is Bachman's extensive use of what can be called the *hard-boiled simile*. Perfected by Chandler, the hard-boiled simile suggests a miswiring—a juxtaposition of two seemingly unrelated objects or ideas. Once more, language and experience do not quite align in the world of noir, as slick words signify something that is untrustworthy. Chandler once described "spring rustling in the air, like a paper bag blowing along a concrete sidewalk" (*Farewell* 99), or, in perhaps Chandler's most famous simile of all, detective Philip Marlowe notes, "I felt like an amputated leg" (65). A cursory list of sample similes from *Roadwork* will suffice to show how Chandler's stylized similes infiltrate Bachman's text: the governor's car sparkles "like a chrome-inlaid eight ball in the summer sunshine" (8); ammunition looks "like penny candy" (12); Dawes's mind becomes "unstrung like an amateur's guitar" (39); shoppers are "like clay ducks in a shooting gallery" (121); road workers behave "like little boys playing with trucks" (144); a wrecking ball does its work "like an artisan's hammer shaping a sculpture" (173); a car "shudders" on its springs, "like a dog that had been kicked" (292–93). Beyond generic lineage, Bachman's highly stylized diction reflects a noir insistence that, in modern-day America at least, the surface of things has been radically decoupled from a substratum of meaning.

Recycling the critique of materialism that frequently occurs in the hard-boiled tradition, *Roadwork* aims to expose the superficiality of contemporary American culture. Whatever the cause (Bachman is more inclined to blame the shifting faces of capitalism than the encroaching threat of communism, so he bends toward Chandler's political ideology instead of the more conservative hard-boiled writers such as Mickey Spillane), Dawes heroically refuses to submit himself to the logic of industrial growth and limitless monetary gain. His comments concerning American consumerism again echo Cain's Huff, who acerbically observes that American living rooms include "nothing that any department store wouldn't deliver on one truck"—this overpriced detritus comes "right out of the same can" (Cain, *Double* 106). Dawes defends his home because he values something other than wealth, the gross engine that appears to drive everyone else, including his soon-to-be ex-wife. When Dawes rebuffs attempts to purchase his home, he starts to look to America's uncynical eyes a bit unhinged. "I haven't taken their money yet," he reasons, "ergo I must be crazy" (248). Elsewhere, he thinks to himself, "Either the world has gone crazy or I have" (128). The thing that characterizes hard-boiled heroes like Chandler's Philip Marlowe is their primary status as outsiders: their pride that marks them as alien to mainstream values and priorities. More specifically, it is their enduring indifference to their material status that identifies these individuals as heroic in the first place. Whereas most Americans seem lost in a maze of mindless consumerism fueled by credit—a longing to emulate empty-headed celebrity copycats, a yearning for artificial needs stimulated by a barrage of constant advertising, and the existence of bourgeois identities tied up with the ownership of luxury goods—hard-boiled heroes avoid these base temptations in the pursuit of ideals that have come to seem un-American at best, crazy at worst.

At the same time, the hard-boiled holdout can be classified as equal parts radical and conservative, progressive and nostalgic. Dawes laments the steady invasion of modernity by gesturing at a "better era" in which small businesses devoted themselves to loyal workers and the nuclear family reigned supreme. Like Cain's Huff, he resents the new business ethos, which has robbed him of a larger purpose. On his early career, Dawes bemoans, "They were fucking *great* days" (69; emphasis in the original). He goes on to remark, "I'll just scream now, I think. For lost things" (74). What is at stake in this gap between a consumer mindset and the kind of antiquated chivalry embodied in the likes of Barton Dawes? Dawes goes to visit his boss in a scene that closely mirrors all-too-familiar scenes from the hard-boiled novel: the boss's house, set back from the main drive, looks as if it should have a California kidney-shaped pool; the boss comes to the door in his cord jacket "with patched elbows and burgundy slippers" (45); and the disgusted hero outwits his wealthy, and not so secretly villainous, host, thereby exposing the audience to the vapidity of the criminal one-percenters. More significantly still, Bachman's *Roadwork* underscores the essential materialism of the American Dream, with its surfeit of petty pleasures, by contrasting it with the life of an honorable loner who remains defiantly unfulfilled. The hard-boiled hero invariably stakes his ground in an unremarkable corner of the city, in a shabby office surrounded by squalor. Dawes too remains driven by "lost things," and so he plants his feet stubbornly in his eminently quotidian ranch house. He consequently moves much closer to "the truth" of the matter than the individuals who orbit around him, blissfully unaware that none of these material goods will deliver on their promise of happiness.

To illustrate modernity as a disease, Bachman's novels confront cancer as both a serious epidemic and a cultural metaphor. The Bachman novels are riddled with characters suffering from various stages of cancer and cancer-haunted subplots. This metaphorical disease haunts the landscape of *Roadwork*: Dawes's child dies of the disease, and it also takes a friend of his mother-in-law (King would repeatedly return to cancer as a metaphor in many of the texts written under his given name; for instance, he nearly used the disease as the name of a novel that eventually became *Dreamcatcher*). The child's illness is a vicious illustration of nature's cruelty and indifference. At its core, Charlie's inoperable brain tumor underscores the helplessness Dawes feels at the hands of a hostile nature as well as modern society's mad rush into the future. The personal loss of his son—through a disease that is largely beyond human control—becomes the filter through which Dawes interprets the recent events of history and the changes in his larger society: "That collection of bad cells, no bigger than a walnut, had grown down deep inside and was growing larger every day. . . . Today a walnut, tomorrow the world. The creeping unknown. The incredible dying son. What has there to understand?" (464–65). Susan Sontag argues that cancer is the most modern of illnesses; it serves as a metaphor for our times and our society's quest for material abundance and out-of-control accumulation.[6] Its presence in modern life reflects the Western desire for instant gratification, a willingness to pollute and degrade the natural environment in exchange for chemical materialism and cheap and abundant foodstuffs shot with antibiotics. It is the shadow attendant to the affluence Americans cherish and continue to pursue. In *Roadwork*, progress and cancer are inexorably linked: one cancer has killed Dawes's son; another is destroying his home and nation. Both appear as inevitable conditions, inoperable realities that are foisted upon Dawes even as he refuses to accept them. Like the hard-boiled detective, Dawes remains painfully cognizant of the illnesses that surround him, both as a metaphor for his times and the literal by-product of a culture addicted to the mania of owning things.

Yet to depict *Roadwork* in this fashion may leave a false impression in the reader that Bachman depended upon noir tropes as only a subtext, as the stuff of ambitious conjecture. In fact, the novel foregrounds its relationship to crime fiction, thus rendering this connection to be of the utmost importance. Bachman channels crime fiction with his numerous references to the gangster film. For example, Dawes cites *The Godfather* as one of his favorite films; but illustrating the range that embraces the term "crime fiction," Bachman also gestures at thrillers like *Dial M for Murder*, the emergence of the police procedural on television, and even earlier permutations of the genre: "It was like stepping into the last chapter of an Ellery Queen mystery" (174). Crime fiction orients *Roadwork* at a foundational level. At one point, Dawes lies in saying, "'I don't watch cop shows'" (85). However, Bachman's reader knows better—cop shows are ostensibly the *only* thing that Dawes consumes. Bachman's antihero spends a good deal of the text defining his own actions in distinctively generic terms, which is to say, he relies upon formulaic patterns to comprehend his motivations. He stands at arm's length from the laced-up police procedural when, in the beginning of the novel, Dawes laughs at an interview with television star Lorne

Greene in which Greene is being asked about his latest cop show. Greene wears a shocking silver wig, and Dawes chuckles at the idea of snatching it from his bald head. In multiple moments, Dawes moves to distance himself from the police procedural: a buttoned-up typology that remains too close to the state apparatus for his comfort. Similarly, Dawes bristles at the notion of being bundled together with the archetypal cowboy (the journalist misreads Dawes in precisely these terms when, upon Barton's death, he labels the event "Dawes's Last Stand"). The archetypal cowboy strikes Dawes as entirely too good. When he sees a western on television, he observes that the star, David Janssen, best known for playing the lead role in the television series *The Fugitive* (1963–67), among other hard-boiled heroes, "made a shitty cowboy" (176). Pushing himself away from the police procedural and the western, Dawes prefers his own narrative to be read in a different generic register.

Dawes identifies with the protagonists of crime fiction in related but distinctive veins—as noble misfits that straddle the line between the police and criminality, like the gangster or the hard-boiled detective, Dawes turns to a Vegas gangster named Sal Magliore to procure the explosives to blow up his home, taking control over his own self-destruction and depriving city renovators of the pleasure. In these exchanges, it becomes clear that Dawes is drawn to the gangster story: a narrative formula that centers around so-called criminals that uphold their own version of a moral code in the face of a society that has long abandoned any semblance of ethics. Emulating his mentor Magliore, Dawes increasingly operates in the seedy underbelly of his community, but in so doing, he, like Magliore, clings to a certain code of conduct, which is much more than can be said of the novel's well-apportioned members of the consumer class: "In his mind's eye he saw [Magliore] and himself eating linguini in a small Italian *ristorante* with dark-toned walls and scarred wooden tables while the strains of *The Godfather* played on the soundtrack" (225).[7] Magliore recalls that other "cheap hood" from the Bachman books, Ginelli of *Thinner*. These caricatures of Italian mobsters expose the latent brutality of innocent suburban men. At least part of the identification between Dawes and Magliore can be attributed to King's long-standing affinity for postmodern tropes, visible already in the earliest works of Bachman; one must read Dawes's gangster posture as being symptomatic of his own conditioning by his hypermediated age. As much as he outwardly resists a world that orbits around the broadcast values of television, Dawes has obviously been channel surfing because his entire personality relies on references to generic storylines. In the final shootout with the police at his home, for example, he frames the encounter as if it is lifted directly from a gangster film, "the last reel of a Jimmy Cagney movie" (295). Even at the height of his emotional arc, Bachman's protagonist recycles canned dialogue from crime fiction. Dawes's generic framing devices underscore Bachman's commitment to generic storylines.

What links the conventional gangster story to the hard-boiled detective tale is primarily their shared insistence upon a respective moral code unique to themselves: a code so uncommon in early 1980s America that it resides only in the shadows—the jurisdiction of King noir. Like the gangster, the private investigator straddles a line between the upstanding (although criminal) realm and its criminal (yet upstanding) counterpoint. Dawes flirts with the darker half of his society because he recognizes that virtue is no longer available in mainstream American culture; in response, he maintains a strong—if highly subjective—ethical code. To quote Magliore, "'It ain't a matter of money. It's a matter of principle'" (255). Dawes not only forfeits the opportunity to strike it rich; he also refuses to press his advantage with an innocent young woman (more on this issue later), and he refrains from killing any police officers during his climactic shootout. Living a monastic lifestyle, the hard-boiled hero reclaims the romantic promise of chivalry for an age that has long abandoned the ways of the knight. At one point, Dawes watches a private investigator (P.I.) get hit over the head by a thug on television; still, despite the odds against the P.I., Dawes "thought that the private cop had [the thug's] number" (117). Dawes repeatedly proves himself akin to modern knights of noir. Magliore asks, "'You must be Effa Bee Eye or a private detective. Which is it?'" To which Dawes responds, "'I'm not a cop . . . I'm not a crook, either'" (84).[8] In his ostensibly evasive response, Dawes provides a relatively direct answer: according to Magliore's formulation, Dawes aligns himself with the fabled private detective. After all, private detectives are neither cops nor crooks. Hard-boiled heroes like Dawes walk a thin line between old-school ethics and a latent bond with the criminal.

Crime fiction stresses the ambivalence at the heart of modern America. On the one hand, Dawes lacks a noble design; he has lost the faith, and not only is his rebellion self-serving, but it is also ultimately suicidal. In the final defense of his home, the last enclave in a world that has lost sight of moral values and respect for the individual, Dawes emerges as a kind of ironic patriot facing his last stand: defending forsaken American principles and asserting himself in the fundamental defense of private property. It is ironic because Dawes's demolition of his house and self essentially completes the work of the state; his psychological destruction parallels the state's commitment to the demolition of his house. Nevertheless, his final act of defiance—although merely a gesture—is the last act of the free individual. It is in his suicide that Dawes exercises a modicum of control over a destiny that has thwarted his autonomy since the advent of his son's terminal illness. Despite an overwhelming sense of fatalism, the hard-boiled hero soldiers onward.

"I do it this way because it's the only way," a stranger tells Dawes. "I'm locked in" (273). Film noir foregrounds the fatalistic character of crime fiction in its various permutations. In the 1947 noir film *Out of the Past*, a nearly defeated character asks, "Is there any way to win?" The protagonist replies, "There's a way to lose more slowly." Film noir thus returns to the timeless theme of fate: how can a person "win" in a game that has been so glaringly rigged against her? In Freudian terms, on which noir as well as Bachman so heavily relies, the Oedipal scene serves as a sort of master narrative. Even though the character's (and society's) doom has been spelled out from the beginning, audiences watch as the character struggles "to lose more slowly." The hard-boiled Dawes must face down his own "doomed fatality" (Naremore 45). It is no longer about saving society; such a grand purpose is the stuff of a faded past. When Dawes manages to set ablaze some of the roadwork equipment, the government declares that it has been set back perhaps a month or so. Thoroughly deflated, Bachman's modern knight confronts "the invulnerability of systems everywhere" (112). In noir, "the standard picture is of people 'trapped,'" writes Robert Pippin, "by a vast purposeless play of uncontrollable fortune" (11). Barton Dawes's name, with its emphasis on property and home, spells out the inevitability of his undoing: etymologically, "Barton" signifies land that has been reserved for a lord's use. "Dawes" may be a reference to the (in)famous Dawes Act, in which the US government regulated the use of lands held by Indigenous tribes. When at last Dawes appears to have triumphed over his oppressors, and his story of struggle has been broadcast to the public, Bachman's noir sensibilities rise once more to the surface: "The new track is just like the old track." "Meet the new boss," the British rock band The Who once proclaimed, "same as the old boss." Dawes appears condemned to walk the path fate has given him, no matter how much he resists. In the noir tradition, if the individual can snatch victory from the yawning jaws of cosmic defeat, it is only by cultivating a moral position against the ever-pressing expansion of evil. Bachman's Dawes will not succumb to the materialistic, hedonistic hellscape that is all around him. Although he knows that "something evil

[has] tainted everything," the tentacles of evil have somehow not yet claimed him (268). Dawes "loses," of course, but not before proving his mettle and perhaps setting the stage for a brighter future by relaying his prophetic tale to Bachman's audience. Again, King maximizes the value of his chosen character names: "Dawes" also means "son of David"—David, that imperfect monarch who nonetheless overcame the odds to defeat Goliath; David, that enduring deliverer of prophetic words. A fatalistic lineage, yes, but not a lineage without a kernel of dignity or hope.

Still, King's Constant Reader finds in *Roadwork* the seeds of Bachman's undoing, the first shovelful of dirt to be thrown down upon his metaphorical coffin. The (mis)handling of the *femme fatale* in *Roadwork*—if, in fact, we can use these terms to describe her—indicates *a generic dead-end*. Intimately tied to the fatalism of noir, the *femme fatale* typically entices the hard-boiled hero only to be rebuffed and, on some occasions, destroyed. She is the embodiment of the craven materialism that threatens to swallow the protagonist whole. Dawes meets the wayward Olivia as a hitchhiker and a would-be *femme fatale* whose raw sexuality reawakens the moribund middle-aged man. Olivia's presence is the last challenge for the monastic modern knight. Ultimately, the relationship between Dawes and Olivia does not map easily onto convention, since Dawes strikes the reader as more paternal than libidinal. Olivia is not for Dawes what the widow Phyllis Nirdlinger is for Huff in *Double Indemnity*: unlike Phyllis, Olivia does not tempt Dawes into the ultimate transgression (murder), and she is more associated with life-giving energy than with an unsavory link to death. Olivia's presence underscores the figurative impotence of the hard-boiled hero—a connection that could push the reader to double down on the fatalistic impulses of the novel. However, Dawes proves to be neither impotent nor all that chivalrous. By resisting modern temptation *and* being revived by a hypersexualized young woman, can Dawes have his cake and eat it too? Can Bachman operate both inside and outside the generic confines of crime fiction?

Like the rest of his society, Dawes caves to his carnal impulses in his quest for a balm to sooth the ailments of modernity. Simply put, even in his Bachman guise, King is willing to push the moment to its climax, to take the tensions felt by a dissatisfied protagonist and "solve" his feelings of incompleteness through gratuitous indulgences: drugs, sex, and generalized good feelings. He eventually escapes from this mortal coil with an epic (and eroticized) explosion. As we have seen, Dawes's ambivalence mirrors the ambivalence of the private detective, who compensates with his slick patter in place of the existential drift of modernity that threatens to leave him in its wake. We call to mind Huff, staring into the boat's wake at the close of *Double Indemnity*, contemplating his own self-destruction. Yet King's *Roadwork* pulls away from the brink and drifts into surplus and sensationalized portrayals of consummation. Noir defines itself by the *opposite* of this sensationalized surplus, in the form of self-masochism, flagellation, and a monastic moralism. Unfulfilled desires shine against the backdrop of an exorbitant material realm. In contrast, King allows his hero (and his reader) to achieve release, that is, to achieve something like a climactic resolution. Even when King is writing as Bachman, then, his characters find satisfaction within their dissatisfaction, and so King noir is never quite as noir as it initially seems to be.

BURYING BACHMAN

King was eventually forced to bury Bachman—symbolically, in *The Dark Half*'s effort to confront and rebury this "Not a Very Nice Guy" with his "rainy-day" perspective (25), and, literally, after the Bachman pseudonym was revealed to the reading public. But another part of what King buried in disposing of Bachman is his overt indebtedness to crime fiction, especially in its shadowy, fatalistic forms. Eliminating Bachman brought King "back toward the light," providing him with other fictional opportunities such as the last-minute rescue of Wendy and Danny in *The Shining* or Red and Andy's hope of a glorious reunion in Zihuantanejo at the terminus of *Rita Hayworth and Shawshank Redemption*. The future according to Bachman is devoid of love, stable relationships, and any kind of sociopolitical freedom; it is a world that in many ways stands in contrast to the optimistic core of King's corpus. The pseudo-noir energies of Bachman's gangsters and hyperbolic criminals find their counterbalance in the humble affirmation of *The Shining*'s Dick Hallorann, the Losers' Club of *IT*, and Bill Hodges in *Mr. Mercedes*, each of whom is committed to sustaining the values of human life and love. One might take this opportunity to conjecture why King chose to repress Bachman, going so far as to postulate that the author might have been better off letting Bachman live. In the end, how much more engaging is it to read about George Stark's half-mad exploits compared to his thoroughly bourgeois alter ego, Thad Beaumont—the latter a good, albeit rather dull, husband and father? If *The Dark Half* is meant to be a metaphorical indication of how strong Bachman's pull presented itself on his inventor, then we might well read Richard Bachman in terms of an addiction. While the Bachman books are certainly less polished than the rest of King's canon, their roughness, or grittiness, seems somehow more real, more *authentic* when examined in light of the crucible of the 1970s and '80s when King forged his career as a writer. Bachman helped King push his writing to the extreme by conjuring the poetry of fear in books (both authored under Bachman as well as those belonging exclusively to King) that are every bit as terrifying as they are genuine. Without Bachman, King's poetry of fear would be a good deal less potent.

Of course, it could also be said that the Bachman experiment succeeds because it adheres to the sort of ideological work that defined so much of hard-boiled fiction, especially in its constructions of a (supposedly) virile masculinity. Bachman may appeal to some readers because he extends the "cultural fantasy of the 'realness' of hard-boiled masculinity," and, as such, his books succeed in "eliding [their] very status as fantasy" (Breu 11). In other words, when Bachman insists that his reader confront a grittier reality beneath the artifice of modern life, he effectively masks his own complicity in reinforcing America's most toxic fantasies: a vision of tough-guy masculinity that pretends to be "real" against the superficiality of everything else. As Bachman, King participates in a long-standing literary battle in America over who has access to "the real." Critics must not ignore the cultural impact of these claims.

Bachman's melancholy musings are thus too much like crime fiction (in their affirmation of unpalatable cultural norms) and not enough like crime fiction (in their unwillingness to embrace fully the dissatisfaction of, say, the *roman noir*). Nonetheless, King's Constant Readers might continue to eulogize Bachman because he kept alive a set of noir principles that energized King's prose and gave it a political, ethical, and philosophical bite that arguably dulled in Bachman's wake. On a parallel track, King's many efforts to downplay or dismiss the importance of Bachman's voice speak to an America that would go on to undervalue its affection for crime fiction in the 1980s and '90s (those twin decades of consumerism run amuck with rampant consumerism, decadence, and denial). Bachman's fingerprints can be lifted from every corner of King's canon; his impact is felt in every subsequent King plot or character that can be linked to crime fiction as well as a broader noir sensibility. At the close of the day, Barton Dawes of *Roadwork* embodies Bachman's emphasis on fatalism as well as prophecy. He, like Bachman himself, represents the necessary dark half of Stephen King.

Chapter 5

THE OPEN-AND-SHUT CASES OF *MR. MERCEDES* AND *HOLLY*

THE 2014 NOVEL *MR. MERCEDES* WAS BILLED (ALBEIT INCORRECTLY) BY its author as well as his critics as his first hard-boiled book. As a bestseller and the source material for a successful limited television series, the novel remains perhaps the most successful offering to date from the crime side of Stephen King. The novel provides fertile ground for exploring the noir aspects of post-9/11 America: its seedy underbelly, rampant corruption, and chivalric posturing on the global stage. We begin by surveying how King returns to certain hard-boiled themes and tropes to reflect the liminal space between criminality and heroism in the contemporary United States. Yet the crime fiction of Stephen King concurrently engages in a thorough metacommentary upon the strictures of this particular genre. This chapter will attend to the ways in which King employs these themes and tropes—and, in the process, how he once more uses what he calls the portable magic of writing to thwart the cynicism of his age. In the final tally, it is King's *rejection* of cynicism, alongside the novel's appetite for intuition over deductive reasoning as well as for an illusion of full transparency, that ultimately undermines the hard-boiled premise of *Mr. Mercedes*.

Let us start, though, in the shadows. Throughout the present study, we have continually referenced the affinities shared by the criminal and detective, both in King's work and in the commingling of the horror and detective genres. Bill Hodges and Brady Hartsfield would appear on the surface to be oppositional figures—*Mr. Mercedes*'s protagonist and antagonist, respectively—the forty-year veteran detective who finds it difficult to function since retiring from his profession, and the narcissistic loner who seeks to destroy whatever social fabric Hodges has spent his adult life trying to sustain. When the novel commences, however, Hodges bears more in common with Hartsfield than he does with the former detective he has left behind. They are both trapped in a *Weltanschauung* that closely resembles what we find in the universe of King's deceased pseudonym Richard Bachman (see chapter 3). Hartsfield finds nothing of value in his job, his community, America, or himself. What motivates Hartsfield's nihilism is a complicated admixture of childhood psychosexual trauma, social alienation, and an urge for revenge to "cut the skin of the world," along with a superiority complex fed by his desire to transform into a Nietzschean *Übermensch*: a unique being who exists beyond the sophomoric morality of the masses (28). Of all psychopathic demigods that populate the King multiverse, Brady Hartsfield is perhaps the most volatile because he exhibits traits of a white supremacist as well as being a nihilist committed to killing as many people as he can in making his final statement:

> Off you go into the universal null set that surrounds one lonely blue planet and all its mindlessly bustling denizens. Every religion lies. Every moral precept is a delusion. Even the stars are a mirage. The truth is darkness, and the only thing that matters is making a statement before one enters it. Cutting the skin of the world and leaving a scar. That's all history is, after all: scar tissue. (391)

Early in the novel, when King introduces readers to Hodges's relationship to Jerome Robinson, his young African American neighbor and friend, the writer informs readers that "Hodges believes friendship is overrated, and in this way, if in no other, he is like Brady Hartsfield" (114). However, the retired detective shares plenty more with Hartsfield than just a general skepticism about friendship. Hodges looks at his life as it has narrowed through post-retirement into watching insipid afternoon television and discovers a vision of America and the world not far removed from Hartsfield's own conception of it. Their mutual pessimism is born from lives of questionable choices, resentment, and loss of meaning. Hartsfield targets the unemployed and working-class poor in his mass murder at the City Center job fair. His victims represent the dregs of society who are, in his estimation, undeserving of their bare lives: "He imagines all the kids on the West Side dropping their packs and their precious cell phones while the blood poured from every orifice" (103). The members of the underclass that Hartsfield mocks and victimizes could easily be protagonists out of the Bachman novels. In Bachman texts such as *The Long Walk* and *The Running Man*, poverty has reached such a level of desperation that young people are willing to engage in life-and-death athletic contests where the odds are stacked severely against them, but competing in these deadly events becomes their only option to the promise of food and money. Moreover, the level of class antagonism, perhaps only slightly less desperate than in the Bachman books, also finds its way into Hodges's television programs; the banal individuals who wallow in choreographed sexual confessionals and petty jealousies on the afternoon talk shows he watches serve as a mirror into Hodges's own recent isolation and purposelessness: "Hodges eats this diet of full-color shit every weekday afternoon, sitting in the La-Z-Boy with his father's gun . . . He always picks it up a few times and looks into the barrel. Inspecting that round of darkness. On a couple of occasions he has slid it between his lips" (22). Even Jerome at first appears to have deserted him in neglecting to mow his lawn.

Recapturing the atmosphere of the Bachman books, King's American portrait in the first few chapters of *Mr. Mercedes* is without redeeming qualities: because he has entered a vacuum on weekday afternoons in contrast to his years spent engaged in intense detective work, Hodges now confronts in retirement a society and a self that appear to be, at least initially, beyond rescue. Both society and self turn out to be as depressed and depraved as Brady Hartsfield envisions. But while Hartsfield is lost in his narcissistic nihilism, Hodges's retirement has not yet pushed him into a similar state of despair. The televised images of America may reflect his own suicidal emptiness, but Hodges is still capable of recognizing the differences that separate him from both Hartsfield and the afternoon vacuity televised on Channel Seven. Instead of the suicide Hartsfield recommends in his derisive letter to the ex-cop, Hartsfield's mocking hubris pulls Hodges away from the edge and back into operational mode. The letter—a condescending reminder of the fact that the criminal has so far thwarted capture and gotten away with his crimes—reawakens the dormant detective: "Hodges wonders what he [Hartsfield] would think if he knew he had given this particular 'ex-Knight of the Badge and Gun' a reason to live, instead. At least for awhile" (37).

As part of the evolution signaling the detective's re-emergence into life, Hodges finds sex and romance with Janey Patterson, who revivifies Hodges's libido at the same time as her violent death, which was meant for Hodges himself, supplies the detective with further motivation to track down Hartsfield. On the two occasions when they have sex, Hodges is so stunned by his good fortune that he can barely function; embarrassed by both his age and weight, he becomes a passive participant following Janey's commands: "Stay still, I said. Next time you can move all you want, but this is mine. I deserve it" (224). Her complicated positioning in this hard-boiled detective novel forces audiences to question: does Janey serve in the role of the requisite *femme fatale*? Hodges dismisses as "ridiculous" the thought of her as representative of the genre's "tough-talking blonde" (142), just as he finds it awkward wearing the fedora she gifts him. Yet it is clear that Janey enjoys playing the role of the seductive blonde who hires the detective and experiences vicariously through him the hunt for the criminal. Much of the complication that Hodges experiences is that Janey and Brady Hartsfield come to interface within Hodges's psyche. Years of police work have taught Hodges to recognize that part of Hartsfield's problem is psychosexual in nature. As he explains to Janey, "'Look closely and you'd probably find sexual confusion and upbringing were major players'" contributing to Hartsfield's emerging psychopathology (231). It is curious that Hodges also warns her "not to get lost in stuff like that. It's not profiling, it's analysis" (232). The detective's own exploration of Hartsfield's illness suggests, however, that it is the criminal, far more than Janey, who preoccupies Hodges's concentration. The woman's role in *Mr. Mercedes* is neither taboo nor engaging enough. As E. Ann Kaplan argues in *Women in Film Noir*, "The postmodern *fatale* utilizes sex to deliver death"; Janey only conforms to the *femme fatale* paradigm, then, to the degree that her "dangerous sexuality is the explicit cause of several deaths" (172). Ironically, it is Hartsfield even more than Janey's eros that brings Hodges back to life, enticing him with a revivifying life force in every way other than through physical sexual contact. Janey's dying allows Hodges to make his relationship with Hartsfield exclusive, and vengeful.

    The phallic symbol of Hodges's gun, in other words, goes from being inserted in his own mouth to turning outward once again, toward the bad guy. The stylistic confusion that Hartsfield exhibits in confusing "perk" with "perp" in his first letter to the detective underscores the level of Hodges's involvement, as the retired cop is "perked" back to life because of the audacious criminality of his "perp." This confusion reveals the perversity of the detective's task: for a detective like Hodges, the perp *is* the perk—that is, Brady Hartsfield is the real perk of the detective's job, since he is precisely what gives Hodges pleasure and brings his existence renewed purpose (arguably even more than Janey's sexuality does). Brian Kent sums up the cat-and-mouse game the mass murderer establishes with the retired detective in terms of their mutual obsession with watching and surveilling one another—via constant Internet tracking as well as optically—especially important to recognize because in the novel they never actually meet face-to-face. Their contact occurs exclusively from a distance and thereby is allowed to blur into the realm of unconscious urge and visual fetishism: "King's trilogy and Kelly's [television series] production explore through the two men the relationship between the compulsion to *watch* and the impulses of the unconscious, or the relentless demands of the id" (Kent 122). As he has so often done throughout his career, in *Mr. Mercedes* King meditates once more about the psychoanalytical underpinnings of crime fiction, especially on questions of perversity and desire.

King crafts a milieu that borrows much from the world of the hard-boiled sleuths. Like the alleyways of a noir Southern California, Lowtown is the place where both Brady Hartsfield and his unemployed victims reside. At first glance, *Mr. Mercedes* may not appear to bear strong similarities to the fiercely urban and industrial locales typical of the hard-boiled detective genre. Yet, set in an unnamed rust belt city in the Midwest, possibly Cleveland or Detroit, much of the plot's major action occurs not in the neat Harper Road suburb where Hodges and Jerome Robinson live nor in the upscale microcosm of Olivia Trelawney's Sugar Heights "twenty-room McMansion" (71). Hartsfield stole the titular vehicle from Trelawney, and her secret relationship to Hartsfield drives much of the plot. In contrast to both these locales, Hartsfield lives "on the city's North Side." The house he inhabits with his alcoholic mother was "built between Korea and Vietnam, which means they all look the same and they're all turning to shit" (111–12). Borrowing heavily from the environments of the earlier Bachman novels and riffing on the industrial wastelands of traditional crime fiction, *Mr. Mercedes* remains sharply bifurcated between two socioeconomic spheres. In turn, Hodges and Hartsfield, for uniquely different reasons, share much with the underclass poor massacred at the City Center in the book's startling opening chapter. Hodges chooses to meet his former partner Pete in a favorite restaurant, DeMasio's, located in the bowels of Lowtown; as the name implies, it is in the lowest part of the city, a place that every hard-boiled cop knows all too well: "He knows that if he walked under [the overpass], he would smell the sour reek of cheap wine and whiskey. His feet would grate on the shards of broken bottles" (58–59). Like Poe's C. Auguste Dupin, Hodges frequently represents the triumph of sense over urban chaos: a sometimes-successful effort to exert control over the city's dark labyrinth.

Reflective of the hard-boiled tradition, Hodges knows better than to seek to change society; his wish is only to patch it up and persist. The four teenage boys Hodges encounters in Lowtown after his lunch with Pete are a reminder to the reader—and perhaps to Hodges himself—of Hartsfield's earlier attack at the City Center. Three older boys bully, threaten, and attempt to rob a younger child. Just as Hartsfield seeks to impose his violent will over those weaker than himself—first through the murder of those who are unemployed at the job fair and later in his plan to murder an audience of teenage girls attending a rock concert—Hodges understands intuitively that it is his role to intervene to stop such acts of unreasonable cruelty. In this case, he notices the unfairness of the three bullies threatening a lone boy. "'Three-on-one pisses me off,'" the renewed detective insists (92). Hodges's intervention in this scene has less to do with being an ex-cop than it does with his identification with the personal and subjective code of hard-boiled detective chivalry, as Hodges, like Philip Marlowe and his other noir brethren, imposes his own code of justice over the multiple injustices that he encounters. John Paul Athanasourelis describes the gap separating the rugged individualism of the hard-boiled detective from the rusty machinery of the legal system: "Contemptuous, not only of the police but the entire legal system, which he denigrates as 'the tedious process of the law,' he rails against agreed-upon communal standards, underscoring his personal connection to the victim in order to justify his vendetta. The detective himself is someone who must gather within himself not just the law of the jungle but sole, absolute authority" (41–42). In fact, King's ex-detective's aggressive intervention violates civil codes of police behavior even as it affirms his own capacity to commit acts of violence if he feels it justified. Hodges swings the Happy Slapper "at the side of Troll One's neck in a tight, flat arc, careful to steer clear of the Adam's apple; hit a guy there, you were apt to kill him, and then you were stuck in the bureaucracy" (91–92). Expeditious justice that proves so motivating for the hard-boiled detective could not be meted out if "you were stuck in the bureaucracy." Hodges acknowledges to himself, without a hint of embarrassment, "I'm old school" (174). And it is for this reason that, at the end of the novel, Hodges neither wants nor expects a key to the city nor one of the medals presented to Holly and Jerome. His satisfaction occurs because he has done what he knows to be right, in his own fashion (the fact that he arrives at a place of satisfaction also separates him from the traditional hard-boiled sleuth—but more on this point later). Like the noir detective, Hodges ostensibly plays by his own rules. After Hartsfield has murdered Janey in a car bomb explosion meant to kill Hodges, the retired policeman has Jerome send the murderer a cyberspace warning: "I'm no longer going to catch and turn you in to the cops. Why should I?

I'm not a cop anymore. I'm going to kill you" (355). Although it is difficult to imagine Hodges caring much about legal protocol, even when he was a cop, the murder of Janey activates a spirit of vigilante justice that links him directly to those noir detectives, such as Mickey Spillane's Hammer or Raymond Chandler's Marlowe, who have as much (or more) in common with criminals than with other cops. The embodiments of King noir thrive in the murky dredges of Lowtown, where they can operate in a crude state of exception.

The bond that Hodges shares with criminality, a personal shading that reminds us immediately of the connection Poe's Dupin shares with Minister D— (see chapter 3), parallels King's own deeply professed admiration for the fiction by his contemporary fellow horror-crime writer Thomas Harris, whose work confounds easy and conventional notions of genre.[1] Both *The Silence of the Lambs* and *Red Dragon* merge the genres of horror and detection equally and seamlessly, providing audiences with multiple detectives who forge intimate bonds with the psychopaths they pursue. In spite of their unwavering dedication to placing themselves in opposition to the destructive madness of the serial killers they hunt, Harris's detectives—Clarice Starling and Will Graham—are deeply shaken by their close contact with evil. Graham even spends time recovering in an asylum after his encounter with Hannibal Lecter, no doubt the result of acknowledging the latter's repeated insistence that their affinities are so close that the detective must consciously work to repel its implications: "'Do you know how you caught me? The reason you caught me is that we're *just alike*'" (*Red Dragon* 86; emphasis in the original). Indeed, Graham makes himself so valuable an asset to authorities because of his ability to "empathize" with psychopathic murderers. The merging (and blurring) of criminal and detective is one of the many qualities that make Harris's novels so engaging, as in the relationship between Lecter and Clarice Starling. Their association serves to "balance" the young FBI trainee by teaching her as much about criminality and sociopathic propensities as anything she learns from her time at the FBI Academy. Further, the one character in Harris's canon that comes closest to embodying the criminal-detective amalgamation is Lecter himself, the definitive split self in contemporary American fiction: just as the doctor is a gourmand and a cannibal simultaneously, he is a psychopathic murderer at the same time he is a cryptic criminologist willing to play *quid pro quo* games that provide tortured insights for Starling and Graham as they struggle to solve their respective cases. In the end, it is the muddling of oppositional personalities that pulls Harris as well as

King into the realm of noir drama. While a close and thorough reading of the intriguing connections between the fiction of Harris and King is still to be authored, the complex interwoven tissue that connects Harris's criminologists so intimately to the criminals they pursue has undoubtedly shaped King's detectives, most notably Hodges.

    This blurred border between psyches is also reflective of urban capitalism's economic disparities, exemplified by the crowd of unemployed people lined up in a parking lot when their collective desperation leads them to an early morning job fair. Humiliated and wretched, a woman in this crowd admits that she is "a single unmarried mother with no job. I want to apologize to everyone, for everything" (6); in a society that values wealth and security over human dignity, her impoverished status forces a turn inward where she can summon only shame and a personal sense of failure instead of blaming the "belt tightening" that remains a chronic element of capitalist economics (4). Because Hartsfield proves himself to be a sociopath incapable of empathy, he fails to acknowledge a class bond with people such as this struggling woman. Instead, despite their shared economic rank, Hartsfield disassociates himself from his prey. Although the novel does not explore the political implications behind his selection of "the Gray Lady," a Mercedes-Benz owned by a woman of extreme privilege, as his murder weapon, it indicates his not-so-unconscious identification with both class status and Nazism's systematic program of racial and ethnic terror. As he confesses in his first taunting letter to Hodges, "Most people are fitted with Lead Boots when they are just little kids and have to wear them all their lives. These Lead Boots are called A CONSCIENCE. I have none so I can soar high above the heads of the Normal Crowd" (28). At the same time, his selection of a "a two-ton piece of German engineering" (14) highlights the irony associated with his character: like all white supremacists, he has no rational justification for feeling superior to anyone. While the mother in line for a job at the City Center allows her poverty to translate into personal shame, Hartsfield's translates into an unfocused fury either incapable or unwilling to recognize an unfair and oppressive system of wealth distribution. Had Hartsfield come on the scene after 2016, he might well have identified with the MAGA Republicans who found a voice in the politics of Donald Trump. His anger is directed at those more like himself than he is willing concede. The novel is set in the aftermath of the 2008 recession, so King's omniscient voice describes an aging and crippled America: the Deepwater Horizon oil spill continues to pollute the Gulf, home mortgages have put private properties underwater, unemployment is rampant, the stock market has tanked, America's overinvolvement in the Middle East continues to bleed the country's treasury and global reputation, and Hartsfield's only social reference point is as a competitor with other recent mass murderers, such as those at Columbine and Sandy Hook. Simply put, King's sociopolitical context informs his revival of a certain hard-boiled ambivalence.

In the early twenty-first century, horror and crime fiction bled together profusely—as they have always done.[2] Noir serves as a crucial bridge, in form as well as content, between the detective's imposition of order and an all-pervasive monstrosity. During the City Center massacre, Hartsfield wears a mask "very close to the face of Pennywise, the clown in the sewer" (74), which both disguises his identity from the public and serves as an homage to the monster from King's 1986 epic *IT*. Hartsfield and Pennywise have much in common. They are both narcissistic and braggadocious to the degree that they feel entitled to impose their supreme will over others while preying on the most vulnerable in their respective cities—Hartsfield on unemployed and poor people and female teenagers attending a boy-band concert, Pennywise on the children of both genders in Derry. Hartsfield emerges as a shrouded figure of the post 9/11 underground who fits the profile of a lone domestic extremist. At the end of the novel, he even shaves his head and then assumes the role of a disabled man who uses a wheelchair. The attempt to disguise his identity, however, ends up unwittingly disclosing his connection to white nationalists—skinheads— and while his personal nihilistic narcissism may not allow him to identify explicitly with any of their underground organizations, he shares their racist sympathies.[3] Pennywise is of course a supernatural phenomenon while Hartsfield is not, the former a vampire-like figure that attains its greatest pleasure in bleeding Derry, slowly savoring the fear it instills in the town's children. Every twenty-seven years, the clown feeds off the town's progeny to the point at which it has "become a part of Derry . . . only It's not a matter of outward geography, you understand, but now It's inside. Somehow It's gotten inside" (*IT* 503). But in the end, each monster exists as a product of their respective American societies. Both live in the shadow world of the cities they inhabit: Pennywise thrives in the underground sewer system that honeycombs the bowels of the town, representative of the collective subconscious of Derry's past and present, giving vent to the violence the adult world maintains towards its own children; Hartsfield fits many of the current profile points associated with American adolescent male alienation that is fueled by underground (i.e., parental basement) social isolation and the hyperaggressive stimulation of game world technology. Instead of attending college, finding a job that brings him meaning, or dating a woman his own age instead of his mother, Hartsfield spends his time collecting explosives, fantasizing about his next act of mass destruction, and selling ice cream.[4] He owns half a dozen computers, but they only serve to deepen his isolation in the darkest corners of the Internet. His attraction to committing spectacular acts of mass murder fails to mask his own compulsion toward self-annihilation. Like Pennywise, he is a serial mass murderer suffering from social anomie so profound that it propels him toward committing random acts against complete strangers: "*When you gaze into the abyss*, Nietzsche wrote, *the abyss also gazes into you*. I am the abyss, old boy. Me" (53; emphasis in the original). Yet Hartsfield is also a home-grown, particularly American phenomenon insofar as he seeks the fame—that is, infamy—that comes via the celebrity status accorded to serial killers and mass murderers in popular culture. It is worth noting that his obsession with perpetrating mass murder events occurs in the novel's chronology[5] about the same time as the slaughter of the children at Sandy Hook Elementary. His desire to kill the most vulnerable members of his own society—unemployed people and teenage girls at a concert—appears to follow a pattern recurring with frightening frequency among young white American male mass killers. Hartsfield enjoys the publicity he has attained in thwarting the police and mocking their attempts to capture him, and the thought of the violence he has already committed at the City Center and intends to commit again at the rock concert fills him with excitement that crosses over into the realm of a singular, distorted sexuality.

Per usual, King wants to examine the role of mediated images—*even his own*—in this larger destructive pattern. The banal world of commercial television that nearly succeeds in swallowing Hodges early in the novel has helped to create the monster that is Hartsfield. Kent implicates the consumer's prurient fascination with "watching the ugly achievements of the abyss in human behavior" (122) for feeding Hartsfield's warped desire for infamy, the real-life events of serial and mass murdering that replicate themselves in America so that they are never far from our collective consciousness: "They'll remember me, [Brady] thinks . . . highest score ever. I'll go down in history" (*Mr. Mercedes* 436). The fact that King never reveals the specific "midwestern American city" where the events of *Mr. Mercedes* take place suggests a purposeful anonymity. As the twenty-four-hour news cycle illustrates, disaffected men like Brady Hartsfield are everywhere and capable of surfacing at any time. The cyclic nature of Pennywise's reappearances is always connected to various gruesome outbursts of communal injustice and violence in Derry's history, its "unusually high rate of every violent crime we know of, not excluding rape, incest, breaking and entering, auto theft, child abuse, spouse abuse, assault" (*IT* 504). The clown's reemergence is both reflective of Derry's violence and a kind of cosmic reverberation that echoes its unleashing, as the clown attacks random children who venture too close to its lair. Similarly, Hartsfield mirrors the faceless violence of urban America, as he muses to himself, "Can he be blamed for striking out at the world that has made him what he is?" (*Mr. Mercedes* 390). His personal mix of familial dysfunction, social anomie, and untreated mental illness fits the profile of the contemporary American monster: the mass murderer-domestic terrorist whose mission serves no god or political ideology—only the determination to foment chaos (the actual word he employs as his computer password) and as much destruction as possible: "If I was over there in Afghanistan, he thinks, dressed in a head-rag and one of those funky bathrobes, I could have quite a career blowing up troop carriers" (127). Such a statement reveals that he has no allegiance to culture or country; like Trashcan Man in King's epic *The Stand*, he is a visceral embodiment of noir—a face for the existential chiaroscuro that has long plagued America's disenfranchised.

Beneath the surface anarchy of King's most vicious fictional monsters, there is always a strong element of autocratic oppression. They conform to the theory that underneath every Nazi is a narcissist. Brady Hartsfield and Pennywise join other King autocrats—Randall Flagg, Greg Stillson, the Crimson King, Andre Linoge, even the patrician ghosts in residence at the Overlook Hotel—as warnings about the inherent fragility of democratic society and as a means of highlighting the importance of *resistance* against such forces. Standing in opposition to these oppressive figures are King's underwhelming characters who fight back against authoritarian principles and persuasion through the simple assertion of their directness, fierce independence, and the persistent, intuitive understanding of the difference between wrong and right. Included in this group, as we have traced elsewhere in this study, are King's detectives (and his detective-like protagonists). On the one hand, then, Brady Hartsfield maintains an illusion of total control as he meticulously orchestrates his crimes of anarchy. Bill Hodges, in contrast, plays the part of the hard-boiled hero, dropping into a sequence of chaotic events that he cannot comprehend.

When Hodges sits back to intuit—switching off his conscious reason in favor of gut feelings and imaginative speculations—he makes important advances: "He tries to think about nothing, because that's how you open the door so the right idea can come in" (311–12). It is his uncertainty and commitment to his personal credo that ultimately redeem Hodges. When he expresses confidence that he has achieved mastery over the situation—when he reasons his way to the conclusion that Hartsfield is not likely to target the concert—Hodges fails. In other words, in King's estimation, the greatest asset of the hard-boiled hero is not his unlimited reservoir of knowledge (à la Sherlock Holmes or Dupin), but his awareness of his acute limitations. Unlike Hartsfield, Hodges possesses the ability to release control and "fake it" until a better idea occurs to him—the kind of intuitive spontaneity shared by a creative writer, and the skill that Hodges's ally, Holly, will perfect (as we will address later in this chapter).

ON WRITING

A crucial distinction emerges between Hodges and Hartsfield: Hartsfield remains overconfident in his "real life" when, in truth, "scenes from movies [are] also scenes from inside Brady Hartsfield's head" (384); in contrast, Hodges admits to the "unforgivable" mistake of clinging too tightly to formulaic expectations and he therefore evolves as a character, achieving a degree of distance from the role that he was initially meant to play (392). In this way, Hodges anticipates King's Billy Summers, from the novel of the same name: criminals fall back into predictable patterns, while true heroes innovate. As King notes, "It's all on the table, all up for grabs. Isn't that an intoxicating thought?" (*On Writing* 196). Hodges confesses, in the final pages of *Mr. Mercedes*, that he has watched entirely too much television and it has made him lose track of his "essential self" (367). But at this point, an important question arises: how precisely can Hodges, or King's reader, isolate his performative identity (as hard-boiled hero) from his so-called essential self? How is King's Constant Reader supposed to make sense of the slippery border that supposedly divides Hodges's generic façade from the invisible heart of the matter?

Mr. Mercedes confronts this pressing question by turning to an issue of great interest to King, in his fiction as well as nonfiction: namely, *Mr. Mercedes* proves to be yet another tract on writing. The intersection of detection and writing surfaces repeatedly in other chapters in our book, especially in discussions of *Misery, Billy Summers,* and *Dolores Claiborne*. Indeed, writing is, as King observes in *On Writing*, a "uniquely portable kind of magic"—it is his return to his "craft," and all that it implies, that marks Hodges's return to health and happiness. This theme has autobiographical significance to King, of course, who suffered from a horrific accident in 1999 and has publicly acknowledged the value of writing in helping him to rehabilitate.[6] As a sort of stand-in for the injured King, Hodges must re-learn how to be two things at once: a detective as well as a writer. King therefore uses the detective genre to ruminate on the relationship of the writer and the reader (and vice versa)—a tendency that dates to Poe's Dupin stories. Upon misplacing his beat patrol notepad, Hodges picks up a yellow legal pad, one of the main tools of the aspiring writer, and as a result he re-enters the dual profession of detective-author. Like Dupin in "The Murders in the Rue Morgue," Hodges capitalizes on the possibilities of writing to assemble information as he scours the neighborhood interviewing potential witnesses while assembling a "profile he has fleshed out on his yellow legal pad" (419). The art of good writing aids Hodges the detective in his effort to defeat Brady Hartsfield.

King's novel ostensibly knows what "good writing" entails—although it never quite sorts out the demarcation between assumed authenticity and rhetorical gamesmanship. At its most basic level, *Mr. Mercedes* remains a pseudo-epistolary novel, in which the criminal and the detective launch missives back and forth "Under Debbie's Blue Umbrella," each trying to trick the other and gain the upper hand. Hodges spends an inordinate amount of time commending Mr. Mercedes, Hartsfield's *nom de plume*, for his skill as a writer. While certainly not "high-class literature," Hodges acknowledges, the letters from Mr. Mercedes are "better than the dialogue in shows like *NCIS*" (35). Mr. Mercedes has a "good vocabulary," and he's "able to turn a phrase" (142). In what follows, Hodges rehearses many familiar talking points that King has provided for would-be writers: Mr. Mercedes writes "outward" because he learned "with others" and wrote "*for* others" (35; emphasis in the original); Mr. Mercedes, unlike less persuasive writers, keeps his prose "direct and clear" (41). Later, Hodges ruminates on his own strengths as a writer: he employs a "consistent" style, he recognizes the value of keeping the prose "short," and he holds that "thinking too long about writing doesn't work" (164). On the one hand, both Hodges and Hartsfield sharpen their skills as rhetoricians to manipulate their respective readers. Hodges writes, and rewrites, and polishes his prose on his trusted legal pad (167); Hartsfield, meanwhile, artfully crafts a prose style that is "completely different" from the voice that he employs to express his so-called essential self (43). Of note, the automobile with which Hartsfield assaults the job seekers is nicknamed "the Gray Lady," a well-known moniker for the *New York Times*. In a sense, then, Hartsfield —like writers at the *Times*—exploits the power of rhetoric to manipulate his audience. With "the Gray Lady," Hartsfield's rhetoric becomes quite literally weaponized. In response, to be a successful writer, Mr. Mercedes as well as Hodges must always stay one step ahead of the detective-reader. At one point, Hodges "kills" the television and shifts his attention to his legal pad: a dramatic turning point, in the novel as well as the case. This vital choice of an alternative medium transforms Hodges from the consummate consumer—a passive receptor of televised talk shows—to an active creator, a move that empowers him to make invaluable progress in his mission to restore order.

In turn, it is Brady Hartsfield's failures *as a writer* that nearly give him away: his stylistic tic that confuses "perp" for "perk"; his slip-up in which, due to his heightened anger, he writes a letter to Hodges without judicious revisions. A clear sign of his deteriorating grasp of the situation comes when he starts to write poorly, when he "can't think of any other similes. Or are those metaphors? Maybe, he thinks, I just ought to kill myself now" (243). In *Mr. Mercedes*, "good writing" remains a necessary skill if one hopes to win at the detective's game of cat and mouse. To lose that skill, as Jack Torrance discovers in *The Shining*, prompts self-destruction in more than one sense. Most importantly, while Hodges creates content for the good of his community, Hartsfield can only destroy the world (literally and figuratively). In ways both subtle and overt, *Mr. Mercedes* restates a truism found throughout the King canon: critics, especially those mired in a hypercritical mindset, cannot hope to outwit the creative writer. That is, critics often lack the ability to keep up. While Hodges busies himself trying to keep their electronic conversation going to save future lives, Hartsfield wants to end it once and for all.

And this distinction between generative creator and destructive critic bleeds over into a case being made by King against overconfident detectives. Hodges understands implicitly the delicate dance that unfolds between an author and her audience; he knows that he can neither fully grasp Hartsfield's meaning without sustained reflection, nor can he plot, with absolute certainty, the response of his intended reader. Hartsfield, on the other hand, holds that he can effortlessly "read" Hodges—in more ways than one—and he treats his own missives like a blunt instrument to bludgeon his victim until he acquiesces and commits suicide. At stake here is a distinctive take on the act of writing (as well as reading) that King has spent most of his career honing. Hartsfield's literary "style" works on "poor guilt-ridden Olivia Trelawney" (53) for the same reason that it fails to persuade Hodges: Hartsfield understands enough about Olivia as an older, privileged, and insulated woman that he can manipulate her as a reader, weaponizing language to forge a bond of culpability between them: "If you hadn't left your key in your ignition, that little baby and her mother would still be alive . . . your carelessness made my terrible act possible" (138). By emphasizing collusion, his masked plaintive voice successfully preys on Olivia's naivete and instability. It is also reflective of Hartsfield's fundamental misogyny as he manipulates Olivia's vulnerability as a woman living alone in the absence of another person to help her evaluate accurately his poisonous rhetoric: "Pushing the Trelawney bitch over the edge had been the greatest thrill of his life" (190). When he tries "to get the chief investigator in the case to kill himself" (190), however, employing language designed to goad Hodges by identifying and mocking his life's recent failures, the detective proves to be a far more sophisticated reader than Olivia. Hodges penetrates Hartsfield's rhetorical persona and views the self-destructive humiliation that Hartsfield proffers as an opportunity to strike back. While Hartsfield employs two very different rhetorical voices and strategies in the prose he authors for Olivia and Hodges, in truth he's really saying the exact same thing to both readers—neither has earned the right to continue living. One sees evidence of his hubris in such judgment, but this single-mindedness also leaves him vulnerable to Hodges's own rhetorical manipulation. The detective's return correspondence deflates Hartsfield's God complex by proposing that the criminal is "nothing but a crank," thereby infuriating him into revealing more about himself as well as his crime (189). Armed with clever banter, thoughtful engagement, and sturdy craftsmanship, strong rhetorical skills remain the hard-boiled hero's greatest asset.

Yet, unlike the major writers of crime fiction, from Raymond Chandler to Dashiell Hammett, King does not seem content with linguistic warfare. There is more to King noir than slick patter. *Mr. Mercedes* instead celebrates the essential self, which is to say, an imaginary self that remains untouched by stylization. In King's hands, the delicate dance of writer and reader frequently gives way to a celebration of wordless communication: a mode of communication freed from the inherent gamesmanship of language.[7] When Hartsfield capitulates to "the kind of typing you do when you're mad as well," the reader might call to mind Truman Capote's famous insult of

Jack Kerouac in which he claimed Kerouac's efforts are typing, not writing. However, is Hartsfield's mad typing actually worse than his "stylistic masking" (202)? Isn't this unwitting exposure of his so-called essential self a sign of his weakness, his vulnerability to Hodges's probing eye as a professional detective and critical reader?

    King frequently lauds simplicity, and he obviously wants to undercut the deception and falsity of online identities—but, as we have seen, *Mr. Mercedes* also depends upon an adroit writer (Hodges) who fools his opponents through rhetorical persuasion. Once more, King underlines a thesis traced throughout the chapters of this book: in *Mr. Mercedes*, King invests in an author who can outwit readers with an unearned sense of superiority. This superior author privileges spontaneity, intuition, gut impulses, and an admission of his own blind spots. King acknowledges that, as a writer, he leans "heavily on intuition" (*On Writing* 164).[8] King's ideal author knows how to misdirect the overconfident critic through carefully cultivated prose. However, the "resolution" of *Mr. Mercedes*—made possible through an omniscient author—may strike King's readers as a bit difficult to swallow. Hodges impossibly straddles the border between expert use of formula and a radical escape from formulaic confines, out into a delusional realm of "essential selves." King captures this impasse in the quotes that open *On Writing*: on the one hand, Miguel de Cervantes states, "Honesty's the best policy"; on the other hand, an anonymous figure offers a prompt rejoinder: "Liars prosper." A similarly complex interplay between honesty and deception is what makes *Mr. Mercedes* such an interesting as well as irksome text.

    Let us consider the evidence. A symptom of its time and place, *Mr. Mercedes* proves to be a novel about identity politics, for better or worse. Hodges's young assistant Jerome Robinson, a gifted Black teenager who struggles with his racial identification, experiences what he calls "identity challenges" (95).[9] Every major character in the novel feels an acute tension between his or her outward appearance, replete with social expectations, and the assumed "reality" behind the façade. The novel opens with a single working mother detailing the many ways that her society casts negative judgment on her based solely on her socioeconomic status and the fact that she is a single mother, alone in the world. Elsewhere, Hodges's love interest, Janey, knows that her family views her as a malicious money-grubber, akin to the "cruel sister" one sees in "old movies" (116). In reality, she's a faithful and caring daughter and relative, willing to split her inheritance from Olivia with her jealous aunt and uncle. Orbiting within the constellation of the detective genre, *Mr. Mercedes* adopts its main impetus—to uncover; to peel back the layers of subterfuge in pursuit of the truth beneath the surface of things; *to detect*—in the name of sorting through what T. S. Eliot once described as the faces we put on to meet the faces that we meet. Said another way, *Mr. Mercedes* revolves around the metaphor of truthful books and deceptive covers, or about how detective-readers must learn to read the objects of their interest a bit more carefully. After all, in a digital world populated by avatars and assumed online identities, how is an astute observer to separate the "good guys" (Janey's moniker for Hodges) from the "aliens," Hodges's final label for Brady Hartsfield (407)?

The stakes of being a bad detective-reader are spelled out consistently throughout the text. Hodges initially misreads the victims with whom he comes into contact: he unfairly dismisses Olivia, owner of the Mercedes that Hartsfield steals, as a "self-pitying rich lady" when, in fact, her story contains crucial clues about Hartsfield's sophistry (59). Later, he misreads Mrs. Melbourne, a local conspiracy theorist, as a "harmless crank" when, in fact, she has correctly isolated the ice cream man (Hartsfield's alias) as a suspicious culprit (339). Hodges repeatedly makes faulty assumptions about individuals who have information pertinent to his case: assumptions grounded in his own biases against women, wealthy people, poor people, and so forth. Although he takes pride in his ability to connect with victims, Hodges is in truth a pretty poor judge of character. It is only at the very end that he can admit, "We were wearing blinders" (296). If King's fictional detective-writer does such a dreadful job of reading people, what hope remains for real-world readers? King's Constant Reader might be led to seek the anonymity of the cynic, or the online troll (to adopt contemporary parlance), since liars do indeed appear to prosper.

THE FEDORA

Part of the struggle described above stems from the prevalence of generic miscues. In King's estimation, individuals regularly base their assumed identities—be they digital or analog—on fictional formulas. His characters routinely derive their identities from American popular culture. Harkening back to the Bachman novels, King's *Mr. Mercedes* highlights how consumers of televised content gradually lose touch with reality and become lost in the simulacra of fantasy worlds. Even Brady Hartsfield, a notorious outlier, anchors his identity to recognizable touchstones: the text incessantly draws the reader's attention to Hartsfield's screensavers from *The Wild Bunch*, a Sam Peckinpah western noted for its gritty realism and displays of violence. Just how much of his criminal identity, then, is derivative of popular culture? As he is a nihilist, it may strike King's reader as a bit strange that Hartsfield identifies his role through lowbrow Hollywood fare. Perhaps even more interesting, he exists as a familiar construct within the King fictional universe: as we have discussed, he assumes the avatar of Pennywise by wearing the clown mask, and throughout the novel he conjures images of Barton Dawes from *Roadwork*. Like Dawes, Hartsfield recognizes that the system is irrevocably broken and pointless; like Dawes, he wants to use explosives to strike against the false face of his consumer society. In short, can King's reader ever fully separate Hartsfield (the man) from the tropes that allow Hodges and the reader to flag him as a terrorist (the archetype)? Is there *anything* beneath the surface, any sign of authenticity, that will reveal Hartsfield to be more than a caricature? Or, for that matter, can King's reader ever separate fully Hodges (the man) from the tropes that assist Hartsfield and the reader in flagging him as the novel's hero (the archetype)?

As much as he tries to resist his preprogrammed fate, Hodges himself may be a byproduct of a culture saturated in cop shows and crime fiction. He moves within a tightly conscribed fictional topography, pulled as if by gravity toward DeMasio's, a restaurant that calls to mind the multiple scenes in Italian restaurants in *Roadwork* and crime fiction in general. In a minor subplot, *Mr. Mercedes* turns to a couple of disposable cops named after characters from the popular television program *Car 54, Where Are You?*, a less-than-subtle reference to which King actively draws his reader's attention. In other words, King forces Hodges—like Bachman's Dawes—to look around himself and recognize how formulaic storylines have hemmed in his horizons. This insight may lead King's readers to consider the degree to which Hodges has been imprisoned by genre. Right away, Brady Hartsfield narrows the interpretive possibilities by labelling him as "a true Knight of the Badge and Gun," a "combination of by-the-book and intuitively brilliant" (21–22). Hartsfield, as well as King's reader, ostensibly has the jump on Hodges: they have seen characters like this before (see our earlier discussion of Hodges as noir detective), and they can expect that he will subscribe to the tenets of the formula. Hartsfield acerbically considers Hodges to be ill-read, a "John Grisham man," rather than a deep thinker such as himself, with his incessant allusions to Nietzsche (45). Even Janey wants to peg Hodges as a stereotypical detective; she buys him a fedora to have him perform for her the role of private investigator (P.I.) and get to the bottom of her sister's torture at the hands of Hartsfield—a performance piece with a sexual subtext. If Hartsfield must wear the mask of Pennywise, the psychopathic clown, Hodges must assume the posture of the hard-boiled detective. "Every private dick should have a fedora he can pull down to one eyebrow," Janey coos (235). The hat becomes a potent generic symbol as every character who dons it must conform to the expectations of the P.I. While wearing the costume, the hard-boiled detective must use ratiocination as well as cunning, and he must keep one foot in the realm of the law and one in the city's criminal underbelly. In other words, the hard-boiled wearer of the fedora operates within and without the legal bureaucracy. At one point Jerome puts the hat on and asks, "Do I look like Bogie?" (235). As a result, what attracts Janey to Hodges is meant to attract King's reader to his protagonist, and the cause is surprisingly flimsy. After all, the hat exists as a purely sartorial object. Janey, like the reader, knows exactly what revs her engine: "That hat she bought him. That Philip Marlowe fedora" (279). After Janey's death, Hodges notes that, in part because she gave him the P.I. hat, he cannot let go of the case. In multiple senses, then, the fate of Hodges has been preordained by the familiar costume of a P.I. His ongoing identity challenges can be traced back to the performative status imposed upon him by Janie's fedora.

Against Brady Hartsfield, who tries to manipulate him into committing suicide, or against the computer programs that run on autopilot, Hodges must attempt to "hack" into plotlines that have been devised for him. "Any system created by the mind of man," Jerome asserts, "can be hacked by the mind of man" (207). Accordingly, the two characters who strive in futility to escape from the confines of fictional formula, Hartsfield and Hodges, display an instinctual hatred of the fedora. Hartsfield sees it as "ridiculously old-fashioned" and "stupid" (284–85); Hodges denounces the hat as "ridiculous" and "not what attracts him" to his line of work (118). When asked to play the P.I. in Janey's fantasy, Hodges demurs and asks that she instead refer to him as a "security consultant" (118). Throughout *Mr. Mercedes*, Hodges subverts—with varying degrees of success—the expectation that he should behave like an archetypal Marlowe character. He critiques *Dexter*, a popular television show in the genre of crime fiction, as "fantasyland bullshit" (191), and at one point he has to remind his collaborators: "'It would make a neat solution for an Agatha Christie novel, but *this is real life*'" (328; emphasis added). When a character like Janey does cling too tightly to the trappings of genre, she ends up eviscerated: it is her choice to don the fedora that leads Hartsfield to mistake her for the retired detective and subsequently blow her up, in yet another fundamental misreading of a book by its cover. Elsewhere, Jerome declares himself to be playing the part of Dr. Watson to Hodges's Sherlock Holmes, a statement that rubs Hodges the wrong way. When Jerome assumes the part of Watson, he appears to wear a "*knowing* smile" that immediately repulses his companion (133; emphasis in the original). In sum, as his friends and lovers become fixed within the hard-boiled formula, Hodges declares his discomfort with such generic expectations. His final heart attack exposes an innate vulnerability rarely seen in the callous hard-boiled hero, just as his embrace of Holly and Jerome transforms Hodges from tough-guy loner to surrogate father. Like his protagonist, King ostensibly swerves around his forefathers in crime fiction as well as his own public persona as America's reigning *horror-meister*.

    The fedora that Janey buys for Hodges is packed with significance. It marks Hodges as the novel's private dick, a deceptive label that, as we have argued, never comfortably fits Hodges. Again, the fedora contributes to Janey's death because Hartsfield errs in identifying it exclusively with Hodges. This mistake is not the first one that Hartsfield makes in his misunderstanding of the retired detective; the killer's fundamental underestimation of Hodges's personality manifests in his belief that taunting the retired cop will lead to Hodges's suicide as it did with the more fragile Olivia Trelawney. While the fedora is a nod to noir detection, its obliteration pushes Hodges out of his romantic idealization of Janey and right back into the violent realism of Hartsfield. Holding true to the fatalism that drives both the Bachman books and the hard-boiled tradition, the destruction of both Janey and the hat narrows the novel's plot as well as Hodges's focus away from Janey, the idealized love interest, and relentlessly back to Brady Hartsfield, the serial killer. After his sobering rejoinder that "This is my fault. If I'd used my father's gun two weeks ago, she'd be alive" (347), the detective represses his guilt over her death for the rest of the book. Hodges's focus is now back where it should be: the detective's game of cat and mouse. He sees through the lie and recognizes what he takes to be the truth. This pivot underscores the fact that King is not truly deviating from the larger trajectory of the genre: his "innovations"—such as the apparent softening of Hodges throughout the trilogy—are really extensions of historical precedents. Leonard Cassuto charts how the genre "becomes more and more sentimental in tone, more inclined toward emotional affect, and more explicit about its domestic concerns" (16), moving steadily from rigid logic to passionate detachment to introspective humility. In other words, King's *Mr. Mercedes* appears to be a departure from generic norms when, in truth, it relentlessly circles back to the basic patterns from which it emerged.

The renewed focus of the final part of the text may indicate a chronic problem in a similar register: despite its early lines of metacritique, *Mr. Mercedes* never fully implicates its reader in its game of cat and mouse, instead affording her a comfortable perch from which to survey the novel's proceedings. Closely allied with neither detective nor criminal, King's Constant Reader lacks introspection as well as strong emotional investment in what will happen next in the story. King's text thus operates on two levels: there is Hodges, frantically searching for a genuine fingerprint or a slip-up that will expose the "real" Brady Hartsfield, and there is King's reader, relatively comfortable in her identifications of the "good guy" and the "alien," who enjoys watching Hodges strives to solve the puzzle *without being implicated in the detective's game.* From its very beginning, the reader is already in on the book's primary "secret" (Hartsfield committed the crime), so the reader can effortlessly narrow her gaze to the ongoing brinksmanship between the two. But this absence of a secret—the lack of a hidden truth that needs to be uncovered by Hodges—dramatically weakens the reader's imperative to inquire into the "identity challenges" at the heart of *Mr. Mercedes*. Despite their protestations to the contrary, Hodges and Hartsfield are both flattened out for King's readers—that is, their "real" identities are fully exposed and available for uncomplicated consumption. At one point, Holly schools Jerome on Poe's "The Purloined Letter" and repeats that story's central message: that the truth is always hidden "in plain sight" (338). There is no need to second-guess, or to read cynically; rather, the wise detective-reader will always find the truth out in the open.[10] It turns out that Cervantes was right, and honesty is, in fact, the best policy. As we have seen, King echoes Poe on several other fictional occasions, but nowhere more problematically than in this particular text. If the preceding argument of King's novel has any weight, the contents of the book must be synonymous with its cover, which is to say, the contents of an individual's identity remain identical to his or her stylized avatar.

The entire motivation for *Mr. Mercedes* has been unconsciously undermined by the fact that Hodges and the reader are being conditioned to do precisely what the evidence suggests they must not. Let us rephrase the conundrum: the reader need not plumb the proverbial depths to isolate a so-called essential self, for Jerome or Hartsfield or even Hodges himself; instead, if King's narrative is to be taken seriously, critics should stop reading too deeply and read things at face value. *Yet isn't this sort of superficial reading precisely what almost derails Hodges's investigation?* Haven't all of Hodges's missteps been connected to his doomed tendency to "read" victims in a straightforward, unnuanced way (the entitled rich bitch, the kooky conspiracy theorist, and so forth)? And doesn't Hartsfield fail because he, too, thinks he can "read" people based on their outward appearance, especially when it comes to their weight or their race? Therefore, if King's detective-reader conforms to the book's wishes and ceases trying to outwit the story, they unconsciously *repeat* the error of King's main characters: they accept evidence at face value by stripping it of any rhetorical complexity. They begin to believe that King has provided them, alone, with unmediated access to a substratum of authenticity.

This critique has ramifications beyond a lone reading of *Mr. Mercedes*; it speaks to an issue that plagues much of King's crime fiction, indeed his entire body of work. Even though King appears to appreciate how hardboiled detective fiction complicates the relationship between writers and readers, he—unlike Poe or even more recent authors like Agatha Christie—does not always press that point to his advantage. Simply put, King rarely trusts his reader enough to leave her to her own devices (a place of uncertainty, from which the reader tries to sort out the case alongside the detective). *Mr. Mercedes,* like its sequel *Holly,* which we will discuss later, lays everything out for the reader from the beginning. There can be no doubt about the state of the "good guy" (Hodges), the "alien" (Hartsfield), or the various elements of the criminal plot. King supplies his reader with heavy doses of character motivation, and he keeps the reader apprised of Hartsfield's sinister plan as it evolves. Where, then, is the suspense? When everything remains out in the open, and there are few secrets to be uncovered, what is left for the reader to do but watch inevitable events unfold in parallel with the novel's relatively numbed television spectators? We contend that *Mr. Mercedes* would be a better novel—or at least a more engrossing one—if it allowed readers to share in Hodges's highstakes interpretation of Hartsfield's missives, unsure of what was behind them, instead of reading these letters with unrestrained access to the inner thoughts of both individuals that composed them. Along these same lines, it is unnecessary for the author to spend two full pages having Hodges speculate on Hartsfield's psychosexual maladjustment based on profile evidence (231–32). The reader possesses enough information to reach most of these conclusions for herself. Yet King apparently wants his Constant

Reader to respect his authorial command over his imagined situations so much that he will not leave them in the dark for very long.

Put differently, the kind of intuition-based mode of reading championed by *Mr. Mercedes* works against its generic purpose as a suspense novel because it leaves the reader with little to do but sit back and admire the craftsmanship of the story as King delivers it. Although readerly deprivation remains a key component of the detective genre, in all its iterations, King seems reluctant to deprive his readers of much of anything. Importantly, it is not as though King is incapable of cultivating uncertainty; as we describe in an earlier chapter, Wendy and Jack Torrance from *The Shining* are both detectives of a sort, and neither they nor King's reader can make much sense of the Overlook's murky history until the pieces eventually come together. Likewise, in a chapter to come, Billy Summers, in his eponymous novel, complicates the positions of criminal and detective through a dexterous *mise-en-abyme* (story within a story). In *The Shining* as well as *Billy Summers*, then, an enduring state of indecision creates a palpable suspense—something sorely lacking in the reader's experience of *Mr. Mercedes*.

While definitively not King's first venture into hard-boiled terrain, as earlier chapters in this book have shown, *Mr. Mercedes* does recycle the genre's grammar in thought-provoking ways. The text restores a certain color palate in its confrontation of American crises, such as a wave of white supremacists and a niggling sense of meaninglessness behind the soft glow of countless computer screens. King paints with nostalgic sepia tones and Venetian contrasts as he depicts a lawless society in desperate need of a modern-day knight to restore order. At the same time, *Mr. Mercedes* reflects on the confines of the hard-boiled formula, as both its hero and its villain struggle to free themselves from the sort of static characterizations common in crime fiction. The novel revives beloved hard-boiled archetypes as well as a recognizable sense of postmodern reflexivity, which is to say, an exercise in the meta-criticism of derivative formulas, couched in pulpy paperbacks. And yet, despite King's agile navigation between earnest revival and postmodern playfulness, *Mr. Mercedes* wears its secrets on its sleeve. As such, the novel does not really allow its reader to play detective: to feel the suspense of not knowing what comes next, or to have her desires fueled by what is missing. Since *Mr. Mercedes* clearly prefers honesty, transparency, and sincerity to the experiential components of noir—in particular, its requisite dissatisfactions—one might call into question how "hard-boiled" this text really is at its core.

CHAPTER 5

HOLLY GETS HER OWN CASE

Holly Gibney is a walking contradiction. When she reappears at the midway point of King's 2018 novel *The Outsider*, she once more offers a promising rejoinder to a grizzled veteran—this time, to Detective Ralph Anderson. Anderson narrowly applies deductive logic; at the same time, he refuses to admit that he catered to the demands of a bloodthirsty mob when he publicly arrested an innocent man. Holly amplifies Anderson's status as "a man of two minds" whose "double vision was driving him crazy" (175). Holly draws out this double vision. On the one hand, she anxiously obeys laws because, she reasons, "laws [are] laws for a reason" (360). She has internalized her overbearing mother's admonitions, and she does not waver in her commitment to a Platonic sense of justice. However, Holly productively widens Anderson's perspective: unlike her male counterpart, she remains open-minded when it comes to the subject of the supernatural, and she regularly acts on faith rather than empirical evidence. In sum, Holly offers a healthy counterpoint to Anderson because she is a traumatized subject who takes Lexapro and prays constantly: "Please help me to stay safe in my car, obey all traffic rules, and help me to do the best I can" (293). As such, Holly exposes King's reader to the detective's vital blind spots. If male detectives, as well as their nemeses, tend to think of themselves as "godlike"—men who are "arrogant" and constantly "overreach"—Holly is a humble, self-effacing, credulous alternative (469). The results speak for themselves: when King's Constant Readers first learned that King was going to give Holly her own novel-length treatment, many of them were absolutely delighted by the idea. Another entry in King's litany of feminist correctives, including Dolores Claiborne and Susannah Dean in *The Dark Tower*, Holly Gibney both highlights and undercuts the generic expectations associated with a flawed male detective.

    Sadly, there is no way around the fact that *Holly*, despite King's repeated admission that he "fell in love with her" and that "she's fun," is simply not a very compelling book (Interview). The novel's aging, evil, semi-retired college professors are never fully developed; they are immediately forgettable, and readers never come to care about their specious dietary motivations. Like holdover members of the True Knot family in *Dr. Sleep*, Emily Harris and her husband, Rodney, are in search of their own brand of "steam" that comes via consuming the flesh and brains of young adults whom they kidnap, dissect, and consume. As King enters his late seventies and the phase of his own life when bodily ailments are the inheritance of daily living, the plots of this novel and *Dr. Sleep* may reflect the urge for relief from the writer's own physical infirmities, as the True Knot and the Harrises share similar compulsions to cannibalize the recuperative and regenerative properties inherent in their young victims: "There are many uses for the brains of their livestock, and such organs as the heart and kidneys, but the liver is what matters most, because it is the consumption of the human liver that preserves vitality and strengthens life" (*Holly* 289). *Holly* is King's attempt to revisit Thomas Harris's *The Silence of the Lambs*—but without the psychological depth and contradictions that make Hannibal Lecter such a compelling personality. Or, more accurately, the novel's contradictions are really just confusions that provide the illusion of complexity. Holly must stick to her gut, to her intuition, in the face of instrumental reason—and yet, at the same time, too much belief (like, say, belief in bunk medicine) leads to catastrophic conclusions. The character of Holly is both everything and, concurrently, nothing.

The detective story embedded in *Holly* does not exhibit the gripping qualities of Harris's famous tome (note King's unsubtle reference in choosing the surname of his professors) because Holly Gibney's quest to solve the crime bears nothing of Clarice Starling's sharpening urge to save Catherine Martin's imperiled life and its psychological transmission to the reader. When King chooses to delve into a character's psyche, as he does so brilliantly with Jack Torrance or Louis Creed, we gain insight into the writer's greatest skill in his ability to produce monsters that are not supernatural, but in fact all too real: people who deliberately hurt themselves and others for reasons readers may not fully comprehend, but nevertheless elicit their deepest sympathies. This novel's focus remains on the selfish quest to regenerate two octogenarian academics whose careers no one seems to respect or remember fondly and who can barely get out of each other's way. The Harrises act as upper-class extensions of Brady Hartsfield's white supremacism. Emily is a blatant racist who refers to Barbara Robinson (Jerome's sister) as a "*pretty little pickaninny*" and "negress" throughout the novel (159, 97, for example; emphasis in the original). Their cannibalism is also reflective of their elitist politics as their attitude of superiority over other humans enables the professors to reduce their captives to mere body parts—mere meat—only good enough to eat or turn into a visceral crème for aching muscles. The young men and women sacrificed in support of the Harrises' belief in the regenerative properties of human flesh are disposable in the eyes of these aging professors; warped by a perverse form of academic narcissism, the couple considers their unsuspecting victims to be no more than a form of livestock, expendable means to extend the lives of two people selfishly desperate to escape death and prolong their own lives. They are uninspired versions of Renfield in Bram Stoker's *Dracula*. Throughout King's canon there is evidence of an out-of-control cannibalistic orality associated with his worst brand of monstrosity. As early as the vampires in *'Salem's Lot* to the True Knot family in *Doctor Sleep* and perhaps culminating in *IT*'s Pennywise, flesh-eating forms a connection among King's fictional monsters, between a rejection of humanity and the assertion of an authoritarian supernatural agenda. Having abandoned any nuanced or moral continuum, they are reduced to flesh eaters, vicious consumers not only aroused by but obsessed with their dietary needs. Even when his reign over Derry is imperiled, the doomed Pennywise continues to assert his autocratic superiority in gastrointestinal terms, "I am the eater of worlds." In the final tally, just as *Mr. Mercedes* reflects on the dark horizons of post-9/11 America, *Holly* reflects on the grim reality of a Trumpian moment defined by baby boomers in a state of abject self-preservation.

But it is the detective plot of *Holly* that is germane to the purpose of our book, and since she is related to Bill Hodges in both training and ratiocinative intuition, her presence in this novel, despite the distractions from its primary storyline, requires discussion. Like many hard-boiled protagonists in the detective tradition, and despite King's own protestations to the contrary, Holly is not a terribly dynamic personality. In fact, one might be permitted to call her methodically dull, which is a big part of the problem with this eponymous novel. Her contradictory and idiosyncratic personal behaviorisms—insisting on the importance of wearing masks and nitrile gloves during the COVID crisis while chain-smoking cigarettes—indicate that she has not thought through the most fundamental inconsistencies in her life: "It comes to her that there's something exceptionally perverse about taking all the proper precautions against Covid and then filling her lungs with this carcinogenic crap" (311). More positively, her training with Hodges has instilled in her a deep empathy for the cannibalistic professors' victims, not just the woman she has been hired to locate, but all their prey: "Penny Dahl is the client, but Holly is now looking for all of them. The missing. What they call *desaparecidos* in South America" (251). Moreover, while on a case, Holly is in touch with her unconscious ratiocinative instincts: "She's curious about everything. It's how she rolls" (76). Hodges has taught her how to follow the tactics associated with police procedurals when appropriate, such as how to conduct a series of interviews with individuals who knew Bonnie Dahl personally or work near where her bicycle was left and where she was last seen before her abduction. Mostly, Holly follows Hodges's pattern of reacting *instinctually* to criminal activity, as he did when tracking Brady Hartsfield and ascertaining where he would most likely plan his ultimate act of mass murder. Readers are introduced to Holly's cognitive process early on in the novel when Bonnie's missing helmet and bike stimulate the detective's process as she assembles information she will later employ in tracking the Harrises: "Holly's nose for a lie isn't as strong as Bill Hodges's was, but she's good at knowing when someone's shading the truth" (42). Although the cannibals have tried to create a scenario in which their abduction appears as Bonnie's choice to run away, Holly recognizes the sophistry of Bonnie's leaving an ambiguous "*I've had enough*" note (43; emphasis in the original) while abandoning both her bicycle and an errant earring in the woods nearby: "What interests Holly is Bonnie Rae's bike helmet. And the bike itself. Both are *very* interesting to her, for related but slightly different reasons" (59; emphasis in the original).

In her ultimate confrontation with the Harrises, Holly reveals her greatest link to both Hodges and the detective tradition (a tradition that ranges from classic detective tale to thriller). Trapped in the basement cage the academics employ to hold their victims, Holly refuses to panic. Quite the opposite: she goads both her captors into coming close enough to the cage to make them vulnerable, taking advantage of their advanced age and fragile bodies, criminal inexperience, and intellectual arrogance. It is the first time in the novel when Holly becomes verbally animated; when "she's chasing the case, her natural timidity disappears" (250). She manages to gain control over the situation by drawing Rodney close enough to cut his carotid artery with Bonnie's missing earring. Later, she similarly manipulates Emily, the former English teacher, into making fatal mistakes of her own. Bill Hodges, now deceased, occupies a silent presence all through this climatic scene: from inspiring the bravery of Holly's verbal provocations, to reminding his protégé to load her gun with five bullets instead of six, to counting the wasted shots as Emily overreacts to Holly's commentary, to the violent act of "grabbing [Emily's] head and breaking her fracking neck" (430). Holly recalls and yearns for more of Hodges's sage advice throughout this novel, but it is clear from the way she handles herself after she becomes one of the Harrises' captives that the young woman has rediscovered the cool she exhibited earlier in *Mr. Mercedes*, *End of Watch*, and *The Outsider*, and she has graduated as an "apt pupil" from the school of hard-boiled detection.

Even as Holly spends the better half of the book methodically tracking the fates of the kidnapped victims, the narrative interrupts itself with long discursive excursions into Barbara Robinson's effort to define herself as a writer, a poet whose talents are encouraged by another retired academic who once taught with the Harrises, Olivia Kingsbury, "a shrunken doll-woman soon to be a centenarian," who is herself a widely published and respected poet (221). The two storylines seem to be an excuse for King to connect once more the art of detection to the art of writing. The text keeps detouring from its central action into diatribes about what makes a good poem (Barbara's brother Jerome is also pursuing a career as a writer). Although Holly "wasn't a good poet, no matter how much she desperately wanted to be" (84), she proves to be an able "reader" by channeling the many lessons that she has learned about detection from Hodges. Becoming a good reader or writer—like becoming a good detective—involves coming to terms with one's own trauma, not to make the world "understandable" or "less crazy" for audiences but to scratch a kind of existential itch for oneself (183). Poetry "runs on every unresolved experience—every unresolved *trauma*, if you like—in your life. Every conflict. Every mystery" (206; emphasis in the original). What separates Holly from her peers in the sleuthing industry is her unique ability to process her trauma and then use those insights to solve the case at hand. In *Holly*, King obsessively returns to the fraught relationship between reader and writer via a battle between a savvy detective and a ruthless criminal.

This type of self-interrogation isolates Holly from the villainous Harrises, especially Emily. Emily, a failed poet who published a couple of books of literary criticism but none of her poetry, believes in total control over her surroundings: she thinks that her opinion alone matters when it comes to literary matters, she feels that she can "read" the thoughts as well as the motivations of others, and she harbors godlike delusions. Contrastingly, Holly doubts herself; in fact, self-doubt remains her Achilles heel: "I need to learn to trust myself more" (412). Yet self-doubt also makes Holly an enduring character. While she may not produce poetry, she knows how to accept what she cannot control, and she knows how to strip away her own egotism when it comes to interpreting her environment. Consider the postcards she exchanges with her absentee father, written in Latin. Although her Latin skills remain subpar, Holly keeps struggling to make sense of them in order to connect with a loved one. One critic (Emily) cravenly cannibalizes her prey; the other critic (Holly) admits that she can never know everything. *Holly* reinforces King's distaste for overconfident reviewers of his work—those overanalyzing professors of English.

While *Holly* ruminates on the art of detection in interesting ways, it also has some of the problems that we have discussed concerning *Mr. Mercedes*. For example, the reader knows from the beginning who committed the crime, and the process of deduction plays a limited role in what unfolds. True, Holly doubles with the hard-boiled hero in that she too must confront a fatalistic world: "There's no end to evil" (442). Like Hodges, who now serves as her literal conscience, she recognizes that "the systems are breaking down" (124), and, in response, she must persist in her pursuit of justice: "What cannot be cured must be endured" (145). However, Holly does not subscribe to the naturalistic worldview of Emily Harris, in which "survival is the prime directive" (92); instead, Holly maintains a stubborn faith in the unyielding goodness of the universe. Her only substantive connection to the hard-boiled detective, then, is her smoking habit—a return to the familiar semantics of noir, perhaps, but not to its primal syntax.

Even though Holly maintains that "*closure is a myth*" (126; emphasis in the original), King defangs the unknown by protecting his reader from genuine secrets. *Holly* is about a persistent belief that everything happens for a reason; it clings to self-help mantras and affirmative statements from groups like Alcoholics Anonymous: "Grant me the serenity to accept the things I cannot change" (164). It ultimately proves to be an open-and-shut case. As such, Hodges and Holly tend to operate in a rather suspenseless state, and King's readers must plod through the platitudes of their well-rehearsed, middle-class morality. Holly lacks the subversive qualities of another female alternative to the patriarchal detective, Dolores Claiborne (discussed in chapter 6). The trouble with *Holly*, in the end, is the essential liability inherent in much of King's crime fiction: the novel flirts with the tenets of noir, but it refuses to confront its characters (or its readers) with an abyss that it cannot overcome.

Chapter 6

FEMME NOIR

Misery and *Dolores Claiborne*

RESPONDING TO CRITICISM THAT HIS FICTION LACKED CREDIBLE FEMALE characters, a position that King himself viewed as accurate,[1] at the end of the 1980s the writer challenged himself to explore writing about women and domestic situations in an effort to create more human and less stereotyped female characters. Beginning with Annie Wilkes in *Misery* (1987) and continuing through the 1990s with the publication of *Gerald's Game* (1992), *Dolores Claiborne* (1993), *Rose Madder* (1995), and *Bag of Bones* (1998), King began to address the critique leveled against his first two decades of writing wherein his women protagonists were little more than sexualized Barbie dolls, maternal figures, and marginal characters in male-driven story lines populated almost exclusively with heroes rather than heroines. Like other contemporary writers toiling in the hard-boiled vein, King began to interrogate postwar fantasies of masculinity that had long been upheld by tough, laconic, male detectives.[2] Although *Misery* is not a feminist text, as it stages an anarchic, potentially castrating conception of women, its female character is a prototype—at least in terms of her independence, intelligence, and angry resolve—for future fictional females. The novels immediately following in *Misery*'s wake attempt to correct the misogyny implicit in the novel, reversing its gendered situation and siding with the woman's point of view (*Claiborne* remains the representative text for this perspective across King's works). In turn, King contributed to a growing body of literature that revisited the archetypal male detective in search of a radically different way of looking.[3]

Misery and *Claiborne* are inextricably connected texts. Both have been adapted into highly successful films, each featuring the actor Kathy Bates in the titular role, and it is now nearly impossible to think of either Annie or Dolores without seeing Bates's face. Both novels and films have been interpreted exclusively by critics in terms of what they reveal about gender—specifically, female and male struggles for power and control—with a heavy reliance on elements of autobiography. This chapter continues this line of discourse as appropriate to understanding the texts in question, but it will also propose a nontraditional interpretation by reading these novels and films *as detective stories*. Considering how the main characters in *Misery* and *Claiborne* employ elements traditionally associated with detectives not only enriches the texts, but it also adds a level of interpretation that is crucial to explaining the behavior and survival of their leads. On a fundamental level, these stories feature women who must be decoded and deciphered; they foreground women who are both criminals and criminalized at the same time. And while there are functioning (and malfunctioning) lawmen in these films and books, who will be analyzed in depth, we will also explore the ways in which characters who are not detectives nevertheless define themselves through acts of ratiocination, including the titular heroines themselves. As a key element in his self-defined feminist turn, King juxtaposes *bad detectives* (shown to be power-hungry, narrow-minded agents of the patriarchy) with *good detectives* (characterized as self-reflective, humble, and definitively "feminine"). King thus participates in a broader feminist revision of the detective genre by exposing how "restoring order, ensuring that the aberrant conforms to a securely perceptible routine, is an endemic feature of societies still founded upon patriarchal ideology" (Bradford 96). Simply put, by instructing his Constant Reader on how to read like a "good detective," King effectively challenges dominant patriarchal perspectives.

THE PURLOINED PAUL

The novel *Misery* has no detective, at least not in the literal sense. It does, however, include a young state trooper who is killed by Annie Wilkes in a horrific danse macabre in which he is first stabbed in the back by a wooden cross and then mutilated by Annie atop her Lawnboy: "The cop looked like a big doll that has been badly treated by a gang of nasty children" (244). The use of detective characters in King's universe serves multiple purposes, some more apparent than others: they are present to explain complex or unexpected plot lines, to provide the reader/viewer with a moral compass, and to help get audiences more involved in the solution of the text's central problem. Although King's heroes are almost never agents of the law (Alan Pangborn, whom we discuss in this book's conclusion, is a notable exception), they often operate like characters in Hitchcock's films—Sam in *Psycho*, Roger Thornhill in *North by Northwest*—who find themselves enmeshed in circumstances not of their own making but requiring them to act in the role of a sleuth to resolve the chaos of their situations. A detective's duty is to extract information and tie facts together to discover the truth. The detective is inherently relatable because, like the reader/viewer, they seek to pull together and understand events that appear initially disconnected. Thus, Buster (Richard Farnsworth), the sheriff in Rob Reiner's film version of *Misery*, begins the search for the missing writer Paul Sheldon (James Caan) by interviewing the innkeeper at the lodge where Paul was last seen. Buster then has his wife, Frances (Frances Sternhagen), drive the same road down from the Silver Creek Lodge that Paul did, while he focuses on the landscape to the right side of the mountain, eventually noticing a snapped pine branch that indicates where Paul's car veered off the road during a recent snowstorm. He suspects this broken branch may indicate where Paul's Mustang is buried, but is thwarted by the depth of a snowbank in his effort to uncover it. Still, he persists in his quest for a rational explanation, trying to make sense where there is only chaos, accidents on a snowy road. On two separate occasions, Buster employs a helicopter to search the area around where he noticed the broken pine branch, and his diligence is rewarded when he finds Paul's overturned Mustang in the snow. The Colorado State Police spokesman immediately "presumes that Paul Sheldon is dead" because the troopers cannot find him in the vicinity around his abandoned car (all quotes in this discussion of Buster are from the movie; subsequent quotes from the novel are accompanied by page numbers). The police in Reiner's adaptation assume that if someone had found Paul, "they would have taken him to an area hospital," and therefore decide to put off further searching for him "until the first thaw, that is unless the animals get to him first, which is a distinct possibility."

To read *Misery* as a film about detectives is to read against the generic grain. Indeed, the choice of the name "Buster" suggests a cowboy, especially since *Misery* is set in Colorado. Yet his lineage as a cowpuncher aligns him with the typical detective because he follows his gut and doesn't necessarily adhere to bureaucratic procedures. Buster "busts" the opinions expressed by bureaucratic police officers. He is a kind of hard-boiled outsider, as the movie quietly underscores that even though he was the one to find Paul's car, he is ignored by the greater authority recognized in the

State Police and the fawning television reporters who dismiss Buster and never bother to interview him, much less seek his insights into the case. Like Edgar Allan Poe's Dupin in "The Murders in the Rue Morgue," Buster distances himself from the police on the case because he recognizes the limits of their deductive skills. Instead, he illustrates the power of analysis, observation, and speculative insight. What Poe would call the ratiocinative mind comprehends what other, more limited minds cannot: "He [Paul] might well be dead," the sheriff tells Frances, "But not the way they say." The police in both film and novel fail to comprehend the importance of searching for clues beyond the locked room (or car) mysteries that leave them baffled. Dupin begins his investigation by surveying the entire Parisian neighborhood, including the outside of the edifice where the crime took place, which reveals the presence of a lightning rod and its proximity to the third-floor window and thus the possibility that the perpetrator entered the apartment from above. He follows the links of his chain of reasoning to a nail: the clue to the means of entrance and egress from the locked chamber. Similarly, Buster goes airborne by commandeering a helicopter, and then, by paying attention to the crowbar dents on the Mustang, he reaches the conclusion that Paul is likely still alive because "someone pulled him from that car."

Most importantly, through pursuing the local library's newspaper records and his own bedtime reading of several *Misery* novels, Buster makes the connection between Annie Wilkes and Paul Sheldon's fiction when he reads the line that Annie the "Dragon Lady" quotes after her arrest. Because of his own research, the sheriff uncovers the crucial nexus between Annie and her favorite writer. After he comes across the line—"There is a justice higher than that of man, I will be judged by Him"—that appeared initially in one of the *Misery* novels and then was restated by Annie on the courthouse steps as part of her defense, he takes the next step in realizing that Annie is capable of transgressive behavior. Like Poe's Dupin, the detective has to learn to be more of a poet, to become a good and careful reader. His hunch is confirmed when he interviews the general store owner who supplies Annie with copies of the latest Paul Sheldon publications and, more recently, writing supplies. These individual moments of insight born from investigative work that the sheriff pieces together lead to his decision to visit the Wilkes farm in pursuit of what his research has revealed about the connection between Paul and Annie, even if this revelation ends up costing him his life. Once inside the house, Buster and Annie engage in a cat and mouse game that frequently crosses over into the comical (perhaps the name "Buster" also is a reference to Buster Keaton?), as they periodically exchange glances separated by rooms. Her goal is to distract him from the basement, which houses the drugged writer, with hot chocolate and awkward banter; he, on the other hand, while also maintaining a friendly guise under the ruse of a neighborly visit, takes every opportunity to search both floors of the farmhouse. Although at first he does not find Paul, Buster's instincts lead him to suspect foul play, assuring Annie that he will return. Both these characters understand the truth hiding under each other's lies, but because the visit is more an exploratory venture than a mission to arrest a criminal, both characters hold their cards close to the vest. At first the viewer thinks that Buster has saved the day when he arrives at Annie's front door, so the audience is shocked and disappointed when he is shot in the back. Although Buster gets killed in the middle of the film, his death continues to drive the plot after that because the detective has been the only one operating from a belief that Paul remains alive. After Buster dies, viewers become even more anxious about how the writer will escape. After all, what is to be done in the absence of the law? In some ways, Buster's interaction with Annie reminds the viewer of Poe's Dupin in "The Purloined Letter" or Sherlock Holmes in the tales in which he is opposed to Dr. Moriarty, as the detectives engage in surreptitious actions that emerge because of their intuition into criminal behavior. In addition to their tacit denigration of fumbling police methods of inquiry and solution, both Holmes and Dupin share with Buster a reluctance to disclose whatever information they possess as well as the design of their investigations, observing and searching for evidence to exploit further the weaknesses of their opponents. Poe and Doyle provide their private detectives with ratiocinative abilities of superior observation as well as the ability to place themselves in the mind of the criminal, thus providing insights unavailable to inferior minds, such as those of the police. After noting Annie's temper at work when she barely avoids an accident outside his office and learning that she has a peculiar attachment to Paul's *Misery* novels, Buster is not fooled by Annie's sophomoric attempts to convince him that she has turned one of her rooms into a writing studio and she has "spent the last four weeks trying to write like Paul Sheldon." On some bizarre level, Annie's efforts to screen Paul and place his writing tools in plain sight are like Poe's Minister D— depositing the Queen's letter undisguised upon his desk.

Buster emerges as another type of detective found frequently haunting the King corpus: the literary sleuth. Although he appears as a down-home good old boy, he resembles other characters found elsewhere in the King universe, such as Thad Beaumont (*The Dark Half*), Ben Mears (*'Salem's Lot*), Andy Dufresne (*Shawshank*), or Mike Hanlon and Ben Hanscom in *IT*, who may not be actual detectives, yet operate in detective-like roles because they are readers and decipherers of personalities and written texts. These characters are alert to the madness that is always attendant to a uniform groupthink or bureaucratic institution. They are fiercely independent thinkers who, like many detectives beyond King's fictional universe, defy institutionalized thinking and thereby discover avenues for freedom and the vulnerability to evil. It is the reader-writer's job, as well as the detective's, to reassert order amid madness and destruction. In *IT*, Hanlon and Hanscom study the relationship between Derry and Pennywise through Hansom's library research (especially evident in the recent Muschietti *Chapter 1* film version) and the adult Hanlon's personal diary entries (especially evident in the novel). Elsewhere, Ben Mears, in *'Salem's Lot,* engages in similar investigative research as he writes a history of the Marsten House, which grants him a certain power over the house. All of these literary sleuths uncover dark secrets that lurk in the small towns and domestic tragedies that King is famous for exploring; their job is to unite characters with similar orientations and see that justice is done. Buster has a long lineage.

Buster is not, however, the only detective-reader-interpreter in Reiner's *Misery*. Paul is forced to become a kind of detective to save himself from Annie. He must pay close attention to her every mood and mannerism and use the things that he learns to make his life as her captive less miserable while also creating an escape plan. Because Annie keeps him restricted to one room, he pays close attention to her facial expressions and to her physical routines within the house that contains them both. As viewers watch a kind of recycling of what occurs during Buster's visit to Annie's farmhouse, Paul's exploratory journeys through her home reveal to him a place full of contradictions and evidence of the severity of Annie's personality disorder: her phone is a hollowed-out shell, present only for the sake of establishing normal appearances; her ceramic penguins all march in the same direction; her "Memory Lane" scrapbook is full of evidence that documents a devolving history of psychopathology and murder; her propensity for anger and physical violence is barely contained beneath her love of Liberace's music and shrine to Misery Chastain, the lead character of Paul's novels. The omnipresent gold cross Annie wears around her neck, the purity of diction she insists that Paul must adhere to, and her belief that the murders she has performed in the maternity unit as head nurse were "mercy killings" indicate the level of distorted, counter-intuitive reasoning that Paul uncovers and is forced to contend with. But beneath the surface, Paul also "saw the woman she might have been if her upbringing had been right or the drugs squirting out of all the funny little glands inside her had been less wrong. Or both" (282). The discipline Paul has cultivated as a writer and his research into Annie's personal history enable him to restrain himself from lashing out at his captor or making any attempt to overpower her physically until he is able to do so successfully. When Annie leaves for protracted periods of time, Paul explores the house and discovers a cache of pain medications. Even more important, he discovers the "Memory Lane" scrapbook that contains her dark history (recalling another of King's textual sleuths, Jack Torrance, as he pores over the scrapbook in the basement of the Overlook Hotel). The painkillers present Paul with a new level of power insofar as he can now regulate his own body, but it is the scrapbook that provides evidence into the psychopathic personality with whom he is dealing. His diligent sleuthing allows him to recognize the seriousness of Annie's mental illness and the seriousness of the predicament that confronts him. He gains insight into what he needs to do to keep his jailor happy and to prevent her from killing him for as long as possible. In an act of desperation, his ratiocination skills take him into Annie's personality, where he uncovers enough about her to save himself.

As both a film and a novel, *Misery* is at its essence a story about a man under constant assault. The novel version of Paul awakens in a new world: he is transformed from a world-famous novelist, a man of status and confidence, enormous wealth, and masculine privilege to a man who barely recognizes himself. Kidnapped, "raped full of her air" (5), and held in jeopardy by his "Number One Fan," Paul finds himself after the accident with both legs broken. Annie completes his dislocation by adding to his physical pain and torturing him psychologically, injecting him with sedatives against his will, amputating his foot and thumb, and reducing him to the status of an infant, "'Just like a baby'" (18). Meanwhile, the film makes ample use of extreme close-ups of Annie's face as it bears down on Paul, on several occasions completely filling the screen. The effect aligns the spectator's point of view with Paul's, making the spectator aware that Annie's face is yet another intimidating intrusion into Paul's personal space, usurping what he sees and hears, even the air he breathes (fig. 6.1). The actions Annie takes against Paul, both physical and psychological, must be read as symbolic emasculations. To make the point emphatically, after

Fig. 6.1. One of the close-ups of Annie Wilkes that fill the screen.

the novel version of Annie amputates Paul's thumb, she says, "'You're lucky I didn't cut off your man-gland. I thought of it, you know'" (251). Annie makes Paul dependent on her for his very survival by feeding him, supplying him with Norvil to relieve his immense pain, introducing him to the dimensions of his new world, and challenging him to find a way to survive and escape: to Paul, these actions "made her seem utterly monstrous, something he *must* escape. She really *was* an idol, and if she didn't kill him, she might kill what was *in* him" (26). Both film and novel document Paul's subtle transformation as a writer and a human being. Nearly his last words in the film are a self-acknowledgment of the bizarre debt he owes Annie: "In some way, Annie Wilkes, that whole experience, helped me." His agent may be baffled by such a pronouncement, but "that whole experience" teaches him a deeper respect for the literary craft he had formerly taken for granted in viewing it solely as a meal ticket. Ironically, he is rescued by the fictional heroine whom he has spent his career exploiting and has grown to despise. A parallel therefore exists in the film between the figuratively castrated state policeman and dynamic detective Buster and the figuratively castrated popular writer Paul and his revitalization as a detective-writer.

Paul has spent his publishing life exploiting women who share Annie's reading tastes in order to make money. His nearly exclusively female readership is entranced by the character of Misery, and he exploits that for his own gain. He has lost touch with what it means to create something new, to experiment and pursue artistic challenge instead of following the scent of cash. By escaping Annie and everything she symbolizes, Paul succeeds in finding his lost self, the self that was drawn to the act of artistic creation in the first place. This is the reason why King frequently associates Paul with the stories of Scheherazade, whose storytelling skills in *One Thousand and One Nights* manage to delay the execution of a sultan's wife (Poe, too, was interested in this story). Blunted by years of affluence and ease, "married and divorced twice" (6), drinking, smoking, and womanizing, living alone in a New York townhouse, "empty, bleak, unwelcoming" (14), Paul has, like the character Harry in Hemingway's story "Snows of Kilimanjaro," apparently "gone soft" by selling out his real writing talent instead of challenging it. Indeed, the car accident during a snowstorm occurs, in part, because he failed to pay attention to weather conditions on the mountain and because "he had also been quite drunk" when he began the drive (12). A reader should also be alert enough to ask why is it that whenever Paul finishes writing a new book, his habit is to celebrate its completion *alone*? To an extent, the author of the Misery Chastain books has fallen asleep at his typewriter—he keeps writing the same book in the same genre featuring the same characters and following a similar plotline for each instant bestseller. In bringing Misery back to life, Paul is reborn into a renewed respect for his narrative skill, his readership, and the character of Misery herself, whose protracted fictional ordeal ends up literally saving his life.

    The novel version of Paul also becomes a more serious reader-detective through the act of writing *Misery's Return*, which Annie forces him to write during his confinement. In developing the sequel, he learns to "read" Annie's moods and plot predilections, to provide acceptable responses to a given situation, while her many lessons in humility serve to "feminize" him by teaching him to moderate his "masculine" temper and language (neither the novel nor the film challenges the gendering of these characteristics in a sustained way). Annie unwittingly teaches Paul to ignore the weather at his own peril: "The climate inside her, he had come to discover, was like spring-time in the Midwest. She was a woman full of tornados waiting to happen, and if he had been a farmer observing a sky which looked the way Annie's face looked right now, he would have at once gone to collect his family and herd them into the storm cellar" (64). He learns that "she was strangely vulnerable to these concepts of discipline and behavior" (229), an indication of the ease with which Annie is capable of losing control over herself, at the same time as his insights also underscore the disciplinary skills required of a novelist. In the process, Paul turns himself into a kind of detective. While Annie reveals herself capable of sudden and random bursts of emotional turmoil, Paul relies ever more on patterned responses of self-control, in his writing choices and his personal interactions with his jailor. Like a hard-boiled detective in a spot of trouble, Paul understands that if he is going to survive, it will be the result of his own actions (not rescue from an outside source), based on what he understands about his current situation.

Although it is on Annie's insistence that he resurrects Misery, in doing so the novel version of Paul shifts the power dynamic back in his favor, as Annie falls under "a certain passive hold. The power of *the gotta*" (230; emphasis in the original), or the skill of a writer to command and entrance his reader: "*The gotta* had kept them both alive—and it had, for without it she surely would have murdered both him and herself long since" (226). The detective part of Paul has consciously studied Annie and knows how to recognize her central weakness: her inability to separate herself from the power of narrative, from a gripping storyline centered on the imperiled plight of her favorite literary character. The film affirms the power of Paul's art of detection: unlike the state police and even Buster, who exits the film with only a superficial understanding of Annie's character (or else he never would have turned his back to her), Paul has done the hard work of exploring Annie's psychopathology. So, after several aborted failures, the novel version of Paul sets out to write a story certain to captivate his reader and reingratiate him in her eyes after the "failure" of the *Fast Cars* manuscript: "Something in her attitude as she stood in the doorway fascinated him. It was as if she was a little frightened to come any closer—as if she thought something might burn her" (137). Paul's "reading" of Annie enables him to access her drug of choice—the story of Misery, as powerful as Paul's addiction to his dosage of Norvil. "'Shall I go on?' he asked. 'I'll kill you if you don't!' she responded, smiling a little" (137). In producing *Misery's Return,* Paul writes a metatext of his own situation as Annie's hostage. Less explicit in the film than the novel, where the reader can see excerpts from the manuscript itself, Paul uses his own "gruesome frame of mind" (137) as motivation to produce a plot that is both a reflection and an analysis of his own entrapment. Thanks to Annie's terrorizing, Paul can act as both detective *and* hostage, criminal prosecutor *and* crime victim.

One of the more engaging aspects of King's novel is that it transports readers into the actual composition of *Misery's Return*. Readers come to operate in the role of quasi-detectives by identifying with Annie (surrogate reader) as well as Paul (meta-author of *Misery's Return*), particularly when King reveals excerpts from Chapter 32 of the manuscript, wherein readers find Misery encased in a suit of living bees: "She seemed almost to be wearing some strange nun's habit—strange because it moved and undulated across the swells of her breasts and hips . . . only her blue eyes peered out of the mask of bees which crawled sluggishly over her face, hiding mouth and nose and chin and brows" (215). Only the steady, sonorous beat of the African drums and the absolute self-control Misery has over her "womanly hysteria" keep the bees, "giant African browns, the most poisonous and bad-tempered bees in the world," in a state of sleepy, suspended animation so they do not sting the novel's intrepid heroine (215–16). As the insects crawl over the length of her naked body, Misery is centered in both her book and Paul's plight: each must be alert to every movement, careful not to utter any sound that might provoke their respective captors. It is impossible not to parallel Paul's fictional protagonist with her author's own dangerous situation; as Annie's prisoner, he establishes an identification with Misery herself—naked under the omnipresent gaze of his own Bourka Bee Goddess, he lives in constant bondage, alert to the fact that the smallest infraction might activate his poisonous "Dragon Lady." That Misery is naked under her living jumpsuit is a violation of her modesty as a Victorian heroine at the same time it underscores the level of invasiveness and bodily exposure that Paul has experienced via the multiple personal intrusions imposed upon him by his captor. The beat of the African drums produces a steady drone that parallels the sound of his typewriter as he labors to keep Annie quiescent in her reading and under the sedative drug of "*the gotta.*" He knows that the composition of this new novel buys him time.

By drawing his captor into the newest episode of Misery Chastain, Paul blunts the sharp edges of Annie's personality under the hypnotic power of his art; he perhaps even deepens a bond of trust with her, making her happy, less unforgiving, and mostly enthralled in the fiction that Paul uses to manipulate her. By assuming the role of an undercover detective, Paul puts himself in a position where he can launch his escape plan by burning the new novel before Annie has a chance to discover Misery's fate. The creation of a sequel saves Paul's life: he is kept alive only to enable him to finish the story. The writing, on the other hand, while at first Paul's single card in Annie's stacked deck, emerges as his sole connection to life and sanity. As King himself acknowledges in "On Impact," an essay he wrote in 1999 after his near-death car accident, "For me, there have been times when the act of writing has been an act of faith, a spit in the eye of despair.

Writing is not life, but I think that sometimes it can be a way back to life" (85). Skills required to be an artist are similar to those a detective employs to establish control over the chaos and darkness that threatens modern humans' stability. In Paul's imagination, Annie represents the primitive Bourka Bee goddess—with the addition of being insane—but Paul is not, and his refusal to sacrifice either his art or himself at the altar of this unreasonable deity creates meaning out his suffering, triumph in the eye of despair. The novel's detective elements thus trump its immanent drift into a brutal Gothicism.

Annie's level of criminality bears much in common with the forces of social conformity and madness born from excessive discipline and oppression that we find throughout the King canon. We need only nod at a few of the major purveyors of an institutionalized world view in other characters—Warden Norton, Flagg, the Crimson King, Greg Stillson, Andre Linoge, Mrs. Carmody, Pennywise, the Tommyknockers, Leland Gaunt, Brady Hartsfield, the vampires in *'Salem's Lot*—to confirm a similarity of behavioral traits that are reduced to the same thing: a demand for conformity so rigid and relentless that it crosses over into the realm of madness. Annie Wilkes is a murderer who has somehow evaded criminal prosecution as the "Dragon Lady," but she also exposes her criminality by imposing her indomitable will over others. As we will argue later in this chapter, if Vera can be interpreted as both Dolores's id and superego in *Claiborne*, the same can be said of Annie, who emerges as the puritanical lawgiver and the consummate lawbreaker. Like Warden Norton in *Shawshank*, Annie wears an omnipresent gold crucifix that belies her true status as a violently disturbed sociopath whose oppressive dominance always threatens to break through the exterior of her giddy, adolescent fan worship of Paul. Fortunately, King's sleuths manage to thread the needle between a dull yet oppressive state police and a monomaniacal and oppressive criminal mastermind. These would-be detectives use deductive reason as well as expansive empathy to endure their darkest days.

Yet it is important to note that the detectives in both versions of *Misery* decidedly identify as male—although Paul's "castration" may mark him as symbolically feminine. Moreover, Annie's alignment with both ends of the spectrum, conformity and abject madness, imprisons her within an oppressive angel/madwoman binary, examined in detail by feminist critics Sandra Gilbert and Susan Gubar. Can Buster's and Paul's brand of ratiocination be extricated from a chronically patriarchal way of viewing the world? And, on a related note, why doesn't Annie, the novel's only substantive female character, display the characteristics of a "good detective"? King himself attempted to answer that question when, five years after the publication of *Misery*, he released a related-yet-revisionary novel, *Dolores Claiborne*.

DETECTION IN *DOLORES CLAIBORNE*

Beyond their status as novels in which King attempts to rectify his stereotypical portrayals of female characters, there is a subtler, and arguably even more intriguing, parallel that connects *Misery* to *Dolores Claiborne*: the fact that each narrative subverts the conventions of the traditional detective story. On the one side, we might pair the film version of *Misery*'s Sheriff Buster with *Claiborne*'s John McAuliffe (given the sobriquet Mackey in the film version). With varying degrees of conformity and success, each agent of the law attempts to use his powers of deduction to solve a crime. Undoubtedly, Buster—because he trusts his gut and has a softer side—is King's preferred model; McAuliffe/Mackey remains entirely too driven, too singularly focused, and too self-involved to achieve enlightenment. Also, as discussed earlier, McAuliffe/Mackey closely resembles the police in Poe's detective tales. McAuliffe/Mackey relies on procedure instead of poetic intuition, and, without evidence, he is convinced of Dolores's guilt. He is therefore a "bad detective." Still, all of these detectives arrive at dead ends for the same reason: *they don't see the literal and metaphorical hole in the ground until it is too late*. Unable to recognize his own blind spots, McAuliffe/Mackey cannot access the figurative and actual wells in which Dolores has buried her secrets. Said another way, because he does not grasp the blind spots of his own perspective, he surely cannot comprehend the inner workings of Dolores's unconscious—the allegorical hole in her backyard. Buster mirrors McAuliffe/Mackey because after he circles around the truth and gets dangerously close to uncovering it, he trusts his own skills as a sleuth too much. Like the detective-analyst in *Claiborne*, Buster tries to peer into the hidden cavity—in his case, the cellar of Annie's house—without first checking his blind spots. Annie takes advantage of this oversight by stepping into his (literal) blind spot and shooting him with her shotgun in his back.

In contrast, both books elevate a *better detective*, that is, a detective who possesses a fuller, deeper understanding of how knowledge and mastery really work. In both versions of *Misery*, Paul learns to read Annie, to interpret (and eventually manipulate) the mote in her eye, just as he learns to recognize his own limitations by seeing what he missed in his earlier presumed mastery over his gullible reader's psyche. In short, Paul becomes a more thoughtful reader, which simultaneously makes him a more sensitive writer, just as he cultivates an appreciation for the dynamic interplay between criminality and morality (in Annie as well as himself). Observing Annie's self-censored, self-righteous personality, Paul starts to read for signs of his caretaker's psychosis: the darkness that rolls in like thunderheads. At the same time, knowing that Annie is always watching for signs of his disobedience, Paul realizes that he needs to hide his transgressive inklings—to play the part of the pet writer while secretly plotting to violate the rules of the house. He slowly sharpens his skills as reader and writer, prison guard and prisoner, to survive his ordeal.

In *Dolores Claiborne*, the eponymous heroine follows in Paul's footsteps by incorporating into herself the astute observational skills of a detective. Unlike the narrowmindedness displayed by McAuliffe/Mackey, she recognizes that *both criminal and detective have blind spots*, and so instead of getting lost in a futile power struggle or hoping in vain to escape from it, she intuitively understands the inner structure of the criminal-detective game that she has been forced to play. By probing into these pairings (Buster and McAuliffe/Mackey; Paul and Dolores), this section traces the outline of what King considers to be a "good detective": a detective who knows from the start she will always lack mastery and therefore opts to pursue something other than an illusion of total control.

Maureen Reddy suggested in 1988 that an alternative, "feminine" way of looking could revitalize the increasingly stale hard-boiled detective genre: "If women, because of their socialization, read the world rather differently than do men, then it stands to reason that a woman detective might read clues differently than a male detective" (10). In other words, since the system at work in traditional hard-boiled detective fiction routinely taught all readers and audiences to look at the world the way a man would, one method for revising the genre's patriarchal tendencies is to introduce the so-called female perspective as a crucial corrective. Jennifer Friedlander asks, "How should women look in order to avoid both the masochism of taking up the position of man as well as the narcissism of identifying too closely with the fetishized image of woman on-screen?" (49). If, as Laura Mulvey famously posits, classic Hollywood cinema routinely insists upon a "male gaze" to master an objectified female figure—a penetrative gaze akin to the classic hard-boiled detective's—then the feminist response should be for a new kind of cinema, complimented by a new kind of detective.

Making a Lacanian turn, Taylor Hackford's film version of *Dolores Claiborne* interrogates blind spots instead of registering (and re-registering, as King does) the mastery of the male gaze.

Claiborne marks an intersection of three intimately related phenomena: an antagonistic relationship between critic and author; the oft-combative dynamic that unfolds between, as well as within, troubled psyches; and a ubiquitous detective formula, in which something called truth must be relentlessly pursued into every dank corner of seaside hamlets and labyrinthine minds. While the detective formula remains our primary quarry here, we cannot overlook the equally rich role that aesthetics and psychoanalysis play. Indeed, this triad directly informs our thesis concerning the two iterations of *Claiborne*. On the front end, King's novel, although providing one of his best characterizations to date in Dolores, succumbs to the very logic that it aims to critique: even as it lambasts the all-penetrative, bad male Freudian gaze, it holds to a sort of armchair Freudian mastery in which the Truth (with a capital T) appears to fall within the omniscient narrator's bailiwick. On the back end, Hackford's film adaptation distinguishes itself from King's novel in a Lacanian fashion by reflecting the inherently structural nature of truth (with a lower-case t)—that is, the paramount role of mediation, relationality, and the difference between the symbolic realm and concepts being represented. Whereas King's novel tracks an introspective detective through a process of self-discovery, Hackford's cinematic version more deftly handles the complexity of the mature detective's task, replete with poetic caesuras and layered ways of seeing.

To begin, it may not be immediately evident why we have chosen to read *Dolores Claiborne* as a detective novel. But once one knows what to look for, the evidence is everywhere. In conformity with formulaic standards, King's text unveils its crimes right away: Dolores's murder of her husband, Joe St. George, and the suspicious death of the woman for whom she works as caretaker, Vera Donovan. With Dolores's criminal acts foregrounded, the town police officer, Andy, a direct surrogate for the reader, must listen to her first-person confession and then deduce whodunit and, even more importantly, *why*. King structures his narrative in line with the template for traditional detective tales. First, the uninitiated reader, alongside the more agile-minded detective, encounters the aftermath of a crime; second, the reader must piece together the relevant information to "solve" the case (when, where, how, and so forth). Furthermore, given King's proclivities for dabbling in metacommentary on the detective story, a propensity that we chart throughout this book, readers discover in *Claiborne* a willingness on

Fig 6.2. Car headlights double as the interrogation lights used to grill suspects.

King's part not only to follow the blueprint of his forebearers in the genre, but to reflect on its limitations. For example, King's book extensively relies on *mise-en-abyme* (stories within stories). Numerous writers' commentaries on the traditional genre, including several by King, place a stand-in for the detective in the position of interrogator, and the individual being interrogated must rehearse her version of events under grilling lights: in the case of *Claiborne*, Dolores being interrogated by Vera; Dolores interrogating her daughter, Selena; Dolores being interrogated by McAuliffe/Mackey (and so on and so on). By placing plots of this type within other plots of this type, *Claiborne* in both its text and film versions underscores latent aspects of the detective formula, especially the powerful but inherently problematic dynamic of suspicious inquisitor and ever-evasive witness (fig. 6.2).

On this front, King's novel closely parallels a seminal detective novel, Mary Elizabeth Braddon's *Lady Audley's Secret* (1862).[4] Braddon's *Lady* is one of the earliest detective stories to explore the fraught dynamic between suspicious inquisitor and evasive witness. Note the many parallels: Braddon's novel features a barrister and would-be detective, Robert Audley, "a pitiless embodiment of justice" (231), who suspects that his aunt Lady Audley, a poor governess turned wealthy aristocrat, murdered her former husband by leading him to the edge of an old well and allowing him to fall into it. Like King's *Claiborne*, Braddon's *Lady* is a detective story that doubles as a commentary on gender and class. It too involves a misogynistic male detective who wants to portray women as shrewd, money-hungry, and inherently deceptive. Yet King's text ostensibly offers a much-needed feminist revision of Braddon's Victorian novel: whereas Lady Audley ends up locked away in a madhouse, like so many oppressed women in Victorian literature, Dolores ends up redeemed in the eyes of the reader, innocent, and vindicated for her choices. At its most interesting, *Claiborne* revives as well as revises the thrusts and parries between suspect and detective—what *Lady Audley's Secret* deems to be a psychological "duel to the death" (Braddon 234)—that define Braddon's foundational detective tale.

In a similar vein, *Claiborne* focuses on psychoanalysis by examining the underlying dynamics of analyst and analysand—an interrogation, or grilling, of a somewhat different sort. King very often borrows from and lambasts Freudianism, and this novel proves to be no exception to that rule.[5] A character vocalizes King's apparent antagonism to Freud in one of his short stories: "Freud offended me" ("Morality" 170). *Claiborne* exhibits a wariness of Freudian approaches since King populates the novel with overzealous interpreters trying to delve into the concealed recesses of a guilty party. Indeed, "The figure of the [male] psychoanalyst doubles with that of the detective, as an agent bent on interpreting class and symbols, a figure of power who applies ratiocinative skills to a particular text" (Munt 147). The subject conceals her genuine emotional state from self and other; meanwhile, the analyst probes into the deceptions, looking for signs of what the subject *really* means when she speaks: "How things look and how they really are" (King, *Claiborne* 134). Unwilling to take anything at face value, the bad Freudian violates what King depicts as the mysterious, even sacred, internal space of a female mind. Similarly, the death scenes of *Claiborne* instigate a kind of dream analysis: Dolores presents the deaths of Joe and Vera, and her culpability in these deaths, as though they were the stuff of her nighttime fantasies. As her account spills out of her, she admits that witnessing the deaths "felt like a dream" (221). It thus becomes increasingly difficult to disentangle the outside—her personal story, the symptoms of her condition—from the inside—her inner life, her imagined essence as a woman, mother, friend, wife, and human being. The reader/analyst is forced to make a choice, one that has clearly been made for him in advance: doubt Dolores's account and insist upon uncovering the truth behind her lies and therefore act as a bad Freudian (in King's estimation, at least), or believe Dolores and therefore eviscerate the supposedly domineering, patriarchal assumptions of psychoanalysis (again, according to King's appraisal). In a variety of ways, then, King's critiques of the detective genre and psychoanalysis reveal themselves to be co-constitutive. For a prime example of these overlapping concerns, let us turn to the foil of the novel, John McAuliffe, the county medical examiner sent to ascertain answers regarding Dolores's part in Vera's demise.

With his Scottish brogue, similar in effect to the German accent of the oft-caricatured Freud, and his status as a doctor who wants to cut through the appearance to the reality, Dr. John McAuliffe serves as the text's principal Freudian authority. Dolores says that he has "a mind like the lamp that shines outta Battiscan Light . . . you felt like he was staring right into your head and puttin the thoughts he saw there into alphabetical order" (289). His patriarchal look penetrates as he tries to tease to the surface Dolores's confession. He attempts to get Dolores to rush ahead in her narrative so that she might stumble into an admission. Much like Dolores, who lures her drunk and abusive husband into falling into an old well, McAuliffe hopes to trap her unexpectedly in a difficult spot, to cause her to fall into a metaphorical hole within her own account. Once she falls into the figurative hole, McAuliffe can shine his metaphorical light down into her unconscious. But he is not just a medical examiner; he also fashions himself as a private eye, a man who "fancied himself just like the amateur detectives in the magazine stories" (303). Playing the part of detective-analyst, McAuliffe instigates a cat-and-mouse game with Dolores, similar to the one played by Sheriff Buster and Annie in *Misery*. McAuliffe and Dolores circle around each other, mentally thrusting and parrying, "duellin with [their] eyes" (300). McAuliffe almost succeeds in drawing out Dolores's untold part of herself, but, like the unfortunate detective saddled with a rather dim Watson (in Conan Doyle's Sherlock Holmes stories) or, more appropriate still, an inept Prefect (in Poe's Dupin stories), the bumbling police officer "assisting" McAuliffe in his investigation intervenes and spoils the session, thereby releasing Dolores from the snare set by the conniving investigator. When Hackford's film adaptation changes McAuliffe from medical examiner to regional detective, it is not a significant departure since the two occupations share several traits. And King's portrayal is hardly a flattering one: while the John McAuliffe of the novel (the John: that etymologically masculine mode of address, occasionally slang for a man who treats women like a consumer good for his own pleasure) reveals himself to be an arrogant and overly aggressive force, Dolores views his partner, the bumbling Andy Bissette, as "tender-hearted" and so, in the final tally, redeemable (307). If McAuliffe had learned to analyze his subject in a more "tender-hearted" manner, he too might have gained greater wisdom and clarity from the case. As things stand, he remains ruthless and unable to move closer to genuine enlightenment. A walking indictment of patriarchal authority of any stripe, King's detective-analyst suffers from a chronic need to assert his mastery over others. The film version of

McAuliffe, renamed Mackey, is similarly obsessed with the past, and his know-it-all attitude blinds him from appreciating the more complicated reality of events. Dolores's involvement in the "accidental misadventure" that killed her husband is the only case Mackey has failed to resolve "to [his] satisfaction." His professional ego will not permit him to investigate how, much less why, Dolores would want to eliminate her husband. Her motivations never enter the dynamics of his investigation. Years later, he is again so far off from understanding the facts of Vera's death that he believes Dolores may have killed her for the $1.6 million inheritance in Vera's will. These failings further link Mackey to Poe's indictment of the police officer in his detective tales and are examples of Mackey's narrowness of vision and his willingness to assume that, as a woman, Dolores is inherently guilty. He never considers that Dolores's threats to kill Vera were part of their lexicon of love, after years of living together. Even after Selena dismantles all his evidence as circumstantial, Mackey stubbornly responds with a textbook example of what is colloquially referred to as "mansplaining": "It's the truth!"

There are better detectives all over Little Tall Island. Dolores's daughter, Selena, for example, differentiates between Dolores's killing her husband years ago and the suicide of Vera at the beginning of the film. Mackey, on the other hand, is unable and unwilling to take that step. All he can do is create a story believable enough to put Dolores in prison for murder. Not only is Selena forced to assume the position of the detective once she arrives on the island, working with her mother to discover the truth beneath Mackey's wrong assumptions, but she is also a journalist in New York City. A major component of journalism, particularly the style of probing interactive journalism Selena practices, is investigating life stories and getting personalities to "open up" (the phrase Mackey uses out of admiration for Selena's interview with Richard Nixon) and reveal highly guarded secrets. Although she is not in law enforcement, nor has she been professionally trained as a detective, Selena most certainly operates as a detective, before and during her stay on the island, and she is the one character in the film who pieces the story together and reveals the whole truth (for herself, Mackey, and the viewer). And she does so by empathizing with her mother—something the arrogant Mackey simply cannot, or will not, do.

As the official face of law enforcement, Mackey uses his investigation to take everything from Dolores. When she goes to get her possessions at Vera's, she finds that he has bagged most of it as evidence. Even her body becomes evidence that Mackey processes, as when he takes strands of her hair to analyze its DNA. His investigation into Vera's death fails to move beyond his fixation on Dolores's past. He violates the first principle of a detective, established under Poe's watch, by failing to remain open-minded enough to follow the evidence instead of holding to his own prejudices. Like the Parisian police officers whom Dupin accuses in Poe's "The Murders in the Rue Morgue" of being locked into procedures that focus on "'what has occurred'" rather than "'what has never occurred before'" and thereby suffer from impaired "'vision by holding the object too close'" (414, 412), Mackey gets swept up into following only the obvious evidence and therefore fails to account for the human elements at play. Like Vera, who scrutinizes Dolores as if she is a bug pinned to a slide, the detective ignores the fact that poetic caesuras, within the self as well as the other, may be real openings for insight. Although his own death is metaphorical (professional) rather than literal, Mackey ultimately shares the fate of Jorge Luis Borges's Erik Lönnrot, from the story "Death and the Compass," in that both detectives obsess over what they assume to be the underlying order of the case until they discover—alas, a moment too late—that they have been running in circles.

Even more interesting, though, is the fact that Dolores has internalized both ends of the detective story, just as she has subsumed within herself the role of analyst as well as analysand: she is criminal as well as detective within her own life story. As she yells out at one point in the film, her narrative *is* her life. Her confession is a tale of victimhood as well as a trap with which to ensnarl her prey; it is an example of self-policing as well as an exercise in excess, in criminality, and in perverse notions involving excrement and incest (see, for instance, Vera's abject behavior as it has been internalized by Dolores). The novel captivates readers because it offers a totalized schema: like viewers of the topographical map of the path of the eclipse included as paratextual content at the beginning of the novel, King's readers are permitted *to oversee Dolores's very being*. Said another way, the detective novel and (bad) psychoanalysis share a drive to make conscious what had been previously unconscious—latent feelings at odds with inhibitions, or the dastardly motive around which the criminal has erected barriers for self-defense. These competing energies are always-already at play within the solitary subject. It is not that Dolores defines herself through external pressures emanating from Joe, her husband (the Oedipal criminal), or McAuliffe (the detective-analyst); rather, actions imputed to others truly belong to her. In the end, every character is a part of herself, just as every detective proves to be already intimately connected to the criminal: he sees through the criminal's eyes, he can access the criminal's secrets, and he operates beyond predictable paradigms established by the legal apparatus and its incompetent policemen. Following writers such as Alain Robbe-Grillet or Ross Macdonald, King complicates boundaries typically assumed to divide detective-analyst from criminal-analysand, and he therefore calls into question the patriarchal premise behind Poe's concept of ratiocination—the hypermasculine basis, or so King seems to believe, for the art of detection as well as psychoanalytical deductions.

As proof of this totalizing schema by the analyst, let us briefly consider the novel's Vera, who wears many hats in King's text. A sly woman, she can pierce through Dolores's stories with the sort of incision later used by McAuliffe: Vera's "eyes seemed to bore a hole" in Dolores's head; she "found a window in my skull," Dolores complains, "and used it to peek right into my thoughts" (187–88). Seen completing newspaper crossword puzzles and known to house stacks upon stacks of jigsaw puzzles in her basement, Vera conducts her affairs as a puzzle master. She considers herself to be the fastidious keeper of order, a standing that Dolores both lauds and despises. As Dolores acknowledges midway through the film, "She did have her ways. I don't know where she got her ideas, but I do know she was a prisoner of them. . . . Mildew was grounds for firing."

Like McAuliffe, the ever-scrupulous Vera is held captive by her own preconceived notions. At the same time, Vera is one of the novel's consummate criminals: cool, calculating, and callous, she dispatches her cheating husband in short order, encourages Dolores to do the same, and then harbors Dolores in her mansion. Dolores holds a special regard for Vera; consequently, Vera occupies a central position in Dolores's psyche, even after her demise: "Vera's voice spoke . . . it was in my head" (270). Equal parts id and superego, Vera figuratively pulls Dolores apart, giving voice to her self-doubts as well as her murderous impulses. In one disturbing sequence from the novel, the elderly Vera plays a cat and mouse game with her caretaker by defecating at exactly the wrong time. Closely resembling the arch-detective Sherlock Holmes, Vera uses her superior logic to get out ahead of her opponent, until Dolores can "catch up" with her and move her own pawn into a more competitive position. But this story also revolves around human feces flung on the walls. Could it be, then, that the detective's game is, beneath its hyper-rational façade, a rather grotesque one, rooted in the basest of human urges to dominate, or mark one's territory, like a primate? Or consider the ominous dust mites that terrorize an increasingly senile Vera: her obsession with orderliness again harkens back to the detective's wit of her youth. In Holmesian fashion, nothing can be out of place in her world. Yet this obsession proves to be a crippling one, as she ends her days cowering in fear from the slightest sign of disorder. Even as Vera knits a web for Dolores in a wily way that demonstrates Vera's acumen and places her in the supercilious position of inquisitor, she simultaneously plants the felonious idea in Dolores's head that Dolores should kill her derelict husband. Like the detective, Vera-as-analyst is both untouchable *and* insidious. She endlessly strives to outmaneuver her opponent, which requires that she stay in touch with the less savory parts of herself that are also trying "to win." Through Vera's dual function in Dolores's narrative, readers must confront the muddy waters prematurely cleared up by the classic detective formula as well as King's account of psychoanalysis. Dolores imagines herself to be chasing others while, at other times, she is the one being chased. The text reports life to be "both things at the same time," and so presumed binaries must be reevaluated (91). King's novel thus undermines two of modernity's most prominent, and acutely patriarchal (or so King believes), modes of interrogation—the detective and the Freudian analyst.

But does King actually succeed in subverting the detective-analyst? There are several reasons to doubt that his subversion truly works. In her defense of Freud against feminist attacks, Shoshana Felman asserts: "The unconscious means that every insight is habited by its own blindness, which pervades it: you cannot simply polarize, oppose blindness and sight," or one "only *reverses* the polarization but does not restructure, undermine, the illusory polarities" (71; emphasis in the original). With the writing of *Claiborne*, King wants to don the garb of feminist to undercut the male superiority of Freud and his followers. It is worth remembering that King dedicated this novel to his mother, who raised him alone after his father's departure. However, King does not grasp that to undercut male mastery, and not simply "reverse the polarities," one must recognize one's own blind spots. Or the game of cat and mouse becomes interminable. King opens his novel with the famous question from Freud's letter to Marie Bonaparte: "What does a woman want?" Yet, in a way that the novel does not recognize, Freud opens this inquiry not to receive a masterful answer, but *to open a need for ceaseless questioning*. The unconscious is a question rather than an answer, that is, the unconscious is a hole, a well that can never be sealed. Felman insists that Freud professed "male restlessness in the face of unsatisfactory male solutions" (99), using Irma's dream in particular to install "a nodal point of significant resistance in the text of the ongoing psychoanalytic dream of understanding" (120).

So too have contemporary crime writers regularly placed nodal points of resistance within their otherwise orthodox stories: voids, caesuras, lacunae that challenge attempts at absolute mastery. One might ask whether *Claiborne* successfully defies what it declares to be Freud's drive to mastery by opening an unfillable chasm—a concealed cavity in the backyard that cannot be permanently closed.

Alas, King's novel does not renounce male solutions; instead, it perpetually outwits its Constant Reader by always staying two steps ahead, just like its guileful protagonist or its caricature of the detective-analyst. To demonstrate this enduring sense of mastery, Dolores, King's authorial mouthpiece, reverses the gaze of King's readers by turning the tables on their surrogate, Andy the policeman: "I c'n read you," she gleefully informs him. "Awful open, your face is" (20, 57). Dolores invites the reader to catch up only to pull ahead once more, effectively proclaiming the supremacy of her authorial position. In so doing, the text simply swaps blindness for sight in a manner that bypasses the structural *necessity* of blindness, which is to say, the blindness inherent to any claim of mastery. One might anticipate this additional turn of the screw when, after the Freud question "What does a woman want?," King's novel quotes from the singer Aretha Franklin regarding R-E-S-P-E-C-T. In other words, unwilling—or unable—to leave the question as a constitutional one, built into its very structure, King's *Dolores Claiborne* persistently provides answers (another example, perhaps, of the "mansplaining" phenomenon).

Rather than leave Dolores's future unwritten, and thereby leave eternally unanswered the question of "what a woman wants"—therefore rejecting the need to insert a man's solution—*Claiborne* includes appendices that fill in the gaps of the story in a neat and tidy fashion that would have made Sherlock Holmes proud. To prove her innocence in the killing of Vera, Dolores insists that she does not want the stunning inheritance that Vera, in her will, has left Dolores. Of course, this point could have been part of a bigger con: a hole in the story that actually empowered Dolores by leaving her secrets unexposed and her depths unplumbed. However, the close of King's text includes a newspaper excerpt revealing that Dolores did in fact donate her inheritance from Vera to a worthy charity. Another appendix reveals that Dolores resolves her feud with her children. Meanwhile, Vera's murder of her husband costs her dearly because, as a repayment of a cosmic debt, Vera's children are killed in a freak car accident. By confessing her crime,

Dolores has "made good" on her own debt and regained what apparently means the most in the world to her (her children). In short order, Dolores goes from the detective-analyst of her own life, haunted by the wells in her proverbial backyard, to a fixed character in someone else's story. As Munt says happens in so much feminist crime fiction, *Dolores Claiborne* produces "a radical change constrained within an overall conformity" (31). Its focus on redemptive self-fulfillment marks the text as very much of its moment in the 1990s; its happy ending strips its heroine of the radicality suggested in its early pages. In short, King's novel affirms a benevolent, essentialist bedrock within Dolores by confirming her alibi. King's readers no longer wonder what Dolores wants; the answer is plain for all to see. Leaving no trace of a doubt, King once more defeats the detective (the skeptical reader or literary critic) by showing this sleuth the danger of his own suspicious, and patriarchal, outlook. Readers should apparently appreciate Dolores at face value. The letter was out in the open all along.

But isn't Dolores worth more? What if King, following Freud in his encounter with Irma, had left Dolores as something of a mystery to his overzealous patriarch? Instead, King falls into the trap of mastery that Felman has elucidated: to outwit his caricature of Freud, he becomes just like his caricature of Freud.[6]

His alternative solution—Dolores redeemed and made singularly maternal—is still a solution, well meaning, maybe, but not qualitatively different from bad Freudianism. By trying to take down the founder of psychoanalysis (defined as King imagined him to be), King does not sustain a method for readers to sabotage his own authorial position. In the final account, King's attempt at a feminist corrective only more deeply re-entrenches his reader within the worldview ostensibly being challenged. There are no gaps, no wells in the lawn, only an omnipotent male perspective (King's) that leaves nothing unspoken and no mystery unsolved.

With that being said, one discovers in the novel *Claiborne* a rather interesting literary device that sets up Hackford's film through the stenographer Nancy Bannister. Nancy is everywhere and nowhere in King's novel. As an invisible laborer, she, like many women, does the dirty work, mostly unseen by male eyes. Nancy functions in *Claiborne* as an essential mediator, a veiled aperture through which Dolores must channel her story for the police of Little Tall Island to consume. Dolores notices Nancy and immediately curries her favor. She recognizes that Nancy, as the only other woman in the interrogation room, may be sympathetic to her cause. Moreover, King's novel closes by drawing the reader's attention to the tool of Nancy's trade, her steno machine: that "cunning little recorder, that rig of yours" (368). Through Nancy, a transcriber so quiet that she effortlessly slips out of the detective's consciousness and into the unconscious of the novel, King's narrative gestures at the structural positions that comprise established truth. That is, Nancy reveals how mastery is not a polarized struggle between falsehood and truth, blindness and sight; instead, mastery involves a complex way of seeing that remains inherently relational. Instead of interpreting *Claiborne* as the confession of a woman's core truth, viewers of the film can, via Nancy's presence, see the story's truths as a layered phenomenon, constructed from a trio of defined positions: the detective, the criminal, and the mediating screen (what we shall soon see as the cinematic machine—a cunning rig in its own right).[7]

Part of this shift into reading the truth as a layered phenomenon involves moving out from the solipsistic confines of self-discovery and into a world dictated by social structures. The film expands beyond the novel's narrow focus (it is all part of Dolores—it is all in her head) to include Mackey, the detective, and Dolores's daughter, Selena. For his part, Mackey tries to exploit long-standing issues between Selena and her mother. He tells Selena, "You know, we're probably more alike than you'd care to believe." He attempts to turn Selena against her mother, to separate physically the child from her mother in order to manipulate her so that Selena continues to do what he has done: assume the guilt of Dolores. Like the Prefect in Poe's "The Purloined Letter," Mackey and Selena at first fail to place themselves in the position of the suspect because they never quite understand the suffering Dolores has undergone as Joe's wife or Vera's closest ally. The film version of King's story amplifies its innately relational qualities and compels viewers to conclude that there is no subject position that isn't always-already defined by relationships. Hackford's ever-shifting camera position underscores this relationality. We only ever know ourselves through the interplay between one another—a fact understood by the historical Freud but overlooked by King's rather naïve detective-analysts.

As we have already seen, King's novel overlooks a famous aphorism from Freud's interpreter, Jacques Lacan: "There is no metalanguage." In critiquing a system based on the mastery of others—the patriarchy, as it materializes in psychoanalysis as well as detective fiction—King attempts to position himself and his Constant Reader somehow outside of the system, as though one can somehow speak from within (first-person Dolores) as well as from without (the appendices). In the novel *Claiborne*, mastery is an immersive game, certainly, but a game from which one can eventually escape by becoming more "tender-hearted," trusting, intuitive, or well informed. In Hackford's film, on the other hand, there is no metalanguage. Instead, the subject speaks from inside the system in question; she remains constitutionally bound to it. The best that an enlightened viewer can hope for is not to take for granted the cinematic structure in which she finds herself engrossed, but to recognize its density and comprehend the inevitable holes in her own field of vision.[8] To understand this crucial distinction, let us briefly turn to Lacan's seminal analysis of Poe's "The Purloined Letter," in which Lacan lays out this argument in detail.

In this illustrative detective story, Poe points to three subjective positions, the occupants of which change as the tale progresses. The King occupies the first position, in that he has no idea of the secret that the Queen is hiding from him; the Queen, meanwhile, believes that she has "outwitted" the King, so she occupies a second, more masterful position, lording over him; and in the third position is Minister D—, who blackmails the Queen, sees the Queen seeing her husband, and thus recognizes her blind spot. With the arrival of the Minister, the Queen shifts into position one, the Minister into position two, and Dupin into position three (and then, the Minister slides into one, Dupin into two, and the reader into three). Why does Poe mark out these distinctive subjective positions? Lacan theorizes that Poe illuminates "the symbolic chain which binds and orients" (28). He adds, "It is not only the subject, but the subjects, grasped in their intersubjectivity, who line up, in other words our ostriches, who, more docile than sheep, model their very being on the moment of the signifying chain which traverses them" (45). The signifying chain precedes the characters themselves. Every character unconsciously slides in and out of the three positions as they attempt to "read" and are, in turn, read by one another. The Minister thinks that he has achieved mastery by reading the innermost thoughts of the Queen, who remains unaware that she is being figuratively penetrated. Yet at the precise moment that he believes he has gained the permanent upper hand and therefore escaped from the prison of intersubjectivity, along comes an even more crafty detective (Dupin), who reads the Minister without the Minister's knowledge and, in so doing, renders the Minister's position synonymous with the Queen's. To say it simply: *there is no authorial position outside of the system*. Everyone must read, and be read, by others. The contents of the purloined letter do not matter; what truly matters is the power structure, the ever-shifting arrangement of interrogator and witness. One errs by trying to pinpoint a single actor within the chain instead of pulling back to recognize that everyone, including masterful authors like Poe or King, has a blind spot. Sometimes you're Joe chasing Dolores, and sometimes you're Dolores chasing Joe, but you are never completely removed from the game, even (or especially) if you are the one writing it down. Lacan might well have been speaking of King's authorial presence in *Claiborne* when he observed, "What does he fail to see? Precisely the symbolic situation which he himself was so well able to see" (44).

Hackford's version of the narrative differs from King's, then, because it attends with a greater degree of sophistication to the structural triad articulated by Lacan *avec* Poe. From its opening sequence, which entices audiences into seeing ever more deeply by moving gradually from the exterior of Vera's mansion to the shadowy interior secrets of her death, the film encourages its viewer to equate vision with knowledge. From the start of the film, the viewer, like Mackey, is provided only partial knowledge, and this knowledge base expands and alters as the film unfolds. The viewer is therefore asked to assume the position of the detective-analyst, the one who must eventually see all. Vera (Judy Parfitt) forever sharpens her penetrating look, stressed by the birds of prey prominently displayed throughout her home (fig. 6.3 and fig. 6.4).

Likewise, the film's detective, John Mackey (Christopher Plummer), lures the viewer into behaving like a detective-analyst: the camera forces audiences to share his eyeline as he peers at suspects, probing for answers. And yet, as the film progresses, it becomes clear that the gaze of the master is not singular but divided into three parts. During the film's initial interrogation scene, Dolores (Kathy Bates) looks at her daughter, Selena (Jennifer

Fig. 6.3. An ice sculpture of a bird of prey appears at the eclipse party.

Fig. 6.4. Another bird of prey is carved into the headboard of Vera's bed.

Jason Leigh), trying to glimpse how she is affected by her father's death and the subsequent investigation; meanwhile, Mackey looks over Dolores's shoulder, looking at her in the act of looking at her child (fig. 6.5).

In Lacanian terms borrowed from "The Purloined Letter," Selena occupies position one, Dolores position two, and Mackey position three. Or consider the scene in which Selena returns to Little Tall Island and encounters her mother for the first time in the police station. Selena gazes at her mother in search of clues. Did she *really* kill Vera? Concurrently, Mackey stands behind Selena, watching her as she observes her mother: Dolores now occupies position one, Selena position two, and Mackey position three (fig. 6.6).

Fig. 6.5. Detective Mackey watches Dolores as she looks at her daughter.

Fig. 6.6. Selena looks at Dolores as Mackey observes.

Fig. 6.7. Mackey at last becomes the subject of Selena's gaze, while Dolores watches.

Finally, in the scene in the makeshift courtroom, in which Mackey attempts to establish Dolores's guilt, Selena returns to act as her defender. The characters once more exchange roles, sliding into different positions: this time, Mackey is the one being looked at by Selena (position one), while Dolores (position three) stares up at Selena (position two), who seems to be seeing things clearly for the first time (fig. 6.7).

In each of these interrogations, the dynamic is not a personal one, in which highly individualized characters enact their will; rather, in these meticulously framed sequences, the detective-criminal relationship reveals itself to be deeply structural in nature. Hackford's characters gravitate to their various positions, unaware of their place in the larger chain of the symbolic. At times, Mackey is the reader; at other times, he is the one being read. And the camera's oscillating orientation moves the viewer through each of the three perspectives. Hackford thus plays with the allure of mastery only to reveal that every assumed position of knowledge inevitably slides into a position of partial knowledge. In one moment, the camera lulls the viewer into a sense of empowerment (the imperious look of Mackey, Dolores, or Selena); in the next moment, the camera pivots, and viewers realize that their self-assured perspective has failed to account for the fact that they were, in turn, being read by the other (e.g., the failure of the mother initially to recognize her daughter and the subsequent awkward hug between them). Slipping between blind positions like ostriches, the detective-analyst struggles to secure her footing.

The shifting triad parallels the constant realignment of sun, moon, and earth during the novel's climactic eclipse. The names of the characters compliment this rotating trinity: Dolores means terrestrial clay, Selena means moon goddess, and Mackey is Celtic for sun god (the hottest grilling light imaginable). Their symbolic names signify a veritable eclipse in which they must orient themselves within the grand cosmic structure that precedes them. Unmooring the audience from the omnipotent look of the auteur, or the objective look of the camera itself, Hackford reveals the intrinsic relationality of human existence. Earth, sun, moon: to know any one of them requires awareness of the others. But in so charting these relational perspectives, Hackford does not fall into the trap of claiming to establish a position outside of the film, a cinematic metalanguage (the trap into which King himself falls in his novel); instead, the film version of *Claiborne* toys with the possibility of looking differently. Instead of telescoping back to impossible heights, akin to the opening helicopter shots of the island, the film attempts to *deepen* the viewer's gaze.

Hackford makes liberal use of depth of field to communicate his distinctive take on King's story. More specifically, he capitalizes on one of the *sui generis* tools of the cinematic medium to revise King's metacommentary upon the art of detection and, in turn, to avoid the trap of male mastery. While King's novel only feigns asking questions—it has the answers in its back pocket all along—Hackford's film uses depth of field to destabilize any sense of firm footing, especially for Mackey as an egomaniacal agent of the patriarchy. Against the gravitational pull of the detective-analyst's clinical mode of looking, Hackford asks viewers to recognize the mediating structure in place: namely, the cinematic machinery. In the opening sequence, Dolores drops her rolling pin (the would-be murder weapon), and it rolls across the screen into a cut featuring a white *New York Times* delivery truck, rolling along the streets of Manhattan. This stark juxtaposition makes Hackford's message about mediation crystal clear: the real weapon here is mediation, or the structural orientation that illuminates or obscures any assumed truth. In the next scene, the audience watches Selena's chauvinistic editor—the audience knows he is a chauvinist right away because he has a salacious magazine openly splayed upon his desk—crumple a story and throw it into a trash can. The arc of the crumpled story on its way to the trash can aligns directly with Selena's entering the office. The editor makes all the decisions; he always gets the final say on what ends up in the trash. When the viewer confronts the presence of a heavy-handed editor, she realizes that she must be ever-vigilant about what is missing from the story being provided. This story will be full of holes, pieces that have been selectively removed or thrown into the existential wastepaper basket. Hackford points out the vital function of montage in exposing the viewer's blind spots. Precisely when you think you have seen it all, you realize that there are caesuras throughout a filmic text.

After all, just as the citizens of Little Tall Island rely on protective mediating boxes to watch the eclipse, the viewers rely on the film camera to mediate what they are seeing. On several occasions, the film *Dolores Claiborne* exploits depth of field to cause the audience to question the assumption of unimpeded access to the truth. The camera lingers on revelers on the docks only to pull back its focus and reveal that the viewer has been peering through a fisherman's net all along. The invisible presence of the net echoes and amplifies Nancy's invisible presence in the novel by reminding the audience that there is no metalanguage, that the subject is always moving within prescribed parameters. The fisherman's snare, that is, symbolizes the trap of thinking that one can see reality itself when, in fact, the subject can only ever see through the apertures available to her. To a certain extent, the spectators encounter a similar dualism of experience as they watch island revelers prepare for the imminent eclipse experience—their general festive mood, dancing at Vera's soiree to the *bossa nova,* and boat horns celebrating in the distance—at the same time as they are sharply aware of the grisly business about to accompany the death of the Claiborne marriage. Hackford uses depth of field again in a brief but important shot to illustrate this structural trap: the camera surveys the ocean surrounding the island, then it recedes and reveals that the camera has been peering through a broken window, and then Dolores enters the frame to seal the window, just as she will later seal the well into which her husband falls. The first position—innocent viewer gazing upon a tranquil seascape with no impediments—shifts into a second position, as the viewer realizes that the first position was entirely too innocent. She is not in the open air; she has been looking through a window. And then, turning the screw once more, the audience watches as this interplay is covered up and hidden, moving the viewer into a third position from which she starts to see how windows are always a trick, a sort of *trompe-l'oeil*: an *illusion* of total transparency. Cinema depends upon its invisibility as an apparatus through which the audience sees its fictional creations. Just when the viewer believes that she has achieved omniscience—the ability to see and understand everything, all at once—she need only pull back the proverbial camera and see the limits of what had seemed, a mere moment earlier, to be effortless. For the uninitiated participant, looking and knowing are denser acts than they first seem to be.

Cinema's depth of field dramatically flattens time and space, allowing the viewer to see in a layered fashion. In a scene that calls to mind the famous moment in Orson Welles's *Citizen Kane* in which the camera slowly draws away from watching an innocent young boy playing in the snow from an open window and it becomes clear that there are multiple, competing layers to any life, Hackford's camera shares Dolores's vantage point as she gazes through an open window at her husband, Joe (David Strathairn) while he drunkenly gazes down at the unknowing citizens of Little Tall Island, blaring their boat horns in honor of the coming eclipse (fig. 6.8). The viewer once more finds her perspective broken into three parts: the innocent citizenry, floating on the waves below; the inebriated master of ceremonies, who foolishly thinks that he has it all figured out; and the one who can grasp from afar how this lout has deluded himself into believing that he has an all-seeing perspective on events (Dolores and the spectator). By actively holding these three positions in tension, *Claiborne* encourages its audience to appreciate how cinema in particular can subvert the mandate of the detective-analyst's penetrating stare.

The film adaptation of *Dolores Claiborne* reveals an opportunity missed by the film version of *Misery*. Hackford's film capitalizes on a layered way of looking by showing the tensions between juxtaposed perspectives; as such, it explores the caesuras that define human relationships (even, and especially, between criminal and detective), because no one can see from all perspectives at the same time. Why doesn't Reiner's film version of

Fig. 6.8 In a shot that calls to mind a similarly layered sequence in Orson Welles's *Citizen Kane*, Hackford emphasizes the importance of depth of field.

Misery elect to do the same? King's source material for *Misery* focuses similarly upon a *mise-en-abyme*, a story within a story: the saga of Paul and the text that he's composing, *Misery Returns*. But Reiner's film never permits the viewer to venture into the world of *Misery Returns*, so it never fully interrogates the gaps that attend any construction of truth: between a text and the so-called real world. The film adaptation of *Misery* allows the audience to remain relatively comfortable, to observe its proceedings from a detached place. Reiner's imagined spectator is not in the end so dissimilar from Sheriff Buster. Spectators are well-meaning, perhaps, but they are not being forced to confront the blind spots in their own patterns of discernment. In contrast, Hackford recognizes his spectator as a would-be detective-analyst, so his film fruitfully teases out the implications of unsettled points of view.

If *Misery* provides the viewer with a clear and unobscured narrative arc, *Claiborne* presents itself like one of those New England cloud covers that blunt nearly every scene in the movie. This is in keeping with the shifting complexities and contradictions of past events that follow and confront both mother and daughter throughout the film. In her assessment of *Dolores Claiborne*, Colleen Dolan argues that "King does not portray

Dolores as a murderer, but rather an avenging angel, who has also died an emotional, spiritual, and intellectual death from abuse, then rises from this death to become strong and whole again" (163, 161). While we agree essentially with this interpretation, it is also important to point out that Dolores is ultimately more problematic than the "archetypical phoenix woman" (161) Dolan makes her out to be. All the flashbacks that occur in Hackford's film belong to Dolores herself—except, of course, the final one that Selena experiences on the ferry prompted by Dolores's taped history of family events. The intensity and frequency of these flashbacks indicate that Dolores remains haunted by selected images of her past; insulated by years spent alone with Vera in her mansion, she has no more reckoned accurately with the past than has Selena. These flashbacks commence when Dolores is forced to return to the house and property she shared with her husband, the unexpected visit from her daughter, and another Mackey investigation. These combine to awaken the restive ghosts from her violent marriage and a reemergent level of guilt arising from her role in Joe's "death by misadventure" that Dolores has been able to repress until the recent loss of her protector, Vera, and Dolores's return to the scene of her husband's "accident." This guilt further explains her obvious lack of interest in defending herself against Mackey's wrongheaded investigation into Vera's death and her concluding admission to Selena that it is finally "time to pay the piper." Unlike *Misery*, *Claiborne* leaves its audience mulling over the convoluted journeys mother and daughter were forced to undertake on their way back into each other's lives—and, most important, it suggests that their journeys can never be neatly resolved because of the existential laws that govern their cosmic orbit around one another.

While the novel version of *Claiborne*, not unlike the film version of *Misery*, ultimately covers up its blind spots to reassert a comprehensive author, Hackford's adaptation refuses to fall into this trap. The film preserves vital openings within its very frame: the tension between different POV shots; the tension inherent to the invisible aperture of the camera's editorializing lens; the subtle variance between the technicolor past, the desaturated present, and the filters through which Dolores mediates the two. In a way its source text never does, the film *Claiborne* understands that the subject cannot escape from the symbolic structures of mastery that force her to read and to be read, *ad infinitum*. But this prison house does not mean that she is doomed to the monochrome of the stereotypical male detective-analyst. Although the subject cannot achieve the impossible perspective of an absolutely cloudless sky, she can still gain greater insight into her own orbital movements. In turn, audiences of Hackford's adaptation might reassess the patriarchal assumptions baked into the detective archetype: "The feminist counter-tradition [. . .] has broken and bullied, honored and loved, in the service of renewing and assuring the form" (Kinsman 161). Dolores might not be able to outrace competing perspectives or defeat the memories that hem her in; nevertheless, Dolores, like her daughter, leaves the film with a more nuanced understanding of her own position in the world—an understanding in part because the subject has been broken and bullied, honored and loved. This final revelation, this moment of renewal, is born from an enduring promise unique to the cinematic apparatus, and we believe it contains within it the promise of a better detective to come.

Chapter 7

THE INCESTUOUS *LATER*

WRITTEN AS PART OF THE HARD CASE CRIME IMPRINT, STEPHEN KING'S *Later* comments in interesting ways upon the detective genre. Jamie Conklin is a young man living with his single mother, Tia, when he discovers that he can communicate with ghosts. His mother's girlfriend, Liz, a crooked police officer, exploits Jamie's newfound powers to solve cases, until she becomes a drug addict herself and kidnaps Jamie to help her gain the upper hand over a drug lord. All of Jamie's detective work proves to be a red herring, though, when at the close of the novel, he communes with the dead and discovers that he is the offspring of an incestuous relationship between his mother and his uncle Harry. At stake in this relatively forgotten book is a deeper understanding of King's twenty-first-century concerns—more specifically, by unpacking the text's unique design and highlighting King's metacritique of the classical detective tradition as well as its offspring (including the hard-boiled detective story), we might begin to understand better King's ongoing obsession with the genre and his recent efforts to innovate. Through its reflection on ratiocination tales, that is, tales based on the powers of reasoning, *Later* gestures at something that cannot be articulated, beyond the self-enclosed templates of its more straightforward predecessors. King's novel orbits around a secret that could somehow remain untold, or deferred in perpetuity, until "later." As such, the text complicates the closed form of the orthodox detective tale, which historically moved in a linear fashion from mystery to resolution. Here, King returns to a question that he ruminated on in an earlier book for Hard Case Crime, *The Colorado Kid*: could someone pen a detective story that never fulfilled its initial promise?

Like the rest of King's corpus, *Later* gestures incessantly at other works, and by so doing, the novel lays down clues regarding precisely what kind of text it is. While the book wears its indebtedness to hard-boiled thrillers on its sleeve, it also makes a number of references to Sir Arthur Conan Doyle's archetypical stories. For example, in the build-up to the novel's denouement, Liz happily declares to Jamie: "Me and you, Holmes and Watson off on another adventure" (191). This allusion should not be dismissed as mere lip service to an obvious forerunner; King's repeated gesture at Holmes tells the Constant Reader that King also wants her to ruminate on the classic detective and not simply mid-century potboilers. Indeed, *Later* ultimately concerns itself with the detective tradition as a whole, and so readers must be prepared to compare the text's semantics (its Raymond Chandler-esque window dressing) with its syntax (the connection between its plot and plots crafted by earlier practitioners of the conventional whodunit). This is a tale, then, of shared generic DNA, generic mutations, and generic incest.

In another sign of the novel's awareness of its Victorian precedents, *Later* repeatedly points to Charles Dickens, a writer with long-standing ties to the detective genre. As Jamie remarks, "Looking back on it, I sometimes think my life was like a Dickens novel, only with swearing" (25). It is not very difficult to spot the influence of Dickens's *Bleak House*, serialized in 1852–53: a major contribution to the detective genre and a novel that King recently named as one of his top ten favorite novels of all time.[1] *Bleak House*, much like *Later*, creates a disjointed sense of time by oscillating from third-person omniscient overseer to first-person narrator. Shifting back and forth between the recollection of past actions and forward-moving feelings of suspense in the present, Dickens anticipates King's tortured temporality in *Later*, and this correlation reveals one of King's primary focuses: to underscore the incongruities of the classical ratiocination tale, in which the detective already knows the ending but must somehow keep the reader interested for the duration of its telling of a twice-told tale—namely, a recounting of the crime being solved. Why does the Constant Reader keep reading, in a state of constant attention, when a shrewd detective has already established the ending of the narrative? By using first-person narration in this fashion, King stresses the thinly buried reality that a detective story is more a rote repetition of the past than an eager anticipation of the future: "Now (later!) I can see it makes symbolic sense" (152).

King's novel is nothing if not supremely derivative—and, we would argue, intentionally so. For instance, *Later* features several references to texts more Gothic in their inheritance than Doyle and Dickens, most notably Bram Stoker's *Dracula*. That novel's presence in *Later* is tied to several of the characters in the narrative: the emergence of the villainous Therriault as a supernatural being that preys on the citizens of Jamie's city, as well as Liz herself, whose only use for Jamie after she breaks off with his mother, is to provide recognition so she can keep her job as a police officer and, later, to obtain drugs. Near the close of the novel, Jamie cements the allusion: "Fresh blood was running over her upper lip, making her look like one of Bram Stoker's vampires. Which in my opinion she sort of was" (218). Liz's behavior is shaped entirely by vampiric impulses; she is willing to sacrifice her former lover Tia and Tia's son, Jamie, to maintain her status as a policewoman and to obtain a large cache of drugs. Jamie counterbalances the destructiveness of both Therriault and Liz in the same way in which Stoker's Crew of Light does battle against, and eventually vanquishes, Dracula. Like Van Helsing, Jamie studies the counterforces necessary to employ against each of these vampires. He comes to appreciate, for example, the Ritual of Chüd as a means for employing a rational set of precepts and techniques in order to confront and control irrational forces (the supernaturalism of Therriault as the mad bomber, the recklessness aligned with Liz's selfishness). He also seeks out Professor Burkett, who operates in a way similar to Van Helsing in *Dracula*: he is there to provide Jamie with the means for controlling supernatural events. Burkett reminds us of Matt Burke in King's earlier novel *'Salem's Lot* insofar as he has spent his life deeply immersed in Gothic lore. Just as Ben Mears and his vampire slayers rely on Matt's book learning to go into battle against the vampiric Barlow, Jamie is a willing student of Burkett and seeks out his wisdom in much the same way as an adult struggling with a difficult personal problem might consult a therapist. In this way, Jamie should be viewed as a kind of detective—perhaps more closely resembling the genre's contemporary examples, such as Clarice Starling in Thomas Harris's *Silence of the Lambs*—in his acknowledgment that he must appropriate the superior knowledge and resources of his friends and intellectual superiors to gain access to the flaws of his adversaries.

More significant for our purposes in this book, *Later* plays with the generic constraints highlighted by Tzvetan Todorov in his seminal study of the detective story. In detective fiction, Todorov contends, there are always two stories: the story of the crime and the story of the criminal investigation. To use the language of the Russian formalist, the detective story can be broken down into the *fabula*, what "really" happened, and the *syuzhet*, the way that events are arranged into a particular order. Todorov explores how these two stories evolve in tandem over the course of the genre's lifespan. In the whodunit of a Holmesian lineage, the detective is always working backwards to piece together what happened before he took the case; in the thriller of the hard-boiled variety, the detective's fate is never so certain, and solving the crime remains secondary to proving the detective's moral fortitude in the face of social corruption. Todorov views the suspense novel as *an eclectic interaction of these two emphases.* The suspense novel, he writes, "keeps the mystery of the whodunit and the two stories, that of the past and that of the present": "as in the thriller, it is the second story which here occupies the central place. The reader is interested not only by what has happened but also by what will happen next" (50). Well aware of this generic interplay, King crafts a metacommentary on the form of the suspense novel, in which the reader finds comfort in a retroactive gaze upon the past even while feeling genuine anxiety at the uncertain fate that awaits her.

Much of what unfolds in *Later* concerns the second story, that of how Jamie gets to the truth—or does not, as we shall consider below. King's text emphasizes its own status as artful deferral, as the art of delayed gratification, which is, in truth, the very essence of the formula. Although filled with smaller cases, red herrings, and precarious situations, the reader knows that Jamie survives to tell the tale, and so the reader spends an inordinate amount of time wondering about *how* Jamie managed to construct the narrative that she is currently reading. Jamie's job, like that of any great narrator of detective fiction, is to hold a line between readerly innocence and the foreknowledge of a detective who has already experienced the events being described. At the opening of the novel, Jamie encounters a ghost, but the reader does not yet know that what she beholds is a phantom; Jamie deliberately places his reader into the unknowing position that Jamie himself occupied at the time of the unnerving scene being described. In this way, King stresses how the detective, somewhat perversely, forces others to relive something that has already happened. In his first case as an amateur sleuth, Jamie must transcribe a story being told to him by a specter; he subsequently relishes his function as designated revealer by refusing to expose the story's central secret to his audience: "I'm not going to tell you what it was. Read the book and find out for yourself. If you haven't read it already, that is" (68). But why would a reader *re-read* such a story once she has discovered the secret—that is, "whodunit"? The entire premise of the genre is wedded to an artful dodging of the big reveal, or that which is already there: the principal story of a crime that has already been committed. King thus toys with the genre's parameters—its hard-boiled angst alongside the disciplined unwinding of its classic clockwork.

THE (W)HOLE STORY

Because the story of the crime—the "real" crime, the crime that King's audience cares about the most—cannot be unveiled until the novel's final pages, or the reader loses her impetus to continue reading, much of *Later* involves contemplating how exactly the story of the investigation is being presented. While the reader awaits the big reveal, King keeps her interested by pondering Jamie's machinations *as a storyteller*. King's *Later* recycles from the detective tradition an extended rumination upon the relationship between writer and reader—a subtext that King has dwelt upon in length (see chapters 3–6). The first of the mysteries to be solved manifests when a well-known mystery writer, Regis Thomas, a client of Jamie's mother, who is a literary agent, dies and leaves his final manuscript unfinished. Knowing that her son can commune with the dead, Jamie's mother, Tia, takes him to the place where Regis died, at which point Jamie speaks with the deceased author and retrieves the remainder of the plot. A second mystery involves Professor Burkett, whose wife dies, after which Jamie assists in locating her valuable jewels (Burkett is, importantly, a scholar of the mystery genre). King thus foregrounds the correlation of reading, writing, and detection by including a mystery writer as well as a mystery reader as key characters in his text. Although these particular characters do not herald the novel's big reveal—that which can only be teased to the surface later—their presence allows King's reader to engage in a degree of self-reflexivity concerning the inner workings of the genre.

The character of Liz likewise signals to King's readers that *Later* is engaged in a kind of metacritique of the detective story. Since Jamie is quite literally a walking text—a transcriber of the truth, an artful narrator of the story that we are reading (the private "I" that embodies the unfolding mystery by giving it flesh)—Liz can be posited as the novel's primary reader. And it is hardly a flattering portrayal of mystery readers: Liz desperately needs for Jamie to give her clues to unsolved mysteries; she hungers for shortcuts to the final unveiling because to her the story itself, like Jamie, is "just baggage," or an obstruction to that which she so desperately needs—a resolution to the mystery of her next big fix, be it money, drugs, or something less tangible (117). She could not care any less about the story of the investigation or the pleasure in "reading" about it; instead, she yearns *to cut to the chase* and grasp the story of the crime in its entirety. In 1928, Father Ronald Knox famously established rules of Fair Play for the detective genre. Liz refuses to play by these rules, going so far as to plant a recording that will explain how she knew a crime had taken place. In other words, she stacks the deck in her favor by inserting clues that will prove advantageous for her. If Jamie's writerly way of engaging with life's mysteries is "natural" and intuitive, Liz's readerly approach reeks of corruption, of unfairness. She eventually tortures and murders a man to utilize Jamie's psychic abilities, revealing just how much she is willing to shortcut morality to gain access to the secret at the heart of the story. Her motivations are strictly self-centered. Not fazed by the possible negative effects her violent machinations will have on the impressionable adolescent, Liz devolves as a character once she leaves the home provided by Jamie and his mother and completes her descent into drug addiction. Liz is both literally and metaphorically an addict hooked to the detective formula. Indeed, one of the formula's most churlish detractors, Edmund Wilson, equates its fans with opium addicts and dismisses the consumption of works in this vein as a "vice." Junkies like Liz, he writes, "get a mild stimulation of the succession of unexpected incidents and of the suspense itself of looking forward to learning a sensational secret." In her urge to scratch this itch, Liz doubles with the early Burkett, who eventually learns to believe in the "magic" of Jamie's story but spends the first part of the novel occupying the role of skeptic. "As a lifetime reader of detective stories," Burkett notes, "I like to know the answers," and "I lean toward the rational, the known, and the empiric" (139, 144). Although neither early Burkett nor Liz truly understands their addiction—as we shall see shortly, *Later* concerns the unconscious drive behind these structural fantasies, not the reader's outward desires—their bad faith hermeneutics implicates certain readers in ruining the holistic, "magical" acquisition of knowledge being practiced by Jamie as yet another psychic detective in the King canon (other prominent examples include Johnny Smith in *The Dead Zone*, discussed in the third chapter).

Due to its extensive metacommentary on the genre, King's *Later* is an example of what Patricia Merivale and Susan E. Sweeney have called the metaphysical detective story. Interestingly enough, Merivale and Sweeney contend that King's *Umney's Last Case* (1993) offers a primary example of this highbrow subgenre moving into the mainstream. They select the term "metaphysical detective story" over other terms, such as "anti-detective story," because even as these stories subvert the blueprint of the classical detective story, they do not outright negate it—that is to say, even as they depart from their predecessors, they nonetheless require the machinations of earlier variants to "make sense." In dialogue with writers such as Jorge Luis Borges, Paul Auster, and Umberto Eco, King's *Later* reveals how the detective tradition provides an important precursor for postmodern literature by speculating about "the workings of language, the structure of narrative, the limitations of genre, the meanings of prior texts, and the nature of reading" (Merivale and Sweeney 7). Metaphysical detective stories amplify the self-reflexive tendencies of the genre, which have been percolating since the genre's inception under Edgar Allan Poe in the 1840s: "They are narratives about narratives, or stories about reconstructing and interpreting the story of a crime, and it is this metanarrative self-awareness that both invites critical and theoretical approaches, and creates the perfect framework within which the genre can endlessly question and reinvent itself" (Scaggs 143). Along these lines, *Later* comments upon the evolving structure of the detective tradition and how it imposes artificial desires, like Liz's eagerness for a quick fix, while exposing the reader's deeper drives, including a need to preserve secrets and to leave at least some mysteries unsolved to serve as a catalyst for the reader's future enjoyment.

The Freudian contrast between desire and drive within King's narrative warrants a bit more consideration. On the one hand, *Later* continuously whets its reader's appetite by offering up one mystery after another; like Jamie's access to the truth (only the dead, the story informs us, cannot tell lies), the mystery promises to fulfill the reader, to give her—we can think once more of Liz's rampant drug use—exactly what she thinks she needs. On the missing Regis manuscript, Jamie asserts: "The book could save us. The book, the whole book, and nothing but the book" (53–54). The illusion here is that the novel's big reveal will offer a kind of palliative. *Later* endlessly provokes the sense that solving its mystery will deliver the fates of its characters and readers alike to completion. "Millions of readers slavered to know the answers" to Regis's tale (48); readers will not be able "to rest" until the solution is made clear (49). The impression of totality beneath the surface may grant solace to troubled readers by suggesting that, once the pieces fit together, there will be a salvific release, a peaceful rest. Regis himself tells Jamie, "I always have *everything* before I write *anything*" (64; emphasis in the original). But this impression of the author "having everything" is only another bait, another bell at which King's reader must salivate. In truth, even as Jamie and his mother claim to possess Regis's "whole book," there is no such thing as a "whole book," only holes within a book that drive its readers onward (66). Per usual, King's choice of names proves illuminating: Regis derives from the word king, and indeed, the text refers to the author as the "jewel" in Tia's crown; meanwhile, Dutton (Liz's last name) means enclosure or settlement and, in Old English,

Burkett means "strong fort." King's names call to mind sacred areas that must be fenced in and defended. Simultaneously, these names/enclosures provoke the reader by goading her into storming the castle, so to speak, and retrieving that most valuable of hidden objects behind fortified walls: what the word means. But the secret is not just a part of the apparatus, or a mere means to an end. Rather, the secret is everything, an end in itself. While readers of the detective formula are trained to desire the big reveal, they simultaneously appreciate, however unconsciously, the importance of maintaining a given text's secret. After all, to solve the mystery would be to lose their purpose as readers and spoil the fun.

By the novel's conclusion, King equates his big reveal with death. As the tagline of the text tells us, a person can only tell the truth and stop lying when he is deceased. Deception—of others and of self—remains an existential constant for living beings. And so the truth must linger just out of our reach, or the game would come to an irreversible end. Similarly, *Later* presents its core antagonist, Therriault, a mass murderer, as a sort of amateur detective writer. Like Liz, he does not subscribe to the genre's assumption of Fair Play; instead, even after he is dead, he eludes the truth by offering Jamie only false clues and misdirection. The truth that he wishes to reveal is macabre and fatalistic. In a note to the police, Therriault writes: "How do you like my work so far? More to come!" (98). The big reveal in this case proves to be an explosion meant to kill hundreds of innocent civilians. King's reader might recall the sign at Regis's home, which boldly warns Jamie: No Trespassing. Better to defer access to the truth, which is, ultimately, the truth of one's own mortality, until later. Always later.

A metaphysical detective story as well as a self-reflexive suspense novel, *Later* urges its readers to juxtapose their desire for order with their unconscious drive to preserve secrets (as the detective's *raison d'être*). In this mostly forgotten little book, King harkens back to another of his forgotten little books, *Umney's Last Case*, to ruminate on narrative as a kind of detection, and he wonders about the limits of the form as well as what those limits tell us about the nature of readerly desire. With this overarching message in mind, it is time to turn to the text's final unveiling, since many of the preceding arguments hinge on King's preferred resolution. Put a bit differently, the specific way King elects to end *Later* inevitably ties together the narrative threads that we have been teasing apart. The big reveal should allow readers to make sense of the detective genre's occasional open-endedness and how it stands in tension with its unconscious compulsion to close the case.

A GENRE WITHOUT A FUTURE

In the closing pages of *Later*, King addresses a question that readers may not have been consciously asking: who is Jamie's father? While the text makes clear that Jamie's father is absent, and Jamie overtly wrestles with his "surrogate father" (the corrupt policewoman, Liz), almost every micro mystery in the text proves to be a red herring. It turns out that the real mystery, the mystery that anticipates the novel's biggest reveal of all, remains one of paternal identification. The last revelation may be a surprising one: Jamie's father is revealed to be his uncle Harry, who has been institutionalized since the beginning of the story. Jamie is thus the offspring of an incestuous relationship between his mother and her brother. We would argue that this "surprise" turn to incest cannot be overlooked as mere shock or titillation; the narrative structure of the text that precedes the revelation depends entirely upon this quilting point. Once King's readers realize that incest is the novel's focal point, the event around which all the other events turn, they would do well to return to the beginning and reread the text with fresh eyes. All of King's textual clues have been oriented toward that outcome. Peter Brooks describes this phenomenon as "the anticipation of retrospection," or the acknowledgment that "what remains to be read will restructure the provisional meanings of the already read" (23). Yet where King's Constant Reader should go from here is hardly obvious. This revelatory moment introduces two interpretive strategies for engaging not only with *Later*, but with much of King's corpus: one, the incestuous logic compels King's Constant Reader to reread the novel as evidence of generic or textual exhaustion—a kind of postmodern fatigue that is attendant to the figurative as well as literal theme of incest; and two, the incestuous logic leads King's Constant Reader to reread the novel as a reminder of the deepest secret of all: an affirmation of the permanently Other, the unknowable, the uninterpretable essence that King regularly evokes to stymie his overly enthusiastic critics, who probe into the concealed corners of his work in pursuit of hidden meaning. In the end, however, these ostensibly competing interpretive strategies prove to be complementary.

With his emphasis on incest, King gestures at one of his favorite authors, Ross Macdonald, whose hard-boiled prose dealt extensively with Oedipal themes. In a recent interview, King confessed that, when he was a writer in his twenties, he emulated Macdonald and adopted many of his stylistic flourishes (Brown). One might interpret *Later* as a sort of return to form, then, but to a form that is not King's own. Macdonald remains best known for psychoanalytical detective novels that examine unhealthy family dynamics. In *The Goodbye Look*, for instance, Macdonald tracks a young man who, unaware of his parentage, murders his own father. Fate circumscribes his every movement: "Life is so strange, it seems to go in circles" (108). Perhaps none of Macdonald's novels is more Oedipal than *The Three Roads*, which borrows its title from Sophocles's *Oedipus Rex* and opens with a line from that famous play. In *The Three Roads*, a man loses his memory and gradually realizes, through the process of detection, that he is the very criminal he has been seeking. Along the way, he confuses his wife with his dead mother: "His future was still in the inescapable past, and he was caught in a closed circle" (77). Channeling Macdonald, King recycles Oedipal themes in *Later* to underscore the pervasive influence of the past or the circular logic that drives his typically male reader to repeat, unconsciously, the sins of the father. At the same time, and once again following Macdonald's template, King's detective confronts an incomprehensible deed that disrupts the narrative at a foundational level, one that has forced him to accept, like the detective from *The Three Roads*, a degree of "merciful humility" at the outermost borders of reason—the outermost edge of what can be thought or put into words (254).

Reading *Later* as an overtly Oedipal text requires little interpretive strain. Beyond the obvious correlation—the incest that undergirds the plot's machinations—there are other clues that assist readers in connecting these dots. For one, Jamie expresses an excessively strong attachment to his mother Tia: "It was Mom and me who were supposed to have the secret" (51). It is only because of Liz's insertion into the family unit that Jamie can break this libidinal bond and achieve a "healthy" sexuality. In this sense, King's novel rejects the countercultural possibilities of lesbian detectives, highlighted in works by writers like Barbara Wilson, and it doubles down on a rigid, old-fashioned heteronormativity. King's lesbian detective is a criminal, and, worse still, she emblematizes the story's puritanical critique of "abnormal" sexualities (it conflates a lesbian relationship with an incestuous one as obstacles to Jamie's personal flourishing). Meanwhile, the logic of the absent father drives much of Jamie's decision-making: "I had a soft spot for father, not having one myself . . . I knew I was missing *something*" (77; emphasis in the original). In addition to serving as Jamie's mother's lover—"she stole a lot of my mother's attention and affection that I used to get!" (75)—Liz dominates as the most masculinized presence in the book: "She was like the hero of a movie, the lone wolf who means to solve the case on her own" (106). In addition to taking what she wants from Jamie and his mother by force, her phallic gun, which is often at the center of discussions between the two women, is nearly omnipresent (despite Tia's insistence that the gun should be kept out of sight, hidden inside their home). Of course, as these phallic stand-ins remind us, Liz is not Jamie's actual father, but only ever a surrogate. Liz's ineffectual paternal performance further exacerbates Jamie's sense of what he is ostensibly missing. Macdonald similarly reveals in *The Three Roads* that "the pattern was Oedipean. . . . He was one of those who had formed the habit of loss and acquired a need for it" (85). There is a kind of self-sabotage at work as Jamie rehearses the loss of his maternal ties as well as the recurrent loss of the father-figure. But it is that moment of pure shock, of pure taboo, when Jamie's reader realizes the incestuous truth beneath it all, that serves as the scaffolding upon which King builds his story. The Constant Reader has been on a hunt for what Peter Brooks calls "those shaping ends" that, "terminating the dynamic process of reading, promise to bestow meaning and significance on the beginning and the middle" (Brooks 19). But what specifically does it mean for King to render his so-called shaping end as an incestuous one?

The quilting point of incest demands that King's audience place, front and center, a self-enclosed circuit of meaning-making. Incest involves a bloodline turning inward not in pursuit of progeny but as an unholy attraction to self. Incest indicates a grotesque circle: a metaphorical violation of genetic difference; a figurative rejection of interactions with individuals as well as ideas that exist outside of the immediate family unit. By now, the implications for the detective genre and King's contribution should be clear: the secret at the center of the genre is not external to the narrative, since the narrative does not in fact travel outward in search of answers but remains within itself (and so it is never truly a "secret" at all). In an orthodox detective tale, the end is there from the beginning, and the beginning unveils itself to be the end. With each agonizing loop, the genre preys upon itself, passing off its "novelties" as healthy reproductions when they are only ever more of the same. Jamie's previously webbed appendages underscore the abject quality of *a genre without a future*. When Jamie's mother publishes Regis's last book under her own name, she dedicates it to herself, not her son, in a self-referential move that reveals how insular formula fiction can be. Or, to come at the issue from a slightly different angle, the mass-murderer Therriault, self-described artistic maestro, stages his final crime at the scene of his original crime: "Seemed right to finish where I started . . . [to] complete the circle" (113). In addition to the Oedipal palimpsest of criminality, this moment suggests the perversity of an art form that never matures, moves on, or evolves, but stays largely stationary, appropriately situated within the obsessive mind of a killer. As we have already seen, *Later* does indeed obsess over its own literary heritage, with countless examples of intertextuality on full display. The most obvious example of self-referentiality occurs near the close of the book, when Jamie observes: "Books are a uniquely portable magic. I read that somewhere" (241). King's Constant Reader will likely recognize this oft-quoted line from King's treatise *On Writing: A Memoir of the Craft* (we have cited it several times in the present volume). In other words, at the climactic moment of the narrative, King drops his citations of Holmes, Stoker, or even Macdonald, and elects to quote himself. To return to an inquiry that Jacques Derrida poses of Poe's detective story "The Purloined Letter" (discussed in the third chapter), what are readers supposed to do with a signature that is a quotation—and, in this case, a quotation lifted from one's own work? *Later* is trying to generate something "new" by obsessively gesturing at familiar things; in crude terms, King's text "procreates" with another one of King's texts—a closely related member from the same literary family tree.

King's *Later* thus underscores the incestuous logic of the detective genre. Jacques Barzun, a self-proclaimed fan of the genre, does not deny this indictment: "The art form has reached exhaustion and nothing can be done with it" (578). More than any other formula, the story of the detective has historically followed relatively rigid rules, thereby leaving little room for deviation or experimentation. Such derivative acts, naysayer Edmund Wilson contends, reveal "a fidelity ever more complete," a near-absolute fidelity that never strays far enough from its source material to germinate anything genuinely unexpected. Just as Macdonald cannot escape from his own favorite plot devices, King appears to be fascinated by his imprisonment within this formula. Like Macdonald, King is "holding to [. . .] the sameness," but, in one last creative burst, he reflects on how "the pattern swallows material at a fearful rate," "absorbing [situations and characters] in the same rigid interpretive mode" (Skenazy 11). Even this postmodern revelation has been done before and so it cannot be deemed totally new or innovative.

Of course, we need not read *Later*'s derivative impulses in such generous terms, because King's novel lacks inventiveness even in its moments without metacommentary. For example, one might apply Max Byrd's critique of Macdonald's flat characterization of the detective to King's mode of storytelling in *Later*: "[The detective] remains the same at the end as he was in the beginning, sadder and wiser probably, but not tragic"; "of his own potential he has learned nothing"; "The detective has not yet detected himself" (83). Like many of King's protagonists, Jamie does not "grow up" over the course of the novel; he starts "good," and "good" he remains. In a way, this lack of character development confirms the operative logic of incest—although it would be a stretch to conclude that King intended for his characters to be flat to prove his larger point about the entropic cycles of this generic lineage. Such stagnation is extensive: one could go so far as to say that King fails to live up to even the flat standard set by Macdonald, in that at least Macdonald's detectives wind up a bit sadder or wiser. Jamie's only growth appears in his self-described improvement as a writer, and King's reader will likely struggle to find any concrete proof of this advancement. Even as King foregrounds generic exhaustion as the primary focus of *Later*, he unconsciously (re)commits the sins of his mass-market forebearers by returning to the same stagnant pool of generic questions, in search of the same generic answers. While maybe interesting as lofty metacritique, King's theme of incest justifies the boredom that readers could feel when experiencing *Later* as a work of fiction.

Yet there is a second way to read incest as the quilting point of *Later*: namely, as an incomprehensible, extratextual incident that cannot be explained within any normative framework. The text's central secret remains so unfathomable, so brutally excessive, that no narrative could ever fully account for it. In his analysis of Roman Polanski's neonoir film *Chinatown*, John Belton compares the modern detective and one of the earliest detectives, Oedipus. Oedipus never truly explains the mystery posed by Sophocles, since "its solution lies in the realm of the unnatural" (941). Similarly, the subject of the title of Polanski's film problematically signifies that which cannot be signified, "a world that cannot be understood," or a point at which audiences must recognize a fundamental "resistance to representation" (945). Like the revelation of incest that closes the film, the Otherness of Polanski's exoticized Chinatown reduces the detective, played by a bewildered Jack Nicholson, to a muttering state of paralysis, not far removed from the mutilated paralysis of Oedipus at the terminus of his tragedy. The character played by Faye Dunaway is most affected by the incest, and she withdraws from the possibility of mature relationships as a result. By thrusting his spectator into confrontation with the genuinely unknown, Polanski undermines the expectations of the detective story by confirming the *limits* of reason. "The film brings us into contact with the unnatural," Belton argues, "giving us access to it, but calls attention to the failure of its figural representative of human reason and logic, the detective hero, to produce a rational reading" (949).[2] Like many of King's metaphysical detective plots, *Later* prefers the kind of intuitive reading on display with the psychic detective to the overconfident interpretive muscle exerted by King's critics. "Smart people know a lot," the narrator of *Later* cautions his audience. "And maybe that makes them think they know everything" (166). But how can the detective possibly comprehend, or rationalize, the unseemly deeds of an incestuous father figure? Maybe it would have been better if Jamie had not found out the truth or made his own story whole; perhaps, in the end, he would have been better off preserving that paternal spot as a hole.[3] It is a gap in his knowledge that should never have been filled. For Jamie, as it was with Oedipus, ignorance would have been bliss. Some secrets should never be exposed.

King weaves this warning into the structure of his text by bringing his reader to the brink of revelation and then refusing to cross the threshold. Jamie offers a disturbing retelling of a Christmas party gone horribly wrong, a party that leads to an unspeakable violation of one of humanity's most enduring taboos. At this point, though, Jamie pulls the figurative rug out from under his reader: "Except, hold it, wait one. *That whole story is fiction*" (245; emphasis added). King's rejection of neat and tidy resolution turns the reader from her exposure to a literature of exhaustion to a sudden encounter with something truly unexpected. It is a sort of *mise-en-abyme*, a story within a story, but in true metaphysical detective fashion, the original cannot be found. That which cannot be represented—the sheer excess of the incestuous event—reminds King's audience of the evergreen unknown: an exterior to the symbolic order that cannot be folded back into formulaic algorithms. From this vantage point, *Later* applies incestuous logic not so much as a reflection on its own derivative nature but as an opportunity to rush up against the limits of what a detective (as well as an ambitious critic) can possibly grasp in their interpretive talons. The novel closes with yet another deferral of recognition: "We'll see. Later" (248). Each of King's novels for the Hard Case Crime imprint considers such an unknowable kernel: whereas *Joyland* and *The Colorado Kid* flirt with the incomprehensible materiality of death (see chapter 8), *Later* flirts with the incomprehensible logic of incest.

So why is it that *Later* does not close with something akin to the absurdist mutterings that mark the finale of *Chinatown*, or the unruly self-blinding that occurs at the end of Sophocles' tragedy? Quite distinctively, King's young narrator appears relatively unfazed by the big reveal. In fact, it looks as though he not only survives the traumatic news but thrives. In its remarkably chipper denouement, the novel reports that Jamie has started to have more success with girls at school. Unable to gaze alongside Nietzsche into the abyss long enough for the abyss to gaze back, *Later* proves to be the latest example of King's inability to end the narrative in a way that many readers will find to be very compelling. The incest theme ushers Tia and Uncle Harry back into the story with a conclusion that manages to startle, to disgust, but decidedly not to inspire or challenge. Having "moved on" from the "perverse" sexualities of his biological and surrogate parents, and having transcended the moribund epistemology of his predecessors, Jamie enters into an apparently healthier way of knowing the opposite sex as well as his surroundings.[4] He emerges from Oedipus's shadow and graduates from would-be detective to fully functioning human being. However, is not the entire premise of *Chinatown* and *Oedipus Rex* that there are some limits that no detective should, or even can, overcome? In effect, both Polanski and Sophocles contend that we cannot simply absorb an encounter with Otherness, or exchange it for a more productive state of being; instead, these storytellers set a rigid boundary beyond which the detective cannot pass. At the edge of our perceptual horizon exists something else entirely. By allowing Jamie to improve his lot in life, to become a better lover as well as a better writer, King leapfrogs the authentically perplexing in favor of the temporarily unsettling.

Just as Jamie supposedly reaches beyond the grave to access the truth, King implies that his enlightened reader can overcome the limits of a non-representative unknowable and tap into an effortless connectivity with his book's "uniquely portable magic." Bridging the defining schism that separates secret from detective, *Later* wants to have its cake and eat it too: to maintain the unknowable and, at the same time, render the unknowable as an intimately knowable trope. The Constant Reader is very much "in on" the text's secret; so, unlike other canonical works in the metaphysical detective mode, *Later* puts forth its incestuous solution with little hesitancy and even less concern over its use of incest as a *deus ex machina* to swerve around the thought-provoking implications of other writers working in the genre. Willing to ignore the sincerely disturbing aspects of Oedipal blindness, King's detective finds comfort, even solace, in his own limitations because (of course) they are never really limitations at all, only an excuse for one last turn of the screw and an opportunity for the author to achieve a position of supreme cleverness. Perhaps King's pastoral inclinations pulled him back from the brink (see our discussion of *Joyland* in the next chapter).

Too healthy to gouge out his own eyes, Jamie seems incapable of the existential distress experienced by Macdonald's detective, Lew Archer, much less by Oedipus.[5] In *Later*, as in so many of his other works, King relentlessly reiterates a critique against tyrannies of every type, articulated best by Creon at the close of Sophocles's *Oedipus the King*: "Do not seek to be master in everything" (186). At the same time, King privileges knowledge acquisition that is first and foremost intuitive: a mode of reading without any pretense of interpretive acumen. His Constant Reader must read Jamie, literally and figuratively, just as Jamie reads the various truths possessed by the dead: preternaturally, impulsively, via a so-called portable magic. Although his Constant Reader can never be objectively certain of the veracity of Jamie's narration, King apparently wants her to treat his own authorial designs as akin to the truths professed by the dead. As a result, Jamie neither confronts the torment at the heart of his own existence nor engages in the type of painful introspection demanded of an anguished Oedipus. And the reader lacks the commitment or care to watch Jamie engage in such a quest. We pose the question once more: what is a psychic detective? It is a detective who can bypass barriers to hard-earned knowledge and solve the mystery in a relatively uncomplicated fashion. A psychic detective is not so much modeled on Oedipus but Sophocles's other famous character, the prophet Teiresias. Better, King suggests, to be blind and to "get our knowledge from birds" than to follow in the footsteps of a tragic monarch (Sophocles 134). Yet we must confess that Teiresias may not be all that interesting to contemporary audiences because *he already knows the answers*, and his prophetic abilities alone would not make for very compelling detective fiction. More Teiresias than Oedipus, Jamie—and, vicariously, King's Constant Reader—enjoys ease of access instead of sustained self-scrutiny. The implications of this effortless detection for the rest of King's corpus are profound.

In truth, the Oedipal underpinnings that Jamie discovers are never his own; they are the hang-ups of his relatives. If defining works of metaphysical detective fiction expose the detective to his own repressed failings, Jamie, like many of King's protagonists, emerges relatively unscathed, having improbably held onto a significant degree of his innocence.[6] Jamie did not murder his father; his father dies of natural causes. Jamie never sleeps with his mother; his risky libidinal bond is successfully broken by Liz, and he matures into adulthood, little worse for the wear. King's ostensible reassessment of knowledge and power in *Later* proves to be far more normative than radical.

Jamie's intuitive *modus operandi* proves far more effective as a mode of communication than the language games played by the text's English professor. *Later* is not a mystical *rejoinder* to the postmodern condition, then, but a *symptom* of its generic dead-ends. Jamie can go around incompetent narratives of old and transmit knowledge in a far more direct, accurate, and simplistic manner; he thus behaves in a premodern fashion. His push to access the unobstructed truth of the dead without the messiness that defines existing narrative forms is accompanied by an undeniable sense of the sublime—but we need not let this impression of the ineffable fool us into reading King as some sort of modern-day mystic. As we have shown, the calculated uncertainty at the heart of *Later* remains highly predictable. The "alternatives" that *Later* presents are neither startling nor distinctive.

Although it may not be all that revolutionary as an addition to the growing list of metaphysical detective stories, *Later* does speak to how King values intuitive reading (versus the detective paradigm deployed by some of his critics). The novel's incestuous underpinnings also reveal a dual impulse that surfaces throughout the world of King noir: a dissatisfaction with the status quo alongside a hunger for what he considers to be the unspeakable. At its best, King noir features characters that have—to repeat Macdonald's words—formed the habit of loss and acquired a need for it. Relatedly, King interrogates the prominence of narrative endings, an issue that has plagued him for decades. Can a text ever preserve its deepest secret, the mysterious hole that drives a reader's interest, or must it conclude with its (hardest) case closed? One senses that *Later* wants to work its way out of this box and somehow defer its answer until later. But its so-called secrets are already out in the open, so it leaves audiences with precious little to entice them. "[King] has major problems with [the] unseen," Dara Downey and Darryl Jones surmise, "and with hidden things in general" (229). For several of King's detectives, including Jamie in *Later*, the game is over before it ever really begins.

Chapter 8

STEPHEN KING AT THE BRINK

The Complicated Influence of Raymond Chandler

THE WORLD OF HARD-BOILED FICTION IS RECOGNIZABLE IN PART DUE to its extreme bifurcation. It is an imagined world torn asunder by powerful contrasts. For every angel, there is a madwoman; for every level-headed rationalist, there is a brutal, violent animal. It confirms humankind's essential splits and reaffirms the eighteenth century's counterintuitive energies: the disruptive ruptures of Gothic upheaval versus the promulgated clockwork order of a rational universe. Moreover, the two halves of the hard-boiled sphere are produced by a schism between "what once was"—an imaginary chivalrous social order—and what currently is—the rot of a modern civilization, drowning in sin and abject criminality. On the one side, a private investigator goes through the motions of solving a case because he ostensibly has no choice but to persist in his oft-futile quest for justice; on the other side, readers of hard-boiled tales glimpse the senseless, the shadowy interior, or more to the point, *the dead*. No wonder Stephen King, whose bread and butter has been primarily in the realm of the macabre, is periodically drawn into this cleaved world.[1] It allows him to tarry at the brink.

The cleaved world of hard-boiled fiction offers King yet another opportunity to distinguish the limited realm of reason from an unknowable beyond. Raymond Chandler's *Farewell, My Lovely* closes with detective Philip Marlowe staring out across the horizon, wondering about a woman named Velma who has been killed: "You could see a long way—but not as far as Velma had gone" (292). As King reminds his Constant Reader, "I believe there is an unseen world all around us" (*Nightmares* xxii). This chapter explores how King's would-be detectives confront the vital split between a world driven by rationality, a realm demarcated by the mind with its sense of rational balance, cause and effect, and the province of the body, of raw materiality and, eventually, of death. This split endures regardless of all the hero's frenetic work. However, King seems unwilling (or unable) to leave this gap unresolved. His books compulsively suture these splits back together by enfolding them into his preferred ur-narrative, in a sentimental arc that bends toward equilibrium and cosmic debts paid.[2] When readers peel back the outer shell of King's crime fiction, his hardened borders prove to be softer, more permeable. After all, the term "hard-boiled" implies rigid borders, both physical and psychical; King's texts, in contrast, suggest permeability, connectivity, and an implicit unity. Generically speaking, whereas hard-boiled implies angst at the countless hard lines that cut us off from what we cannot know or to which we cannot reconcile ourselves, King prefers a pastoral geniality. In this sense, King is not alone, since, historically speaking, "the hard-boiled loner of genre stereotype gets gentler and gentler over time" (Cassuto 5). While King sometimes channels the unsettling private dicks of Ed McBain and, most importantly for the purpose of this chapter, Chandler, he sutures back together what he tears apart. He retreats from the brink in search of solid ground.

We begin this examination by gesturing at two of King's recent would-be detectives, Jake Epping from *11/22/63* and Lisey Landon from *Lisey's Story*. Many of King's protagonists search for meaning in nonsensical past events. Still, most critics would hesitate to classify the two protagonists of these novels as orthodox detectives because detective is the official occupation of neither figure, and their respective plotlines do not involve solving a case so much as coming to terms with an inability to resolve their respective mysteries. Nonetheless, Jake and Lisey both closely resemble fictional detectives as they gather clues in the hope of restoring order and coming to terms with ambivalent past events. Their stories underscore an all-important friction between the assumed *modus operandi* of the detective and an alternative world that has been too readily dismissed as quotidian, defined by its overlooked everyday objects, its heightened immediacy in the here-and-now, and its unnerving sense of impermanence (namely, its rootedness in questions of loss and mortality). In interesting ways, King distinguishes a narrative driven by *temporality*—chronologically, the detective references the past to pave the way for a clearer present and future in terms that are both personal and historical—from a narrative driven by *spatiality*—the physical stuff that human beings tend to take for granted or ignore, including office goods, food stuffs, bodily sensation, and, more shockingly, corpses.

In *11/22/63*, Jake discovers a portal to the past and decides to go back in time to thwart the assassination of John F. Kennedy. In certain ways, Jake dons the garb of the consummate detective: he must retroactively piece together clues that led up to a crime that has already been committed (the killing of JFK), and the solution of this crime involves him embodying the role as a man of action, that is, a man unafraid to either take risks or employ violence to make things happen.[3] On the one hand, *11/22/63* involves a hyperactive sense of historicity, as the protagonist (along with the reader) jumps from era to era, moving with relative abandon through America's historical plot; on the other hand, the novel gestures at a stable, firm physicality. Set against the (futile) detective's mobile mission through time is a world characterized by thicker creams, more flavorful, unfiltered cigarettes, and a richer sense of place. Against the heady and speculative dimensions of time travel, King exposes his reader to a much more rigid sense of material reality. Said another way, the fixed spatial realms of *11/22/63* come to conflict with Jake's increasingly frantic jumps through time. This is a technique that King manages to employ in other texts, such as *The Talisman* and *The Dark Tower*, wherein the ravages of a contemporary polluted world, exacerbated by the coexistence of parallel universes, are linked to each novel's reconceptualized (and in many ways idealized) past. The difference manifests right away: at the entrance to the portal in *11/22/63*, a gatekeeper named Al stands as a sentry of sorts, openly displaying a façade that looks "mortally ill" (15). Foreshadowing the end of the novel—King's protagonists almost always know what is going to happen before things start—Jake notes, "Serious illness does horrify us, doesn't it" (15). He comments on Al's hand specifically, "wrinkled, the knuckles big. It didn't look like the hand of a man in his fifties" (20). Here King's reader encounters the mortal vessel, which remains quite solid in contrast to Jake's fluid movement through history. Likewise, Kennedy's body is both everywhere and nowhere in *11/22/63*—it is a singular corpse, the dead material that cannot be changed, despite Jake's desperate temporal maneuvers. "If it's real," he realizes, "it's old" (25). The past has a distinctive smell and, importantly, a distinctive "texture" (32). Even as the detective sorts cause from effect and puts everything into a neat chronological order, he cannot overcome the chasm that exists between his mental labor (arranging events in time) and the sheer physicality of the crime itself, which has already been committed and sits, like a rusty anchor, unyielding in its place. King's detective must learn to exist in a "living, unarmored history," that is, at a point in time that exists spatially, with real weight.

Lisey's Story has an almost identical plot: Lisey must go back into her husband's imagined past and sort through the clues to address traumatic crimes, including his murder. Like Jake, Lisey is a kind of detective. Yet King again draws sharp contrasts between the detective's futile efforts to sort through the past to make sense of it and a world that exists outside of this temporal busywork: "There's a world right next door to this one . . . and *the wall between is so thin*" (346; emphasis in the original). Again, echoing Jake, Lisey must recognize that the detective's project cannot account fully for what remains external to it: stacks of dusty books and a red maple desk, or the ephemera that comprises lived spaces, "the things that lasted the longest" (592). Losing herself in jumps between eras, Lisey requires a piece of cloth, "a bit of anti-magic, a thing to keep her feet on the earth, a ward against wandering" (652). *Lisey's Story* involves two types of character: deluded individuals who try to order their reality (in time) and nonhuman objects that exist in space. King solidifies this contrast by closing this novel with an intriguing line: "The room sighed" (653). There is Lisey, and then there is the room. King's reader thus straddles a crucial line between the world of the detective and a world beyond. In *Lisey's Story* as well as in *11/22/63*, ambitious would-be detectives are chastened as they stop worrying about the past and the future and begin coming to terms with the terra firma beneath their feet.

It is during such moments that King betrays a debt to that most noted of hard-boiled fiction writers, Raymond Chandler. King has compared himself to Chandler on multiple occasions, including the first chapter in this book, where he calls Chandler "the truest artist of the bunch," and reminds us that the writing of *Umney's Last Case* "gave me a chance to do some hard-boiled, Chandler-esque prose." King clearly venerates his predecessor: "Raymond Chandler elevated the detective genre" ("*Rolling Stone* Interview"). And elsewhere, he writes: "When you read somebody like [. . .] Raymond Chandler, you sense that a lot of stuff is going on there" (Underwood and Miller 69). But to understand this debt at a deeper level requires a detour into a recent study of Chandler's fiction by Fredric Jameson, a study that lays the groundwork for our examination of the hard-boiled King. It will come as little surprise that Jameson shows up here, given the prominent critic's propensity to complicate definitions of time and space; indeed, one of Jameson's greatest contributions to literary criticism has been his insistence that readers must think less temporally and more spatially.[4] In his book on Chandler, Jameson distinguishes the typical American detective story, which depends upon "the illusion that life has already been lived" and transforms experience into a "fetish," and Chandler's fiction, which preserves a crucial schism between experience and the comforts sought, though rarely found, by American sleuths (5). Jameson reveals the distinctive character of Chandler's hard-boiled universe to be an "impossible alternative between an objective and abstract lexical knowledge [. . .] and a lived concrete experience" (14). Even as detectives like Marlowe strive to complete a chronology—an objective and abstract lexical knowledge of the events that comprise a case—they run up against a world that will not sit still long enough to have its portrait painted. In Chandler's novels, Jameson posits, readers find a major rift between the detective's busywork and an "irreducible materiality [. . .] that cannot become social" (79).

We have already shown how King similarly juxtaposes the temporality of problem-solving with a physical experience of weighty objects: the unfiltered cigarette, the food without preservatives, the piece of cloth, the less-polluted air and water, the red maple desk. Like Chandler's distinctive spatial imagery, the rooms occupied by King's detectives become characters, at times so palpable as to issue a sigh. In Chandler's words, "Everything else was junk [. . .] a couple of frayed lamps with once gaudy shades that were now as gay as superannuated streetwalkers [. . .] a big new handsome radio in the corner whispered of dancing and love with a deep soft throbbing note like the catch in a torch singer's voice" (*Farewell* 27, 30). And this experience of space, this materiality that cannot be reduced to social fodder, does not always manifest itself in quotidian stuff. Sometimes, this raw materiality ruptures the chronological indices of the detective in more macabre shapes, like deceased bodies in a state of rigor mortis.

Indeed, "Death itself in Chandler is something like a spatial concept [. . .] the outer edge of Being itself" (Jameson, *Raymond Chandler* 84). Chandler's Marlowe spends an inordinate amount of time driving along the California coast, hearing the murmur of the waves and smelling "the harsh wild smell of the sea" (Chandler, *Little* 80). The sea, where the dead bodies steadily decompose, relentlessly erodes fragile barriers erected by superficial American elites living along the coastline. Chandler's *Big Sleep* portrays the Pacific Ocean as a reservoir of death from which innocent young men must be extracted; the sea is a site of "nostalgic decay" (130), which reminds Marlowe that "the world was a wet emptiness" (149). As we shall see, the hard-boiled King follows Chandler in standing at the brink, at the outermost edge of the detective's world: beyond rationality, orderliness, or proper chronologies. The hard-boiled tradition, unlike its Victorian precursor, depends upon the sustained maintenance of this gap—or so Chandler's fiction suggests.

Yet King is decidedly not a one-to-one match for Chandler (a point of contention that Jameson would undoubtedly second).[5] For one, King does not always maintain the rift in question but instead seeks to suture the detective's busywork to the alternative world of material stuff. On this front, Jameson might argue, King proves to be more like Honoré de Balzac and naturalist writers who blur the line between nature and humanity by conflating them into a singular vision, most often of savage survivalism. The unsettling chasm between the historicity of the detective and the detective's spatial encounters disappears, replaced by an idealistic ur-narrative that explains everything. For King, a kind of boyish innocence becomes an ideal way of viewing the world, as the thwarted detective, armed at first with excessive cynicism, must stop trying to outwit and start embracing a mode of guileless reading. As one of contemporary American fiction's most strident idealists, King enfolds these two worlds—one temporal, the other spatial—into a bucolic totality. In *11/22/63*, Jake reconciles himself to a cosmic system based upon harmony and justice: "Everything that goes around comes around" (768). In *Lisey's Story*, King's titular character arrives at a place of healing, in which the power of love triumphs over the breakages in the story caused by her husband's traumatic death. King "solves" these existential cases by allowing his detectives to incorporate and reduce the unsettling spatial experience of the original crime, and of the material world itself, into social fodder. The weightiness of a supposedly irreducible material realm eventually becomes just another thing that has been mastered by the detective as well as the vicarious reader. What goes around invariably comes around. Unlike Chandler, who wants his reader to languish at the brink, King creates a concrete experience of spatialized (and thus graphable) objects of history; these objects—an unfiltered cigarette, a red maple desk, a dead body—remain part and parcel of the ideal detective's toolkit. There is simply nothing that King's benevolent detectives cannot know, and assimilate, into their overall scheme. In truth, they have known it all along. A step, and then one more for good measure, back from the brink.

DEAD BODIES AND *THE COLORADO KID*

From the very beginning of his 1982 novella *The Body*, famously adapted for the screen in 1986 by director Rob Reiner under the title *Stand by Me*, King contrasts the detective's search for chronological answers with a hard-boiled spatial reality, that is, with the gross materials that precede the detective (and endure long after the close of his quest). The protagonist Gordie, an aspiring writer, whiles away his days surrounded by "a pile of ancient *Master Detective* murder magazines" (2). Eagerly awaiting the arrival of John D. MacDonald and Ed McBain novels, Gordie is easily distracted by hard-boiled pulps, including trashy stories like "He Stomped the Pretty Co-Ed to Death in a Stalled Elevator" (6). The fact that Gordie's imagination is fired by these detective stories is of crucial note. First, it's why King raises the topic from both the start of the book (and Reiner follows suit in the film version), even before we know anything else about his character. Secondly, the notion of the detective's quest fuels Gordie's desire to discover the body of Ray Brower, arguably the only thing that motivates the young man during a summer of lethargy caused by the recent death of his older brother. Gordie is initially drawn to the quest for reasons similar to why a detective is drawn to a mystery: he and his group of friends set out on a hunt for Brower's body—a hunt that the young men understand to be an extension of a parallel search being undertaken by the police. In other words, Gordie plays consciously at being a hard-boiled detective who smokes cigarettes, thumbs his nose at authorities, speaks slick patter with his associates, and takes his lumps as he goes. Because Gordie, like Chandler's Marlowe, takes a few punches along the way, King's reader recognizes him as a specific kind of detective: an occasionally violent, Chandler-esque private dick that gets pummeled by brainless thugs to win the day—or at least, to quote the seminal noir film *Out of the Past*, to lose the day more slowly. This line between two worlds, a temporal world and a spatial world, manifests at a heightened moment in which the boys learn of the coveted mystery. As Gordie bends over "to pick up [his] detective magazine," he hears his friend Vern ask: "You guys want to go see a dead body?" (9).

The cinematic version of *Stand by Me* begins with Gordie as an adult in his car, reflecting pensively on the recent murder of his childhood friend. Virtually the entire movie becomes an extended flashback into Gordie's remembered adolescence. What's important here is that from the start we witness Gordie operating in various detective modes, not only through his love of ratiocinative pulp magazines, but also personally: the grieving adult in the present, stimulated by the violent loss of his former best friend, is actively engaged in piecing together the events of a specific moment from their shared past. Gordie conjures Dashiell Hammett's P.I. Sam Spade, who is spurred into action by the death of his partner at the start of *The Maltese Falcon*. Appropriately, the opening scene of this long cinematic flashback features Gordie in a store examining its array of pulpy detective magazines from the 1950s with titles such as *True Detective* and *Crime Detective*. Reiner makes the allusion even more visual than what appears in King's novella, cutting to cover art and story titles from these magazines that cement the connection between horror (the periodical at the far left of the rack headlines a story about a vampire) and detection. Gordie eventually purchases a copy of *True Police Cases* for twenty-five cents. We see enough of the store's other magazine covers, highlighting their lurid contents and photographs from the detective genre, that this scene becomes a kind of signifier to the child's ratiocinative propensity. From the start, it is clear to the audience that Gordie is more interested in detective tales than comic books or horror fiction. Later, in the clubhouse, moments before Vern's interruption, Gordie is pictured reading the recently purchased detective pulp magazine. Reiner's choice underscores the importance the detective genre plays in King's fiction. Thus, Vern's arrival with news about Brower's death creates a juxtaposition that cements Gordie's featured fascination with the detective genre and the proposed mystery of discovering a real dead body. Even before audiences know the name of the central protagonist, both book and film establish an immediate nexus between Gordie's bond with true detectives and King's titular corpse.

Both King's and Hammett's texts feature the detective's quest at odds with something that exists just beyond the outermost edge of that search—namely, the dead body. King details "the dumping-pit": a liminal space that demarcates the land of bucolic ideals, a pastoral lure that, like a siren's song, summons the boys outward from the land of Castle Rock with its heavy, forgotten detritus, which is to say the weighty things that make up bodily existence: "There was so much stuff" (*Body* 53). Of course, the dumping pit merely foregrounds the real element of *thing-ness* for which a detective's chronology cannot account: Brower's body—the title of King's novella and its unsettling nucleus. "We were all crazy to see that kid's body" becomes the true motivation for the motley gang of would-be detectives (125). But when the boys do locate the corpse, their procedural search radically switches gears: "The kid was dead; stone dead" (143). At the outermost edge of their literal as well as imaginative worlds, Gordie must confront death, ostensibly deromanticized and literal and permanent in a way that their hope to find fame and solve the mystery of the missing child never could be. Echoing Chandler, King relishes exposing a chasm between the detective's flimsy temporal world and its hard-set spatial alternative. As Gordie reaches for his detective magazine, dead bodies announce themselves and interrupt the quotidian comings and goings of a young reader who seemingly wants nothing more than to follow vicariously and at a safe distance the story of some adult detective. At the risk of making a bad pun, we venture to call this paradox, between the traditional detective's *modus operandi* and the unaccountable thing-ness of a dead body, "the Gordie-n knot."

Published as a flagship for the new Hard Case Crime imprint in 2005, King's *The Colorado Kid* echoes the dualism at the heart of *The Body*. Nearly a decade later, in 2013, King would offer yet another entry to the Hard Case Crime family, this one entitled *Joyland*. Considered together, these two texts remain the most quintessentially hard-boiled of any King offering, at least subsequent to the work of his alter ego Richard Bachman (see chapter 3). Each novel borrows liberally from the modern detective yarn, including their throwback plotlines populated by unsavory beachfront characters and punctuated by sensationalist deaths. Gerard Genette would also highlight their paratextual elements, such as their lurid and heavily illustrated covers, which reproduce immediately recognizable imagery from pulpy paperbacks and magazines of the 1940s, '50s, and '60s. King and his publisher, Charles Ardai, aggressively evoke a bygone era characterized by the American noir detective genre, thereby fostering in readers an awareness of the genre's halcyon past. As unique textual objects, King's two books for the Hard Case Crime imprint are pastiche: they exist as postmodern artifacts designed to erase the border between time (a pubescent America that existed in the fuzzy "back then") and space (the books themselves compress that temporal distance and make that imagined, pubescent America accessible by turning the American past into a lightweight, fetishized, glossy object that can be purchased and then conveniently held in one's hand or easily stored in a back pocket or backpack). Additionally, the novels in this series eschew the look of the slick, highly crafted book jackets of the hardcover tomes associated with King's current publication output. Moreover, the Hard Case Crime books retail for a fraction of their cost. Writing about the cover art of King's crime novels, Charles Ardai informs us in chapter 1 that "All Hard Case Crime books share a common

 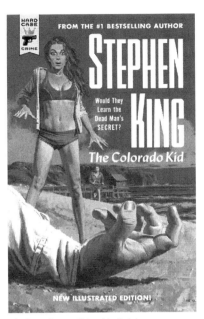

Figs. 8.1 and 8.2. Cover art for King's *The Colorado Kid* reflects the novel's hard-boiled themes.

cover design, which is intended to evoke the look of old paperback crime novels of the 1940s and '50s," noting that "I believe our cover art is a big part of the reason [King] wanted to work with us in the first place." The covers of these novels emulate the covers of the detective magazines we watch Gordie peruse in *Stand by Me*, featuring prefeminist, scantily clad young women in sexy makeup and high heels, who appear distressed and in desperate need of rescue. In form as well as content, then, *Colorado Kid* and *Joyland* juxtapose a world in which King invites his readers to move freely through time, like a detective, with a reified past that he has transformed into a product to be consumed spatially: a concrete thing to be bought and enjoyed (figs. 8.1 and 8.2). King's readers cannot help but identify these novels, from their very first encounter, *as objects*, related to the fictional universe of Chandler and other images associated with noir narratives. Again, Chandler's story world is caught between the detective's delusion—that mysteries still happen, that women are still in need of being rescued, that a shrewd detective could piece the broken puzzle back together, that there is a stubborn permanence to a barren southern California landscape, that hardscrabble lives continue to exist in postindustrial spaces—and the hard reality that death triumphs over all. The danse macabre continues unabated.

The Colorado Kid, has an unorthodox premise: two old-timer newspapermen with auspicious names, Vince Teague and Dave Bowie, regale their intern Stephanie McCann with the only truly unsolved mystery that they have ever covered as journalists. The mystery centers around a dead body found on nearby Hammock beach, affectionately nicknamed the Colorado Kid. Teague and Bowie tease Stephanie with details about the crime even as they remind her that it remains unsolved—indeed, it may be unsolvable. A *mise-en-abyme* (a story within a story), King's *Colorado Kid* is akin to his seminal *Umney's Last Case*, since both texts engage in metacommentary upon the nature of the detective story, and both texts eventually confound the neat temporal logic of the would-be detective by glimpsing something external to it, something beyond its outermost edge.

On this subject, Chandler set the table for King. Chandler's *The Big Sleep* prominently features not one but three dead bodies. There is Harry Jones, a love-struck gangster whose unceremonious offing haunts Marlowe as a reminder of his own mortality: "The little dead man sat silent in his chair, beyond fear, beyond change" (179). In response to this encounter with a dead body, Marlowe unconsciously mimics Jones's rictus and spells out his own burial wishes: "Just a plain pine box. [. . .] Don't bother with bronze or silver handles. And don't scatter my ashes over the blue Pacific. I like the worms better" (191). Chandler also dwells at length upon the dying body of General Sherwood, Marlowe's shady employer: "He looked a lot more like a dead man than most dead men look" (215). Finally, *The Big Sleep* excavates the corpse of Rusty Regan, Sherwood's beloved son-in-law and the *doppelgänger* of Marlowe, from the family oil wells. This climactic reveal underscores the connection between the Sherwood family fortune and its Gothic secrets, buried in slimy residue behind the mansion: "[Regan's] in the sump . . . a horrible decayed thing" (229). The final line of *Big Sleep* speaks volumes: "What did it matter where you lay once you were dead? In a dirty sump or in a marble tower on top of a high hill? You were dead, you were sleeping the big sleep" (230). *The Body* and *The Big Sleep*: these titles indicate that the material corpse doubles as the thing being discussed (content) and the thing being held by readers (form).

Chandler also positioned a dead body at the epicenter of his hard-boiled novel *Farewell, My Lovely*. A patsy named Marriott is murdered while in Marlowe's charge, and the vision of Marriott's dead body plagues Marlowe's mind throughout the novel: "That bag-of-clothes position . . . his face was a face that I had never seen before. [. . .] the beautiful blond ledges were tangled with blood and some thick graying ooze, like primeval slime" (71). Marlowe later recalls "a dead man and a moonless sky" (145); then again, at a later point, he thinks "of dead eyes looking at a moonless sky" (237). Chandler's dead bodies—"beyond change," heavy like a bag of clothes, putrid at the hands of nature—mark the very edge of the detective's quest. They serve as a border that chastens the detective and undermines his unearned sense of comfort or security in his own deductive prowess.

In *The Colorado Kid*, the body on Hammock Beach is posed, like Brower's body in *The Body*: unmoving. It too names the text under scrutiny (the Colorado Kid). These bodies exist as material objects in space; as such, they refuse to be nudged or brought back to life by the detective's ceaseless prodding. Importantly, the Colorado Kid's corporeal form rests against the backdrop of the ocean. Stephanie notes the smell of oceanic decay that permeates the island of Moose-Lookit; that rotting organic material, trapped in the tidal pools and brackish backwater, calls to mind the tangible detritus of the dumping-pit in *The Body* (and Milo's junkyard in the film *Stand by Me*). In his discussion of Chandler's fiction, Jameson highlights the significance of the sea, "that mineral fascination, that radically non-human, cold, even unnatural mystery" (84). As in Walt Whitman's poem "Out of the Cradle Endlessly Rocking," the sea is a stand-in for death itself, as its constant, unyielding presence offers a frightful rejoinder to the detective's systematic thought. "The watery element" that presses in on Chandler's hard-boiled novels does not relent in King's corpus; it continues to mark "the sign of the non-human," or "the other deeper anti-system which is that of Earth itself," or "the seam between a prehistoric nature and the fitful traces of [heroic] history" (Jameson 85–86). The ocean—even more, perhaps, than the brambles of the Maine woods that have nearly enveloped Brower's body—signals a space to which the detective's world cannot be reconciled. "There was loneliness and the smell of kelp," one of Chandler's novels notes. "Below was darkness and a vague far-off sea-sound" (*Farewell* 60–62). The "faint smell of ocean" (239) conjures for Marlowe images of a dead body, while "the huge emptiness of the Pacific" reminds him, time and time again, of the futility behind his own self-fashioned heroism (46). Unlike Whitman's sweet recollection of and harmonious bond with the sea and its admixture of death and birthing, Chandler's detective stands estranged from ocean and death: "I'm afraid of death and despair," he confesses, "Of dark water and drowned men's faces and skulls with empty eye sockets. I'm afraid of dying, of being nothing" (251). This is why readers discover King's Colorado Kid in the sand, in the sediment of countless days, gazing unconsciously at the lapping waves. In turn, Stephanie uses her olfactory senses to recognize the abject Otherness that defines that second, alternative world characterized by its brackish kelp. The world of death periodically pops into her sterilized, clinical account of what, who, where, why, and when. At times, King follows Chandler in asking his readers "to grasp Earth or matter in all its irreducible materiality, even and particularly where we have been thinking about it in terms of meaning and human and social events" (Jameson 80). In turn, "the theme of death [wins] back such power of evocation" (81). Set along the edge of the sea, King's *Colorado Kid* disrupts the detective story by introducing a genuinely unknowable element: the dreadful dirge of a modern-day danse macabre.

This emphasis on the corporeal form extends to the bodies of Teague and Bowie, the geriatric storytellers who hold Stephanie spellbound. Like the gatekeeper in King's *11/22/63*, they appear light in spirit but weighed down in terms of age. Teague's hands are "gnarled with arthritis," and Bowie says, of his withered vessel, "You ran it until it fell apart, patching it up as needed" (28). King's detectives cannot continue their hunt without first facing an unsightly mortality, manifested in elderly border patrolmen. Here death—in all its irreducible materiality—sounds a cautionary note since it alone truly exists outside of the detective's all-knowing gaze. The stubborn fact that these weighty bodies cannot be brought back to life does not stop the storytellers and their attentive listener from striving to solve the case at hand. Despite their occasional glimpses of a second, spatial world, King's would-be detectives—for King, the journalist is always also a detective; recall, for instance, *Dolores Claiborne*, another novel that takes place on the edge of the sea (see chapter 6)—Teague, Bowie, and Stephanie will not (or cannot) forfeit the detective's quest for clarity. And, like Bill Hodges in the *Mr. Mercedes* trilogy, Stephanie carries with her a yellow legal pad, an essential tool for all of King's aspiring detective-writers. While the detectives in his novels are separate from the creative writers found elsewhere in his canon, both groups understand the importance of writing as a tool for both memory and the solving of problems. On those occasions when writers intersect with detection, as in the case of Paul Sheldon in *Misery*, a greater synergy is established. Instead of giving up on the cold case, they persist in their search for clues and their perhaps futile pursuit of closure, for conclusive answers to life's mysteries. Teague asks, "Do real things have a beginning, a middle, and an end in real life?" (177). He is not naïve enough to insist, like most writers of feature stories, that there can be a sense of "closure" (177). Nonetheless, the case of the Colorado Kid has most definitely not been closed. Why not?

King's amateur sleuths appear to be locked in a quixotic pattern. Appropriately, the soundtrack referenced in *The Colorado Kid* is Cat Stevens's 1970 album *Tea for the Tillerman*, a compilation dedicated to the human need to search for greater meaning. King once more turns to the detective genre to probe the nature of narrative: why do readers keep returning to familiar plotlines in search of new solutions to some of their oldest problems, like mortality and existential purpose? Is the continued existence of formulaic fiction proof positive that all human beings are wired to be detectives, which is to say, that they must arrange cognitively random events into causal chains that create order? *The Colorado Kid* illuminates how dissatisfaction drives this repetitive experience: "It was that kind of experience. The kind that's like a sneeze which threatens but never quite arrives" (148). By ostensibly removing its denouement from the start—an impossible gesture, of course, because all texts *must* end—King removes the detective's requisite sense of retroactivity. King's detective suddenly lacks an end point: a final perch from which to survey the preceding events and resolve the niggling unknowns. He attempts to do something similar in his latest contribution to the Hard Case Crime imprint, the 2021 novel *Later* (see chapter 7). At the same time, King asks if a narrative could exist without a cogent temporal order. Could a story be a story without a definitive ending, or a site from which the reader-detective can gaze backwards to understand what they have read? Crucially, King foregrounds this lack of closure right away, thereby forcing his reader to contemplate the very nature of narrative as well as her dependence upon retroactivity in any attempt to make meaning. Teague muses, "You can't get ahead of a story that doesn't exist" (85). At its most interesting, *The Colorado Kid* juxtaposes its own status as a traditional narrative system, with a beginning, middle, and end, and the impossible notion of an anti-system: a story without a story, what King describes as "the-story-that-was-not-a-story" (121). Said another way, King exposes the temporal imperative that orients traditional modes of reading, writing, and detection to be utterly superfluous—a sort of busywork that perpetuates the illusion that things still happen even as it cannot overcome the anti-story at its center, or the revelation that *The Colorado Kid* remains "only a bunch of unconnected facts surrounding a *true* unexplained mystery" (74; emphasis in the original). The true unexplained mystery is a textualized body, resting on the proverbial shore, and it will not divulge its secrets to anyone or comport itself to meet the linear expectations of traditional narrative structure.[6] Again, King's bodies double as the titles of his books in this vein—The Body, The Colorado Kid—and, as such, the text *is* the body. The reader must encounter the text on those terms: as either a detective who can "make sense" of it by establishing cause and effect, or as a dumbfounded human being who can only sense the text/body as a fixture that sits before them.

Still, Stephanie persists in asking questions. She must persist, like her two mentors, even in the face of "a *bona fide* unsolved mystery" (*Colorado* 48). But first, she needs to acknowledge the unknowable kernel at the core of her project, and this acquired wisdom demands that she look at things through a different, child-like lens that presumes readerly innocence. There are certain professional roles that King routinely denounces—including the politician, the military bureaucrat, the religious zealot, the English professor (or academician representing any discipline), the journalist—because each of these roles imposes their own rigid schematics onto otherwise chaotic happenings, further complicating an already difficult situation. Despite the author's dismissal and derision, we would contend that these professional roles fall under the umbrella of detective, the especially overzealous investigator who will not stop searching for a proper chronology, a causal system. Yet, as King so frequently argues, "Curiosity killed the cat." The detective is chastened through his encounters with an anti-system, or the story-that-is-not-a-story. Although Stephanie cannot live without a hunger for narrative structure, she must learn to approach the events of her life differently: she "had been wrong to put on her sociologist's hat. *It was far simpler than that*" (34; emphasis added).

Before we examine this simplicity in greater detail in the next section, we should consider the question of why crime fiction in particular plays such an important role here—and why King has always willingly shifted from the horror end of speculative literature to include hard-boiled tropes (a spectrum that encourages horror and hard-boiled fiction to cross-hybridize, just as their representatives literally appear together on the same drugstore shelf in *Stand by Me*).[7] After all, the Gothic deals with dead bodies and the power of the unknown as well. We hypothesize that King relies upon the hard-boiled tradition, however unconsciously, due to a Chandler-esque split between time and space. Noir detectives in the Chandler mode allow King to concentrate on the gap between a need to sort out what previously happened (a horrible crime) and the immutability of this crime, which exists in a real, tangible space, with actual bodies, and cannot be undone by the detective's relentless drive to index. Teague observes, "You go back to that old business the way a kid who's lost a tooth goes back to the hole with the tip of his tongue" (172). We will consider further King's connection between the detective and a child in the next section; for now, let us focus on the phrase "old business." The hard-boiled detective remains constitutionally bound to investigate events that have already occurred, "old business," and this focus explains why so many protagonists in this literary tradition express a certain conservatism that includes a nostalgic vision of the past. In this regard, Chandler remains unique: Marlowe's agency as a type of time traveler contrasts sharply with the spatial elements that surround him. Marlowe does not succumb to any level of sepia-toned sentimentality because he prefers to dance along its outermost edge, that is, the edge of the story and the-story-that-is-not-a-story. As for "old business"—the crime—a bygone America, Chandler's Marlowe refuses to fetishize the past. Chandler's "old business" endures as an alternative space that exists *regardless* of the comings and goings of society. When King mimics Chandler, he too divides his world between limited human systems and anti-systems—the minerality of the sea, original sin, the irreducible materiality of the arthritic body. When Teague confesses that we are all "'prisoners of the evidence,'" he is not referring to the need for human beings to follow the dictates of causal logic; instead, he is talking about a radically different logic, anchored to a dead body decaying in the sand (132). The "evidence" is a world unmoved by the detective's so-called progress: that old hole in the mouth to which the tongue habitually returns. Jameson draws his study of Chandler to a close with the following poetic passage:

> The underlying crime is always old, lying half-forgotten in the pasts of the characters before the book begins. This is the principal reason why the reader's attention is diverted from it: he assumes it to be part of the dimension of the present, of the events going on before him in the immediacy of his narrated universe. Instead, it is buried in that world's past, in time, among the dead. [. . .] The present fades to little more than a dusty, once lived moment which will quickly take its place in the back years of an old newspaper file [. . .] the reality of death itself, stale death, reaching out to remind the living of its moldering resting place. (86–87)

Lingering in the juxtaposition between a narrated universe and the reality of stale death, King noir ostensibly risks discomforting his Constant Reader. In his preface to *The Colorado Kid*, Charles Ardai recognizes that "at its core the mystery of the Colorado Kid is [. . .] the mystery of the unanswerable" (18). He continues, "The stories that don't answer all of your questions are the ones you remember for a lifetime" (23). Yet a vital question arises: does King *really* want his audience to be so thoroughly disquieted? While Ardai has properly isolated the core conceit of King's contribution to his series, we wonder if the mystery of the Colorado Kid is in fact unanswerable. Why doesn't reading a novel by King ultimately feel much like reading a novel by Raymond Chandler? Is it merely a superficial resemblance? Just what *is* the difference?

King's *The Body* unquestionably rips a hole in the narrative of a detective's quest—from pursuit of the whole to awe before the hole. It divides an irreducible materiality (the body, the dumping pit) from the indexical order of a typical *bildungsroman*. King's dump closely mirrors Chandler's sump in *The Big Sleep*. However, unlike Chandler's text, King's story does not break apart irreparably on this point; in King's telling, "that other deeper anti-system which is [. . .] Earth itself" does not forever alienate his ideal detective (Jameson 85). King invariably sutures the two worlds back together, and it is this suturing effect to which we must now attend.

In *The Body*, King's Gordie-n knot is resolved by the implicit expectations of the American pastoral. Overlooking the hard-edged realism of Chandler, Leonard Cassuto posits, "Inside every crime story is a sentimental narrative that's trying to come out" (7). Gordie slowly reconciles himself to nature through an artful synthesis. Like so many literary figures from the sweep of American literature, from Thoreau to Twain and on to Hemingway and Faulkner, nature, even at its most deadly, is a part of him; the woods heal him by offering a path toward self-discovery, "the magic corridor where the change happens" (*Body* 135). Consider Gordie's eye-opening encounter with a deer in the forest. Or think of the final line: "The river is still around. So am I" (179). It is a narrative journey into the woods that challenges the naivete of the various young protagonists working in a pastoral mode; the events they experience foundationally reshape their identities. King conducts his characters "into the woods" to confront the internal struggles that stew just below the surface. The would-be detective Gordie learns that two worlds are not split but entwined with one another, and he can pass freely between them thanks to his powerful imagination. He can cut through the busywork of the detective and truly experience things again: "And now I sit here trying to recall the best and the worst of that green and brown summer, and I can almost feel the skinny, scabbed boy still buried in this advancing body" (61). King's detectives rediscover a fundamental connection to the natural world, thereby resolving Chandler's gap—or so certain readers might believe. There is apparently no schism between time and space, since time remains part and parcel of a presumed natural order of things (at least, if the detective knows how to look).

There are two major factors at play here. For one, King's hard-boiled fiction is always tinged with the tenets of literary naturalism, which itself subsumed time and space into an overarching survivalist narrative whole: "The pre-adolescent Gordon Lachance that once strode the earth, walking and talking and occasionally crawling on his belly like a reptile" (*Body* 161). A naturalist's logic renders synonymous the human and animal spheres. In this way, a sense of cosmic unity predetermines King's corpus. Secondly, King's hard-boiled detectives must relearn how to see the world through innocent eyes—the gaze of a child (that transcendent Wordsworthian figure affirmed throughout the author's canon). If the detective begins as a hardened cynic, he must revive the naïve part of himself that simply accepts the world as it is. King expects his Constant Reader to embrace the magic of his stories without trying to decipher them, that is, to read without playing detective. A pastoral vision requires that the scales fall from one's eyes. On both fronts, King's reformed detectives eventually rejoin a so-called natural order to cease feeling alienated. What is gone as a result, however, is the real potency of the unknowable, since the pastoral detective appropriates the unknowable within its larger system of knowing things—an echo back to the imperial gestures of nineteenth-century Romantics, such as Percy Shelley and Ralph Waldo Emerson. The impossible alternative is always possible in the sense that it can be incorporated into the status quo. If in Chandler's work "the theme of death [wins] back such power of evocation" (Jameson 81), the theme of death in King's work relinquishes its evocative power, as King transforms encounters with death into moments of inevitable rebirth. And so, the omnipotent vision of King's detectives, after pastoral enhancements, proves to be an all-encompassing one.

Similarly, *The Colorado Kid* promotes a way of reading that aligns comfortably with heuristics developed by America's *fin de siècle* realists and naturalists (we might go so far as to conjecture that Vince's last name, "Teague," conjures the ghost of the titular character of naturalist Frank Norris, McTeague). For example, King's novel prefers the "more realistic" television show *Crime Scene Investigation (CSI)* to the cozier mystery program *Murder, She Wrote* (87). Teague repeatedly drills into his pupil Stephanie that she ought to see people not as characters in stories but as "real people" (122). King prompts his reader to see things "as they are": a project that will not involve dissecting the world so much as it will require a simpler, willfully naïve appreciation of it. The noir detective hunts in vain for conclusive answers; King's "new" kind of detective learns to stop hunting and appreciate the magic of the "real world." Better to hold onto child-like wonder than to sharpen the skills of the analyst. King conveys this preference through his canonical separation of the head from the heart: "[Stephanie's] heart might have been telling her that all along, but her head needed proof to go along for the ride" (160).

King's superficial resemblance to Chandler continues, then, to dissolve the closer that readers look. Beneath the outward resemblance of diction and plot, readers discover a deep-seated idealism. Chandler's Marlowe invariably returns to a state of melancholia, confounded by a corrupt modern society, his own looming mortality, and the cold indifference of nature: "I was as hollow and empty as the spaces between the stars" (*Long* 224). King, meanwhile, has remarked that he learned to write by copying the style of writers in the hard-boiled tradition, but he—like Gordie in *The Body*—eventually had to discover his own voice (a voice, we argue, that more often vibrates at a pastoral frequency).[8] This pivot away from Chandler speaks volumes regarding the ideological work of King's detectives. King resolves the Chandler-esque split between the material world and social fodder by reincorporating the unknowable back into what can be known. Again, *The Colorado Kid* includes stories being told within a story (*mise-en-abyme*), a convention that prods readers into thinking critically about the act of reading. Far more pedantic than Chandler, King's pair of Teague and Bowie spin a far-fetched yarn to instruct the protégé on a hidden moral lesson. These wizened storytellers gleefully recount the subplot of a young aspiring detective being manipulated by two aging detectives—a subplot, readers might assume, that reveals the actual intention of the narrative of the Colorado Kid, which is to impart a lesson about the nature of narrative and, more broadly, the proper art of detection (to be practiced by any self-respecting journalist). It would seem that King dallies with the tropes of the detective tale because he wants his audience to ruminate upon one of his favorite themes: a worldview based on honesty at odds with a worldview driven by cynical investigation.

For King, the detective and the vicarious reader must learn to behave like children. This narrative acceptance is always part of King's ratiocinative process, but readers of the larger canon will recognize the writer's consistent emphasis on the importance of adults recapturing a child-like imagination in books as early as *'Salem's Lot* and *IT*. Child-like exploration allows innocent individuals to spot things that experts employing the most refined, well-cultivated methodologies cannot see. In *The Colorado Kid*, Teague and Bowie laugh "like the world's oldest pair of kids"; Stephanie, in turn, comes to share in their "perfect and uncomplicated happiness" (42–44). From one vantage point, we can see a correlation with the Chandler chasm, as King asks readers to set aside the detective's chronological schemes in favor of a pronounced presentism: a raw experience of the world accessible mostly to the very young (or very old). But King's latent pastoralism does not leave open this schism between a pronounced presentism (space) and the detective's impulse to put events in proper order (time) because it folds everything back into the stuff of a comfortable American mythos, with its hazy focus upon the frontier. Children are always wise; nothing is ever truly out of place. Bowie reassures Stephanie, "Sooner or later, everything old is new again"—a statement that brings Chandler's "old business" back to life and then erases the sheer externality of death by insisting upon a messianic framework (55).

Despite its sometimes-shocking ruptures, King overlays *The Colorado Kid* with the solace of a cosmic orderliness. As such, the weighty Chandleresque world—with its oil wells salty corpses, and irreducible, mineral materiality—is inevitably *re-temporalized*, which is to say everything in King's novel eventually finds its way back into the familiar patterns and cycles of the rest of his fictional universe. The clearest example of this suturing effect in *The Colorado Kid* is the novel's repetitive insistence upon the transactional logic of justice: a logic at the center of King's oeuvre, from *IT* to *Rose Madder* to *The Dark Tower*. Teague compares money to newspaper stories in their tendency to circulate and to arrive, always, at their predetermined destination; through his creative turns, Teague finds a way to redirect money from the hands of corporate elites into the pocket of deserving locals: "I like the way the money goes around and around" (35). In a similar way, Teague helps to redirect the money of an adverse insurance company to the widow of the Colorado Kid. Money and stories have a way of ending up where they need to be, if one only has faith in the internal benevolence of their circulation.

Along similar lines, Teague and Bowie share a kind of telepathic bond. Their thoughts magically circulate, like money, and bring them ever closer together. Everything is connected within the American cosmos. Even during an ostensibly unnatural encounter—with the body in the weeds or the sand—a sense prevails that everything will be, in the final tally, eminently "natural." King thus resuscitates the orthodoxy of the American detective against its hard-boiled drift. The solution to King's Hard Case Crime novels is available before readers can ask the question—not in a tragic or fatalistic manner, as in film noir, but in a pastoral manner that allows readers to redeem the irredeemable and reduce the irreducible. In sum, King gestures to Chandler's vital gap between time and space, between human indexes and the profundity of experience, but King proves to be committed to a uniquely uncynical outlook. An uncynical detective, though, remains something of a paradox: with what, exactly, can a detective busy herself if the unknowable proves to be already incorporated within her existing account of things? The reader's initial, unnerving glimpse of a genuine anti-system, beyond the edge of the detective's *modus operandi*, evaporates, like a shimmering mirage, and leaves us both strangely comforted and unexpectedly uneasy.

THE SECOND SKIN OF *JOYLAND*

King's second book under the Hard Case Crime imprint, *Joyland*, features a young man named Devin Jones who spends a summer working at the eponymous North Carolina amusement park. On the one hand, it is a novel—like so many of its hard-boiled predecessors published by both King and the noir writers who have influenced him—concerned with tragic loss, unexpected deaths, and the dying innocence of youth. On the other hand, it is a narrative about finding oneself and learning to "live in the moment." The resolution of *Joyland* involves solving the murder case of Linda Gray, who dies on a ride appropriately called Horror House. As Devin works to solve Gray's murder, he also struggles to overcome the death of his mother as well as his painful breakup with his first love, his college girlfriend Wendy Keegan. Closely following the template established in both *The Body* and *The Colorado Kid*, King's second installment in the Hard Case Crime family returns to a Chandler-esque split between time and space, between the detective's task and what lies beyond, between a youth's fall from innocence and an adult's reckoning with that fall. Once more, King eventually restores a pastoral orderliness—a comforting suture meant to conjoin the two worlds it has torn asunder.

The novel centers itself, again, in the spatial weightiness of bodies. Gray's corpse, "still warm and pulsing," resides at the epicenter of Joyland, the park as well as the text (36). It keeps resurfacing throughout the novel, "cold and dead" (174–75). When Devin discovers that Gray's killer murdered a host of other young women, he pictures their dead bodies as "gator-bait," effectively "dumped ... like garbage" by the same callous killer (194). The clinical busywork of the would-be detective contrasts sharply with a tangible corporeality that again reminds us of a latent connection that hardboiled detection maintains with horror. As Devin observes, "If you read a whodunit or see a mystery movie, you can whistle gaily past whole heaps of corpses ... but these had been real young women. Crows had probably ripped their flesh; maggots would have infested their eyes and squirmed up their noses and into the gray meat of their brains" (201). Linda Gray—the gray meat of the brain; a lump of flesh, rotting, unmoved by the intellectual exercise of the amateur sleuth. To recognize the difference between a gaily whistling detective and a pile of carnage involves understanding how the mind "defends itself" against its own mortality (89). The pining, hungry detective exists in one world; in the other world, there is the flesh of the body, a physical form that eats, digests, dies, and inevitably rots.

The innermost bodily machinations of *Joyland*, the text as well as the place, depend upon two layers of skin: the epidermis, that which human beings can see and feel, and the musculature, or the tissue and bone that allow the body to move. Beneath the carnivalesque and cartoonish façade, the world of "pop songs" and "Scooby-Doo"—a corporate world that is "too buffed and shiny"—the supposedly real world is differentiated from fantasy. This so-called real world remains defined by its tough, sinewy textures (16–17). A second skin materializes in the glistening, overheated teenaged body of a boy who must "wear the fur," meaning to don the costume of Joyland's canine mascot, Howie. King again characterizes the guardians of this second realm as uniquely aged by paying particularly close attention to the hands of the mature carnies who run the park, which remain "nothing but knuckles," comprised of "gnarled fingers" (57, 84). This second layer of figurative flesh is acutely arthritic: a root system metaphorically couched beneath a "sunken, vein-gnarled temple" (62). *Joyland* comments extensively on minor details characterizing the carnies, from their knotty extremities to their failing digestive tracts. Accordingly, under the figurative dermis of an enclosed as well as artificial place that labors long and hard at "selling fun" (60), King's reader unearths a decaying infrastructure. The novel appropriately labels the carny break room "the boneyard" (71).

Following in Chandler's footsteps, King cultivates what appears to be a class-based spatiality, since his fictional mapping of Joyland, with its glittery surfaces and interior "boneyard," reveals sharp class divisions. A disposable seasonal laborer, whose actual body must suffer to advance a cartoon plotline, Devin finds himself "*buried* in the Howie costume" (78;

emphasis added). The setting of the novel features two distinct spheres—the glitzy world of the uber-wealthy, with their towering homes along the North Carolina shoreline, and the shoddy, behind-the-scenes corners of Joyland, where carnies see themselves as separate from the patrons and speak their own secret language. There is the impossibly large Victorian home of Devin's new love interest, Annie Ross, and then there is the pathetic body of the older carny Eddie, crumpled in a heap after having a heart attack in the shadow of a carny ride. Like King himself and many of his literary protagonists, Devin takes pride in his identification as a working stiff; he earns his blue-collar *bona fides* when he exits from the "Never Never Land" of his college cocoon and willingly resuscitates the unpleasant Eddie, dying at the outermost edge of the vision of coastal elites. For Devin, this blue-collar identification involves *tasting* Eddie—the residue of his stale cigarettes—and Devin dreams of the grotesque feel of Eddie's corpse, with spiders pouring from its orifices. Like Chandler's bodies, Eddie's body has a visceral feel, a texture, to it. Devin comes into close contact with the workaday world as he rests in "the boneyard," out of the reach of well-to-do summer residents sauntering along the gilded surface of the amusement park.

As in *The Colorado Kid*, King sets his detective story on a beach, with its unique stench of organic, mineral decay. The trivial amusements of human experience clash with "the steady, sleepy beat of the surf" (32). When Devin walks the beach, he tarries at "the end of the world," drifting with what lies forever beyond the comings and goings of an existential detective who combs his surroundings for veiled answers, to Linda Gray's murder as well as his future as a brokenhearted adolescent (86). The sea once more represents a profound border between what a human mind can understand (very little) and the vastness of what remains fundamentally unknowable: the depths of a cold and unrelenting ocean. This fact underscores the gap between the mask of friendship and the serial killer who lurks beneath. The sea signifies death; it creates dune-lets that closely resemble "skeleton fingers" (257). Its frigid indifference marks a line that cannot be trespassed—the border between Devin and his deceased mother; the border between Devin and his friend Tom, who will eventually die a tragic death; and the border that narrows the lifeline of young Mike, who will also die before the novel is finished. Like *The Colorado Kid*, this is a novel permeated with death and dying as it stalks both the present and the past. The owner of Joyland, who will also die before the tale is done, may believe that the park is a place that "sells fun," but underneath the carny masks and the smell of grilled hotdogs, the place is haunted by death. Following Chandler, King thrusts his audience into a specific spatial logic—the liminal space of the beach, the openness of an unchecked ocean at odds with the clustered, block-like map of an amusement park—and the chronological index upon which Devin relies in his efforts to make sense of Linda Gray's senseless murder a long time ago.

What is primarily a novel about a twenty-one-year-old's coming-of-age summer only becomes a serious detective story two-thirds of the way through. *Joyland* gradually funnels the former into the latter. After the park shuts down for the winter, the murder of Linda Gray that occurred on the park's "one and only dark ride" (114) becomes the essential focus for Devin, who spends the first half of the book working various jobs inside Joyland while grieving the loss of his girlfriend Wendy, who is responsible for "really and truly reject[ing me] for the first time in my life. She was through with me, but I couldn't imagine being through with her" (90). Readers find much to admire in Devin's genial personality and his genuine love of children, but he also shares something in common with many of Poe's bereft males whose lost women inspire poetry, as well as his dualistic characters, particularly Dupin and Minister D— in "The Purloined Letter." Devin has a complicated psyche that leads him to obsess over a murder mystery that has baffled the police for four years, while his righteous impulse is counterpointed by an unconscious identification with the man who committed the crime. In addition to the recently acquired lovesick melancholia that he nurtures the entire summer, Devin harbors a genuine level of acrimony over his girlfriend's betrayal, which is often the flip side of Poe-esque melancholia. That betrayal fuels an interior pool of resentment and anger: "It was never a constant thing, but I did think of her with a certain malevolence in the aftermath of the breakup. . . . there were long and sleepless nights when I thought she deserved something bad—maybe really bad—to happen to her for the way she hurt me" (44). This is an important revelation because it highlights his loss of innocence and descent into a summer when rage lurks just beneath depression. When Devin is not "wearing the fur," he moons out the window of his room at the ocean or watches his friends, Tom and Erin, spend their days off in each other's blissful company, deepening the fresh wound of his girlfriend's duplicity. He learns, "Love leaves scars" (49). The fact that Devin spends his free time at the boarding house "having those occasional thoughts of suicide" (43) and listening to the music of the rock group The Doors, particularly their song "The End" (92), a violent lament to the loss of hope and love blended with a parallel itch to commit patricide and Oedipal incest, is clear evidence of the noir spirit that looms over the decent young man and threatens to consume his personality.

Thus, Devin is pulled by two contrary, noir-like impulses: he wants to solve the case and redress the harm caused by Linda Gray's grisly death in the Horror House, but he is also drawn into its violence because of his antipathy to Wendy and women in general. His friend and investigative researcher Erin stimulates Devin's desire to probe further into the murder investigation, and she summarizes accurately the profile of "The Carny Killer," Lane Hardy, a serial murderer who has terrorized women over multiple years, by slitting their throats and then escaping capture: "Always in summer. Always as a result of a dating situation with an unknown older man. Always the cut throat. And always with some sort of carny connect—" (208). Apart from the throat cutting, this profile could apply to the brooding side of Devin Jones. Despite Madame Fortuna's warning that "a boy with bad thoughts needs to be visiting a haunted house like he needs arsenic in his mouthwash" (99), Devin's recurrent need to probe the interior of the Horror House ride, the place where the crime was committed, "pulsating red light illuminating a single steel tract and a black tunnel entrance beyond" characterized by "rumbles, flashing lights, and more screams" (116), reveals his obsession with tracking Hardy and his victim to the spot where she was killed. The symbolic layout of the ride networked with secret chambers and labyrinthine pathways spiraling inward into deepening layers of blackness has features that suggest the structure of the human brain. Devin's journey into the ride's interior, marked as it is symbolically as a realm signaling the subconscious, shows him identifying with both Gray *and* her murderer. While Devin is drawn for unknown reasons to the hope of contacting Gray's ghost, as Tom unwittingly does (120), he is at the same time psychoanalytically aligning himself with Lane's criminal design and entering the killer's mind (if you will) by retracing The Carny Killer's footprints on the day he murdered his unsuspecting date. In this way, Devin establishes a bond with the killer, an admixture that reminds us of the symbiotic relationship that so often occurs in Poe's tales, where detective and felon are aligned over acts of criminality. Here King returns once more to the brink: a cut that divides the detective's orderly pursuits from an abyss that cannot be rationalized.

While Devin, unlike Lane Hardy, is not a serial killer, nor does he harbor the same level of misogyny that feeds such acts of violence, he and Hardy emerge as *doppelgängers*, hiding agitated emotions behind placid exteriors. They form a tight bond with each other at Joyland because of their outward friendliness and charm. Hardy, of course, turns out to be far more secretive; like Ted Bundy, he hides behind a mask that disguises his true intentions—a deep-seated hatred for both women and the "rube" patrons of Joyland—and emerges as the illustration for Annie Ross's warning to her son that "Some people hide their real faces. Sometimes you can tell when they're wearing masks, but not always" (276). Devin is certainly less cynical, a sexual virgin whose transparency allows women to intuit immediately his unrequited suffering over a lost first love. *Joyland* puts these two men on a collision course that gradually peels away the false face of their friendship and highlights their core differences.

The novel's climax occurs when Hardy forces Devin to ride the park's Ferris wheel sitting in the same car with him as a tempestuous storm rages around them. Hardy's intention is to kill them both in a murder-suicide, but first he has a need to understand the ratiocinative process that Devin has employed in discovering what has eluded the police. Like the relationship between Poe's Minister D— and Dupin, the criminal and detective find themselves fused together in an unholy bond that will conclude in their division. Hardy, like Poe's Minister D—, seeks only to enhance his power and control over women, his barely repressed violence finally manifested in the very storm where he confronts Devin and reveals his true self to the reader. Dupin, in contrast to his nemesis, wants to solve the mystery more than anything else, but in the process he also finds himself in service to the compromised Queen; likewise, Devin seeks to solve the crime to revenge an innocent woman's victimization. His process of reviewing, enlarging, and rearranging the photographs Erin has supplied him of Hardy and Linda Gray walking together in the amusement park further resembles Dupin's ratiocinative process of assembling evidence in "The Purloined Letter" as well as "The Murders in the Rue Morgue" and "The Mystery of Marie Rogêt": "I sat on the floor and laid them out in a square, moving them from place to place like a guy trying to put a puzzle together. Which was, I suppose, exactly what I was doing" (210).[9]

Through this meticulous rearrangement of images, *Joyland* generates a very particular sort of historicity. Devin clings desperately to a temporal logic as he gathers and reconfigures Erin's photos, at least the ones that would be "admissible" in court, into a coherent scrapbook (110). Like most of King's would-be private eyes, including Stephanie in *The Colorado Kid*, Devin uses a yellow legal pad to document his findings and reconstruct a correct causal chain of events. But there is a different system at work here, too, a kind of anti-system that refuses to bend to the will of these youthful sleuths. An older carny conjures the ghost of philosopher Walter Benjamin when he announces, "History is the collective and ancestral shit of the human race, a great big and ever-growin pile of crap . . . pretty soon we'll be buried under the doodoo of generations yet to come" (64). King's vision of history can be broken into two distinct units: a chronological system, maintained by the naïve scrapbooking of aspiring detectives, and the anti-system best represented by King's dumping pile: a voluminous pile of historical events that have at last been glimpsed in spatial terms.

Said another way, Devin succeeds where more orthodox detectives fail because he alone focuses upon the physical space he occupies—the mighty, if ultimately fetishized, here and now—and ceases to be overwhelmed by the torments of an assumed temporality: what should have been, what could yet be, and so forth. Most obviously, Devin must let go of the events from his recent unhappy past; or to put a finer point upon it, he must recognize that the past as well as the future are pale imitations of a "real," and thus more substantial, world. A second skin. "When it comes to the past," he notes, "*everyone* writes fiction" (43; emphasis in the original). If conventional detectives turn the past into the future through their meticulous problem-solving skills, Devin recognizes that neither the past nor the future truly exists; rather, the future remains unknowable, while the past stubbornly endures, like a corpse or a cold case crime, in a state of suspended animation: "I suppose I could use Google, that twenty-first century Magic 8-ball . . . but to what purpose? Gone is gone. Over is over" (50). In response to this daunting revelation, Devin privileges a pronounced present-ism: a spatialized present with heightened textures and tastes divorced from the vaporous realm of cause and effect. He admits that "the short term is all any of us have" (123). Echoing King's twenty-first-century protagonists, Devin stops pursuing ghosts as he comes to prefer a fully embodied experience.

Following *The Colorado Kid*, King's *Joyland* does not allow its readers to idle for long in Chandler's schism between time and space, or between the world of the detective and the world beyond the sleuth's chronological obsessions. Like many works in the broader detective genre, especially its less hard-boiled variants, *Joyland* arrives at a sense of resolution: "We end with the unmasking of the culprit, whose expulsion will absolve all the rest. To this extent at least, the entire genre is optimistic" (Lehman 2). King once more sutures the detective's world and the exterior world back together, and he does so in two specific ways. First, he returns to tacit patterns established by some of his favorite literary naturalists. Everywhere in *Joyland*, readers uncover signs of a "gloomy realism" (159). Like Stephanie in *The Colorado Kid*, Devin must spotlight the difference between televised detective shows and "real life" (202). In contrast to the neat and tidy roadmap of young employees, elderly carnies acknowledge that all human beings are lost. *And yet no one is ever truly lost in Joyland, either the text or the place.* A clear roadmap endures, as every event in the novel unfolds in accordance with an invisible order. Just as the steady rhythm of ocean waves lulls Devin to sleep, the natural world becomes personified in *Joyland*. The ocean and the wind prove to be active characters in the closing moments of the novel, leading up to the climactic encounter on the Ferris wheel: "The wind gusted and moaned" (199). In effect, King synchronizes the two worlds—the detective's world and nonhuman space, exemplified by the ocean—within an all-encompassing plot that explains everything as part of a vast organic system. When Devin frenetically arranges photographs of his murder suspect on a Scrabble table to solve the puzzle of Linda Gray's murder, his ideas start "crashing together" like "the agitated surf" (251). King's natural world (re)aligns with the human world, and Chandler's radical rupture is replaced by a far more stable and sensical order of things.

Departing from Chandler, King's latent idealism shines through and effectively undercuts the novel's melancholia with a final uplifting message: "Life isn't always a butcher's game. Sometimes the prizes are real" (220). In the end, Devin proves to be more resilient than he thought himself capable. As we traced in this chapter's earlier discussion of *The Colorado Kid*, Devin shares a unique connection with children who visit the park and delight in his spontaneous renditions of the Hokey Pokey dressed as Howie. This special link with children eventually results in his introduction to Mike Ross and his mother, Annie. In the course of this novel, Devin saves the lives of a choking child and a gruff old carny who experiences a heart attack, and he prevents the potential violation of Annie and Mike by the Carny Killer. The owner of Joyland recognizes immediately that Devin is a "seat-of-the-pants-genius" (84), meaning that he is in possession of "magical" attributes, foremost a level of kindness that entertains and soothes children, while likewise attracting them to him. This attachment both separates Devin from Chandler's Marlowe and sustains him as he rises above the personal despair that initially incapacitated him. It is certainly his child-like appreciation of life and his desire for happiness that disconnect him from Lane Hardy, and it may also be what motivate him to right the wrong of Linda Gray's unsolved murder. Just as the antagonist's disdain for innocent "rubes" destroys him, Devin's inner "rube" allows him to emerge from the events of the novel revivified. He and his friends deliberately board the Horror House ride in search of answers. They enter a *"boys' adventure"* as they intentionally "get in line with the rest of the rubes" (111; emphasis in the original). Their shared effort to "see how the other half lives" proves enlightening, since it is precisely their child-like capacity to think "like a rube" (116) that empowers them to solve the case.

The cumulative contrast of King and Chandler could not be clearer: as a morally superior detective, Devin forfeits causal logic in favor of intuition as well as submission to a benevolent cosmos; meanwhile, his nemesis—and Linda Gray's murderer—refuses to adhere to such rules. Unable to occupy the here and now, and repressing a cynicism that keeps him perched at the edge of the abyss, Lane Hardy refuses to make "a rube's mistake" (263). He acerbically dismisses the park's visitors for their naivete: "They're just rubes, all of them. They see nothing" (266). The villain's insatiable "curiosity" will not be easily "satisfied"—such rabid curiosity killed the cat, King once more reminds his audience—and it is precisely this domineering need to know how his criminal self was discovered, his hunger to create a chronological account, that spells his doom (263). A genial dog that delights in the joy he brings to small children; a naïve, childish consumer of trivial amusements; a young boy-man willing to breathe life back into the lungs of a nasty old man with halitosis; an intuitive working stiff who chooses to love the carnal pleasures of capitalism instead of turning into a callous cynic—Devin Jones reveals himself to be a worthy detective in the King design. But Devin's distinctive profile might give readers pause, particularly if they expect to receive the emotional and intellectual pay-offs of Chandler's literary works. An ardent critic of capitalism, Chandler despised the performativity of consumer society: "Life was just one great big vaudeville show," Marlowe moans. "An act is all there is. There isn't anything else" (*Long* 144, 311). Readers can contrast this cynical take with King's *celebration* of the Howie performance—the fact that life is nothing more than a vaudeville show is not meant to fill King's reader with dread; Devin's trivial performance becomes an antidote to what ails an overly jaded world. King therefore softens the hard-boiled tradition by reversing Chandler's logic: no longer an obstacle to resolution, the vaudevillian act provides a degree of solace in a weary world.

King's *Joyland* closes by coming full circle and pivoting into a sort of fantastical fairytale, driven by the fanciful tempo of "once upon a time" (279). The narrative transposes Chandler's gloomy realism—oriented around the inevitable holes in the detective's perception—into a cogent wholeness. Readers of *Joyland* experience something like their own Horror House ride, as a sign pops up that reads "End of the Line" before a secret door "splits open just in time" and the reader/rider can breathe a big sigh of relief (235). Simply put, King lets his Constant Reader off the hook by revealing that the assumed outermost edge of the world, the proverbial end of the line, was just another literary tactic—another trick by another trumped-up carny (an example of King's self-effacement). For King, the brink is only ever part and parcel of an overarching benevolent order. Although "no summer is endless," *Joyland* suggests, in line with Devin's autumnal employment, that an imaginary summer can sustain itself (184). Because Howie the Dog does not waste his time considering the past or the future, Howie's inner human can enjoy a perpetual summer. Similarly, Devin's momentary confrontation with loss proves to be just another thrilling turn along the trackway of a ride that dependably delivers him back to safety, which explains why the adult narrator of this novel is so often capable of looking back at his twenty-one-year-old self and the events of that year as if it occurred to someone else.

But what are the potential costs of this idyllic enclosure? King's intrinsic orderliness undoubtedly complicates the novel's commentary on class. Whereas Chandler exposes a stark divide between the wealthy and the working class—Marlowe jokingly refers to himself as "a beat-up gumshoe with no yacht" (*Little* 195), and he complains, "I'm a romantic. [. . .] You don't make a dime that way" (*Long* 229)—King's class divisions are revealed to be harmless, as the reader/rider learns how to stop worrying and love the trivium of a vapid consumerism on full display at Joyland (the amusement park AND the book). The pitch made by Mr. Easterbrook—his poor man's Disney marketing of fun and the subsequent purchase of happiness, a pitch that sounds much more like a sales ploy than a profound existential commentary—improbably hits Devin's ear as "truth rather than horseshit" (*Joyland* 60). To live in the here and now means, in this context, *ignoring* systemic issues or—even more troublingly—becoming complacent in the continuation of a dangerously insipid consumer culture. This conclusion almost certainly leaves Chandler rolling in his grave.

From a Chandler-esque perspective, King's critique of the detective, his tireless effort to chasten the overzealous sleuth, results in its very opposite: far from encountering the outermost limits of his knowledge, King's detective always transcends his limitations by absorbing what Chandler positions as an exterior world into his impressive knowledge of everything.

Most readers misread Chandler: "They want to be soothed, not irritated," Peter Rabinowitz asserts. "And they do not want to confront Chandler's abyss" (201); readers misinterpret Chandler as stressing the solution to his detective's problems, but he actually stresses "indecisive conclusions" (203). It is only recently that readers, including Fredric Jameson, have started to appreciate how Chandler divides the material realm (dead bodies) from the detective's temporal logic (solving the crime). Because King adopts an intentionally Chandler-esque voice, readers might be tempted to conclude that King likewise invests in indecisive conclusions, or the abyss. Without question, King does tarry with the abyss, as we have seen throughout this volume. Yet King usually upholds a deeper strain of sentimentalism (for better or worse), as characters like Stephanie and Devin cease obsessing over the details of their respective cases and recognize the fecundity of the here and now. A careful consideration of *The Colorado Kid* and *Joyland* therefore allows readers to illuminate how King differs in significant ways from one of his major literary inspirations, Raymond Chandler, and, as a result, to understand why King noir is rarely quite so noir as it initially appears to be.

Chapter 9

BILLY SUMMERS AND THE CRIMINAL'S REDEMPTION

IT IS ONE THING TO ARGUE, AS WE HAVE IN OUR TREATMENT OF NOVELS that King began publishing over twenty years ago for the Hard Case Crime imprint, that King's fascination with crime fiction and the detective genre led to composing his own work in homage to the tradition. Narratives such as *Mr. Mercedes* remain relatively faithful to the formula—that is, a criminal perpetuates felonious activity, and the detective seeks to outwit him and foil his design. This fact alone might serve as sufficient justification for this book, since King's debts (and contributions) to crime fiction are underappreciated and underacknowledged by his massive popular audience as well as literary critics busily analyzing other elements in the King multiverse. But we have also argued that, to read King accurately, it is necessary to appreciate the role ratiocination plays in his novels not ostensibly tied to crime fiction: although *Dolores Claiborne* and *Misery* are obviously texts about domestic abuse and Gothic entrapment, both books can likewise be seen to employ tropes, characters, and plot designs aligned with the genres of detection. Further, the Bachman books dive deeply into the realm of noir while they are portraits of hard-pressed personalities enmeshed in a naturalistic universe struggling merely to survive.

Building upon this foundation, *Billy Summers* is a study in criminality that includes a conflicted point of view belonging to the criminal himself. This is not the first we see of such a dynamic in the King canon. George Stark and Thad Beaumont in *The Dark Half* suture into a singular psyche, a murderer grown troubled by his history of violence; *Dolores Claiborne* is a confessional that complicates conventional divisions between detective and criminal (see chapter 6). And while there is no detective figure *per se* in *Billy Summers,* it is yet another King text that echoes Edgar Allan Poe's core obsession with the self's existential duality, since it contains an explanation for both the impulse toward criminal violence and the need to discover an alternative course. Self-conflict and self-doubt are present in the Manichean impulses that drive its protagonist: an assassin trained by the US Marines who justifies his acts of killing strangers as the removal of "bad people," but a man pulled equally by a desire for vicious retributive punishment and the urge to protect the innocent and vulnerable (the etymology of the name "William" signals protector). As such, the novel's eponymous main character is a slippery and complex individual, a synthesis of the ratiocination dialectic—he is firmly established on the path of criminality at the same time as he seeks redemption for his lifelong vocation. *Billy Summers* confirms and pushes the working thesis of our book to its furthest point: part neo-noir, part gangster novel, part metadetective story, part redemption tale, *Billy Summers* completes the arc of imaginative possibilities this book has traced.

From the opening of the novel, King's readers are alert to its generic inheritance, as Billy enters into a contract to kill a fellow hitman in hopes of a payday big enough to inaugurate his retirement from the assassination business, an occupation that has led to his disillusionment: "If noir is a genre," Billy muses, "then 'one last job' is a sub-genre" (10). Billy later realizes that he is "starring in his own last job story" (26). There are visual cues, too, such as "the misty oblong of yellowish light on the ceiling, thrown by the streetlight" (151), an oneiric image borrowed from noir cinema. Related intertextual threads work their way through Billy's autobiography as he watches the 1950 noir film *Asphalt Jungle*—a frequent reference for King, concerning a heist that ends with someone being double-crossed (and foreshadowing the metatextual betrayal of Billy by the crime figures who hired him). Specifically, Billy processes information by filtering it through the worlds of crime fiction mainstay, and King favorite, James M. Cain, and he "reads" his fellow mobsters as "characters in a Coppola or Scorsese movie" (100). In line with most of King's other work that cross-pollinates with crime fiction, this novel engages in metacommentary upon King's formulaic forebearers. One of the text's so-called patsies "has seen too many movies. Some of them probably in the 'one last job' sub-genre" (15). At another point, Billy grows "a little bored" with the popular television crime show *Blacklist*, arguing that it has exhausted its generic possibilities (291). In other words, even as Billy navigates familiar storylines and uses his evolving writerly skills to retrace the stale patterns that motivate his contemporaries, there is also a kind of fatalism at work here—a point to which we will return. Like a number of King's ill-fated characters, including the titular protagonist from *Umney's Last Case*, Billy may not be able to escape from the prison house of genre.

King's style as a writer adopts many elements from crime fiction. As such, *Billy Summers* can be read in what John Scaggs describes as "the hard-boiled mode," since its characters and setting align with the hard-boiled tradition. The environmental squalor in which Billy spends most of the novel emphasizes the superficiality of the modern condition, comprised of "imitation, artifice, insubstantiality, fakery, and facades"; disenchanted Billy lives in a "kingdom of illusion" (Scaggs 71), harkening back to Barton Dawes from Bachman's *Roadwork* (discussed at length in chapter 3). Stuck with one foot in the morass of modernity, with its cryptic sense of justice, and one foot in the defiant posture of an undead chivalry, Billy slides into the well-worn territory of the mid-century private dick.[1] Similarly, since the private eyes of Raymond Chandler or Dashiell Hammett appear to Billy "like garbagemen with a gun"—little more than thugs peddling their wares to the highest bidder—Billy is repulsed by the very genre that has sustained his life's work (King, *Billy* 5). On the one hand, and due in no small part to the grammar of crime fiction, Billy sets out on "a quest to make sense of a fragmented, disjointed, and largely unintelligible world" (Scaggs 72). King's Constant Reader must follow Billy down this desolate road with a heightened awareness of her own status as a reader similarly questing for purpose in the text before her. Like countless works in the hard-boiled mode, *Billy Summers* "foregrounds its own methods of construction, and invites the reader to become a participant in the construction of meaning" (Scaggs 74). As is the case in texts like *Misery*, *Dolores Claiborne*, and *The Colorado Kid*, King mirrors Billy's readerly and writerly efforts in the task that he sets for his Constant Reader. What changes in *Billy Summers*, however, is the possible *redemptive* qualities that emerge from out of this text, in contrast to, say, some of King's earlier works in the hard-boiled mode, including *Umney's Last Case*.

As always, context matters. King published *Billy Summers* in 2021 in the wake of Donald Trump's presidency, during which King repeatedly denounced self-fashioned "heroic" partisans for presenting themselves as good guys when, in truth, they proved to be little more than criminal thugs. Relatedly, the Trumpian moment involved the unchecked gaslighting of an American audience that did not know where to find "authentic" selves, instead relying upon internet avatars and infotainment to tell them what to believe. *Billy Summers* is a text that highlights, at times quite artfully, the conundrum of living in a post-truth society. But King does not respond to the pressures of the moment by singularly deriding Trump and his supporters; instead, he writes a novel that exposes such simplistic binaries to be the stuff of cartoons. Returning to the noir reservoir, King undercuts the effortless exaggerations of populists, with their paint-by-number evildoers. Swept up in a world of rampant criminality, chronic deception, and a barrage of misinformation, *Billy Summers* offers the art of detection as a redemptive arc in which the reader and writer—or, in a closely related register, detective and criminal—could establish a healthier relationship with one another. When King's figurative detectives start to think like criminals, and his figurative criminals start to think like detectives, King lays the groundwork for a more *relational* state of being than the one on display in a fractured state of Red and Blue Americas (of the kind exemplified in Taylor Hackford's 1995 adaptation of *Dolores Claiborne*, discussed in chapter 6). The blueprint of the hard-boiled detective story provides the audience of *Billy Summers* with a template for greater tolerance and, perhaps, a pathway for coexistence in a sharply divided United States.

A DOSTOEVSKIAN CHARACTER

Billy Summers tells a pulpy crime story about a sniper who makes his living eliminating those he defines as "bad people." But insofar as it is also a story about a middle-aged man striving to come to terms with the destruction he has caused, it has a good deal in common with Fyodor Dostoevsky's canonical *Crime and Punishment*. Dostoevsky subjects his criminals to spiritual contortions; in fact, it should be argued that such contortions are at the core of his commitment to writing. Early in King's book, Billy mentions that he has trouble discerning whether one of the other characters "is a good person or a bad one. Perhaps he's both. Billy has always found this a troubling concept" (99). Turns out that this statement speaks precisely to Billy's own personality as a man fluctuating on the imagined spectrum between good and bad. Like Dostoevsky's Raskolnikov, whose name in Russian means "split," Billy's own dualism—rushing from impulse to impulse, from unselfish kindness to vicious acts of retribution against those he deems deserving of punishment—appears in the form of a violent man who is also simultaneously, semiconsciously, searching for some kind of redemption. This urge only increases as the novel unfolds. King's book is ultimately more concerned with documenting Billy's gradual progress towards redemption than with the numerous criminal acts and underworld activities that have made his quest necessary in the first place. Like Dostoevsky's complex characters, Billy is as much pure id as he is superego: a murderer who justifies his actions as a sniper in Iraq and, later, as a hired killer for the mob by performing jobs that, from his perspective at least, means to eradicate evil from the world.

The reader enters the novel at that moment in Billy's life, however, when this convenient rationale has grown threadbare. In this regard, Billy also resembles Roland the gunslinger in *The Dark Tower*, who initially supports an end-justifying-the-means philosophy that allows him to punish others voraciously in the name of saving the Tower's Beams from the "bad guys" who would destroy them. Like Roland and Raskolnikov, then, Billy is a murderer whose spiritual development can be measured in terms of how he eventually tempers his justification for violence as a result of the interactions he establishes with other people. In truth, this legacy of a moral split conjoins with the formulaic imperatives of the hard-boiled tradition, with its ambiguous leading men and their chronic self-doubts—men who must maintain at least one foot in the dark if they are to endure. Echoing Poe and Dostoevsky, the private dick must operate in a sort of state of exception, identifying (always uncomfortably) with the abject criminals against whom he simultaneously distinguishes himself.

In Dostoevsky's universe, characters such as Raskolnikov and Ivan Karamazov find themselves tortured by their intellectual theories of the "extraordinary man": the individual who is allowed to act without fear of reprisal—even to kill—unrepentant of moral law. Dostoevsky punishes these characters through intense dream experience and deep emotional trauma and distortion (e.g., Ivan Karamazov's Grand Inquisitor and Raskolnikov's array of suffering innocents) to have them question their own theories and behavior. *Crime and Punishment* features a detective, Porfiry Petrovich—a more humanistic Russian version of Poe's Dupin, although both characters are brilliantly sardonic observers of the criminal psyche—who recognizes the need for Raskolnikov to acknowledge the invalidity of the latter's "superior man" theory. Petrovich helps to stimulate the young student's capacity for suffering via intense introspection and a systematic deflation of his intellectual justifications for murder. *Billy Summers* contains no such humanistic detective, nor does it supply its eponymous character with a clear guide to change, but the steady work that Billy performs in his memoir-novel functions in a similar way as it forces him to survey his past actions, what Dostoevsky would have called the necessary "prison of self and conscience," which in turn deflates his hubris and opens the door to a moral awakening. Billy and Raskolnikov both require a reduction of the hubris that has given them the capacity to make decisions over who gets to live or die. And this process includes a level of self-abasement, a degree of emotional humility that Dostoevsky's novels force on his most empathetic characters, from the underground man to Dmitri Karamazov.

To say that Billy Summers is, like Raskolnikov, a conflicted criminal-hero is to understate his psychological status. Unlike King's typically remorseless criminals, such as Randall Flagg, Ace Merrill, Henry Bowers, Brady Hartsfield, or Greg Stillson, who actively participate in greater levels of depravity during the course of the book, Billy struggles to go in the other direction: toward the discovery of some kind of ethical center. Engaged in the process of writing a novel that is more accurately a memoir—an unlikely duty he takes on as part of an elaborate cover while he is awaits his next (and last) assassination job—the act of writing this book reveals to the reader, as well as to Billy himself, the trauma and isolation he has experienced throughout his life, beginning with a childhood surrounded by familial violence that leads to a foster home and then a tour as a soldier in Iraq. His job as a lone sniper, trained for action against Iraqi insurgents, underscores the continued level of this cold isolation. He appears to have only one real friend, Bucky Hanson, who lives a hermetic life in the Colorado wilderness. Bucky is a less lethal version of Billy; Bucky also thrives on felonious activities, and he too "has a lot of connections in different fields" (496), but his more stable moral base suggests that he is an idealized future version of what Billy might have become had he continued his path of personal moral scrutiny and lived longer. Bucky worries most of all about the likelihood of Billy "ruining" (374) a young zealot named Alice Maxwell by corrupting her with a value code that stems from crime fiction. The fact that Alice comes to trust Bucky and returns to his Colorado enclave at the end of the novel signals that underneath his occasional willingness to circumvent the law and ameliorate Billy's criminality, he is basically a "good man."

What begins as a superficial element meant to legitimize Billy's disguise—not much different from the wigs, umbrella, facial hair, and fake potbelly that he dons to avoid visual recognition—the act of pretending to write his life's story transforms into a steady obsession, a near-daily activity that comes to occupy his attention in ways he never would have thought imaginable: "It's not confessional even though it may amount to a confession. It's about power. He's finally tapped into power that doesn't come from the barrel of a gun" (92). The writing process exposes Billy to the raw brutality and alienation that has characterized his tortured history (Detective Petrovich plays a similar role for Raskolnikov). In his fascination with writing as an extension of imagination and power, Billy connects with several of the other writers elsewhere in King's canon; he finds himself recreating his past in his metafictional characters. Like Paul Sheldon in the process of composing *Misery's Return*, Billy discovers liberation and power from the act of assembling his memoir. He also reminds us of Samuel Landry in *Umney's Last Case* and Thad Beaumont in *The Dark Half* insofar as his writing becomes an exorcism for releasing and reviewing his most violent propensities. While his "fictionalized" storyline may not produce immediate transcendent insights into the choices he has made in his life, Billy certainly gains a deeper appreciation into how the events he writes about tie together: "He has never said any of this, not to anyone, and he's appalled to hear that part of his life told out loud. It's sordid and stupid" (384). And like Beaumont usurping the persona of Stark, or even King's own adoption of the Bachman pseudonym, Billy essentially produces a thinly disguised autobiography: "He doesn't make himself sound better than he was and writes it all too fast to come out clean, but it mostly does anyway. It comes out like the water running downhill through the woods when the snow melts" (446).

Just as important as the role that writing plays in the moral evolution of Billy Summers, from a high-priced hitman into an introspective being, is the steady contact he receives for months from his various neighbors while hiding in plain sight as he waits to kill his last assignment. For the first time in his life, Billy is accepted unconditionally by multiple strangers on Evergreen Street, a suburb in the unnamed city he inhabits. From daily moments of simple human interaction with these people, Billy is brought face-to-face with his own displaced humanity. He is nurtured by the authentic kindness of strangers—the invitations to barbeque dinners, sitting on neighbors' porches sharing beers, playing Monopoly each weekend with the neighborhood children, and the easy marital harmony that the neighboring couple, the Jensens, demonstrates—inspiring Billy to "think Don and Beverly Jensen are the really rich ones. Yes sir, really the rich ones. Sentimental but true" (161). These normalized interactions that Billy either witnesses vicariously or participates in directly have been sorely missing from a sterile life spent navigating among duplicitous Mafiosi and carrying out the odious task of murdering strangers for money. Until this point, his adulthood has lacked any sense of community or purpose beyond his job description and the machinations he hides behind to preserve it. In his rootlessness, the various false identities he relies upon, his use of violence as a lucrative solution to making a living, and his studied amorality, Billy has no real identity beyond that of hired gun. As a result of his writing and his interactions with his neighbors, he comes gradually to recognize that he is no different from the "bad people" he has been hired to assassinate.

The novel therefore follows Billy as he embarks on a quasi-Dostoevskian transformation initiated by his bond with the hardscrabble working-class people who live next door or in the same apartment building that serve to revivify Billy's darkened soul and prepares the way for his introduction to Alice Maxwell, whom he rescues in the second half of the novel after which she helps advance his development as a moral agent.[2] For Ivan Karamazov, humans' spiritual contingency is much too great to be limited as it is in the logic of the Grand Inquisitor. Billy learns a similar truth through the anguish of conscience and his relationships with Alice and his neighbors: every man is capable of ascending beyond his former self to a position where all forces within the self merge into harmony: "Meet people, yes. Get liked and like in return, yes. But don't get close. Getting close is a bad idea. Getting close is dangerous" (53). The novel is a study into both a hardened criminal who nearly loses his soul by adhering to this self-protective dictum and an aging man who finally softens enough to lessen the barriers surrounding his hardened soul, thereby giving himself a chance to live in community with others. As Paul Sheldon absorbs a long-overdue lesson in personal humility while serving as Annie Wilkes's house guest, Billy comes to recognize that his criminal persona, and especially his flimsy rationalization that he only disposes of "bad men," has gifted him with less than half a life. As we have seen, in a manner reminiscent of Roland and other King antiheroes, Billy maintains a rather slippery code of ethics that has allowed him to remain a functioning killer, but that code is also responsible for stripping him of his humanity. This killer ethos is steadily challenged by his close contact with and influence by people who do not murder strangers for a living. As a result, Billy reaches a point where he is forced to modify his life code.

Paralleling many of the gendered relationships that emerge in Dostoevsky's novels, Billy's time spent with Alice, a naïve, twenty-one-year-old victim who nearly dies because of a brutal gang rape, puts him in the role of her savior and benefactor—nothing less than a surrogate father to a woman who is fatherless. She's a slightly older and more vulnerable version of Shanice Ackerman, the young Black girl who bonds with Billy during his time hiding out on Evergreen Street. While coming to Alice's rescue jeopardizes his own safety from both the police and the mob, the fact that he refuses to take advantage of her sexual offerings, thinks always of her comfort and protection, and ends up leaving her his amassed illegal fortune so she can attend college highlights both his evolution into a paternalistic figure and his potential for further ethical development. (It is interesting to note that King's hard-boiled characters, including Dawes from *Roadwork* and Bill Hodges in *Mr. Mercedes*, often spend more time as parental figures than sexually charged beings; King's noted discomfort with representing sexual themes puts him at odds with the foundational work of desire in the hard-boiled tradition, that is, the fantasy work that has long sustained the genre—a significance to which we return in the conclusion of this volume.) When Bucky warns Billy that "she's in love with you and she'll follow you as long as you let her and if you let her you'll ruin her" (374), Bucky's operating with a conception of the sniper that proves woefully incomplete and outdated. The novel ends with Billy dying from a gunshot wound delivered from his last effort to right the world through acts of vengeance, leaving Alice to finish the book he has been writing. As the person closest to him, she inherits his quest for transformation, recognizing that he has left before finding "some kind of atonement" (490). Billy's final words to reveal that he has reevaluated the violent code that sustained him for too long: "When you give pain it leaves a scar. It scars your mind. It scars your *spirit*. And it should, because hurting someone, *killing* someone, is no little thing. Take it from someone who knows" (507; emphasis in the original). This is an important change in orientation from a former hitman, now assuming responsibility for his past actions. Billy dies before getting the opportunity to act fully on this realization, to use it as a guide for living the rest of his life, but King's novel provides enough evidence to argue that he has been moving toward this understanding all along. And although he fails to emerge as a fully actualized Dostoevskian character, insofar as Billy is not shown embracing some version of Christian faith or a blood-and-soil tenet about the sanctity of suffering, his consistent behavior with Alice and the impact he has on her suggest that, while his ethical education may have come too late to redeem himself and attain the atonement he desires, nothing has been lost on Alice, who—like the archetypal "good daughter"—is left to carry on his troubled legacy.

OVERLOOKS AND UNDERWORLDS

Let us pause to place this novel within the larger trajectory of King's body of work: *Billy Summers* is a far more engaging continuation of King's 1977 novel *The Shining* than *Doctor Sleep* (2013). All roads mapped on the King topography, in a literal and figurative sense, lead back to Colorado, to Sidewinder, to the place where the infamous Overlook Hotel once stood. Echoing *The Shining*, King's *Billy Summers* recounts the story of a man with writer's block partnered with a woman who has been the victim of domestic abuse. The result, as the first part of this chapter has demonstrated, is a classic *bildungsroman*, a redemption tale. The Jack and Wendy Torrance relationship gets a redux in the healthy bond established between Billy and Alice. At the same time, the fact that Billy and Alice steer clear of any kind of romantic involvement indicates King's desire to plot a different fate from the one that dooms the Torrances and to reformulate what occurred years earlier to this ill-fated marriage and to their son: "[Billy] doesn't need a psychiatrist to tell him what she means to him . . . he doesn't want to fuck Alice. He cares for her, and that means more than fucking" (337). Billy's last name signals a metaphorical shift, from the frigid winter that consumes the setting of King's first bestseller to the great thawing ushered in by summer. *Doctor Sleep* follows the identical path of the Torrance clan, up through the Rockies on its way to the hotel; its journey is one of redemption through an overcoming of addiction and parental abuse. The winding road that carries King's Constant Reader from *The Shining* to *Billy Summers* evinces more of an unexpected generic carryover, as the criminal underworld of *The Shining*—orchestrated by Vito "the Chopper" Gienelli and his unsavory contacts in a mafioso gang—transforms into a full-on crime story in his 2021 novel, reminding us yet again that King has never bothered to draw clear lines between crime fiction and horror narratives. As we discussed in the introduction, the roots of horror and crime fiction are intimately entwined.[3] The tenets of crime fiction allow King to revisit in *Billy Summers* the fictional world of *The Shining*, this time in a different octave. Indeed, crime fiction gave King the tools he needed to revisit the Overlook Hotel in a truly revisionary way.

As we have shown throughout the earlier chapters, King routinely engages in a metacritique of the detective story. The writer came of age in the 1960s and '70s—decades that saw a neo-noir boom with films such as *Klute*, Roman Polanski's *The Tenant* and *Chinatown*, and novels such as Alain Robbe-Grillet's highly experimental *The Erasers* (*Les Gommes*).

This book has charted the influence of these (and other) metacritiques employed in King's writing. In chapter 3, we discussed *The Shining* in precisely these terms: as a unique kind of detective story in which the novel's central characters, Wendy and Jack, must piece together clues concerning the history of the Overlook and the exact supernatural threat they face. It should come as little surprise, then, to learn that *Billy Summers* treads similar ground, literally as well as figuratively. Looming beyond an expanse of the Rockies across from Bucky's cabin, the evil Overlook occupies a haunting visual locus in the novel via its actual physical location, and the site of the former hotel is contained in a painting of its hedge animals, still capable of mysterious animation over Billy's writing desk (367).

Similarly, the surreptitious energies of the Overlook bleed into *Billy Summers* through its fatalism. The literary and cinematic noirs that King consumed in his youth were marked by an acutely fatalistic perspective: an orientation that inspired the composition of nearly all the Bachman books, which dwell upon unhappy would-be detectives who can hope only to delay the inevitable corruption of modern society but never stop it outright. Jack Torrance might periodically resist the allure of encroaching darkness by retreating to a high perch—an overlook—but the pervasive noir of the hotel's underworld *inevitably* swallows him. The best Jack can do (or Billy, nearly fifty years later) is fight to survive in an increasingly brutal environment. The famous line from Coppola's third *Godfather* film—"Just when I thought I was out, they pull me back in"—applies in varying degrees to both Jack Torrance and Billy Summers, with special emphasis for the latter. On this front, both Jack and Billy prove to be melancholy protagonists stripped of any hope for a romantic denouement. In the seminal film noir *Out of the Past*, an exhausted character posits the question, "Is there any way to win?" To which the hard-boiled hero responds, "There's a way to lose more slowly."[4] Or consider Paul Schrader's widely cited account of modernity and its place in the hard-boiled formula: "There is nothing the protagonist can do; the city will outlast and negate even their best efforts" (586). Echoing Jack Torrance, Billy seems to be a cog in the machine for the unscrupulous men who hired him as well as for the formulaic plotline in which he finds himself, and which he struggles mightily to revise. Despite his best efforts to improvise, that is, to riff and employ slick rhetorical patter, the hard-boiled protagonist remains stuck in a vast social order that will not release its hold over him. Nonetheless, a degree of nobility manifests in his (futile) resistance. On the subject of chivalrous private detectives confronted by the genre's characteristic fatalism, Robert Pippin asserts:

"They act anyway" (15). The fatalism of the noir-haunted underworld of the Overlook later seeps into the psychic space of *Summers*.

One might turn back to an even earlier page. Like any conventional detective story, *Billy Summers* implicates its inquisitive reader as a default sleuth who must attempt to "solve" the text at hand, a puzzle designed to challenge her deductive logic. While it may not appear on first glance as though King's book requires much strenuous effort to "solve" the puzzle—the reader knows the guilty culprit from the start (Billy)—things are not quite so simple. The gangsters who hire Billy for executions think of him as a mere tool (marking another similarity with Jack Torrance, whose first name is slang for "tool"). Billy is a man who, to the gangsters who employ him, reads comic books and speaks in broken, abbreviated sentences, while in truth he thinks much more deeply than the hoodlums can conceive, musing that the literary naturalist "[Emile] Zola was—is—the nightmare version of Charles Dickens. He's thinking that would make a good thesis for an essay" (1). The puzzle at hand for the reader involves puzzling out the *real* Billy Summers, which includes an excursion into his literary acumen as well as his spiritual condition.

To uncover the real Billy, King's reader must sift through the multiple texts that Billy constructs as well as the behind-the-scenes account of his composition efforts, which ultimately are revealed to be edited by the inheritor of Billy's manuscript (Alice). So, what is *real* in *Billy Summers*? What, if anything, can King's reader accept as the "authentic" telling of Billy's life? Just as Billy must hunt down the kingpin mobster who dishonorably betrayed him, the reader must track down the real person at the heart of the narrative—if one actually exists. To achieve its purpose, *Billy Summers* once more relies on the progenitor of the genre(s) that it references, Edgar Allan Poe.

As we highlighted in chapter 3, King has long professed his admiration for Poe; indeed, Poe's fingerprints can be found in every odd corner of King's corpus. They are both standard bearers of the American Gothic. Less remarked upon, however, is the influence of Poe's detective fiction on King. Poe generated the detective tale in conjunction with his metacritique of the nascent genre. Even as Poe's prototypical detective Dupin inspires Poe's reader to outwit the story at hand, given Poe's antagonistic relationship to his critics, the story frustrates efforts to locate a so-called hidden meaning.[5] A Dupin story forces its reader to look deeply for answers; at the same time, Poe's texts mock such an effort, revealing that the answers have been available all along, right at the surface—the thesis, in particular, of "The

Purloined Letter." The desired object (a letter being used to blackmail the Queen) is famously displayed right out in the open. *Billy Summers* similarly frustrates overly ambitious readers who want to apply the template with which they are familiar, namely, the familiar patterns of crime fiction, to resolve the tensions at play. The readers of King's book are initially led to think they know what has happened, thereby assuming a position akin to the ur-detective; but they must ultimately confront the possibility that the text is an elaborate ruse meant to undermine their premature assumptions of mastery.

Like "The Purloined Letter," *Billy Summers* is thoroughly textual. Regarding Poe's seminal detective tale, Jacques Derrida argues: "Everything begins 'in' a library"; it is "an affair of writing, and of writing adrift, in a place of writing open without end to its grafting onto other writings" (199). Just as Poe opened his story in a circulation library, King inaugurates *Billy Summers* with overt references to a text that will guide much of Billy's behavior, Zola's *Thérèse Raquin*. Intertextually more adroit than he allows others to perceive, including most readers of his own tale, Billy glides from Zola's novel to Charles Dickens, moving from text to text with literary abandon. Billy then contemplates Archie comic books, slipping into a whole other kind of literary thesis, this one about Riverdale and "how time stands still there" (King, *Billy* 2). It is clear right away that King wants to embed his reader in an idiosyncratic circulation library, and therefore provoke his reader into a specific reading, one that appreciates the richness of intertextual playfulness. *Billy Summers* wanders freely from text to text, and King's audience can never be too sure which text can be categorized as original or "authentic." Every piece of writing is already enfolded in a different piece of writing. Where, then, should an aspiring literary detective put her stake in the ground?

In a related sense, King's book blurs the assumed boundaries that demarcate its cast of characters. Derrida on Poe: "Like *all* the characters," Dupin "occupies *all* the places" (203; emphasis in the original). Consider the proliferation of Billy's alter egos during the King novel; at one point, he juggles four separate identities. Consider too the tenuous lines that separate Billy from everyone else in the book: Billy's target is his double—a fellow assassin—and so he plans to "hit a hitter" (6); to escape after the killing, he dresses like a gay character, Colin White, because Billy recognizes in Colin a kindred performer: "It takes one to know one" (98). In a manner that reminds the reader of the *doppelgänger* relationship of Dupin and Minister D—, doubles are everywhere in *Billy Summers*—at one point, the novel cuts to a newscaster named Bill (a common enough name, Billy muses), unveiling a deep circularity as one Bill comments upon the actions of another Bill. Here Bills circulate, like the world of free-flowing finance that swirls around the text, threatening to destroy concrete referents.[6] These characters occupy the world of Roger Klerke, an obvious stand-in for the former head of Fox News, Roger Ailes. Television screens act as Klerke's "entourage" (453); screens have multiplied and supplanted the world of flesh and blood humans. In this hypermediated world, everything—even the character Billy—reveals itself to be a copy of a copy. A macabre fatalism has taken hold: the slower mode of losing expressed by Dostoevsky is replicated in Chandler's Philip Marlowe and then in King's Jack Torrance and now, yet again, in Billy Summers.

Billy and Alice also mirror one another: first as double-crossed victims in pursuit of revenge, and then as unexpected writers. A business major, Alice is as surprised by her eventual emergence as an author as she is Billy's transformation from "garbageman with a gun" to Faulknerian wannabe (5).[7] And of course the name of aged hitman Bucky, who hides them out in his cabin near the site of the Overlook, closely echoes the name Billy. There is little in King's text that is not a doubling of Billy, whatever this moniker actually means. As Derrida recognizes in Poe's Dupin tale, there are only "doubles without originals," "forgeries without something forged" (204).

We might at this point look a bit more closely at the title of the book: *Billy Summers*. What does the title signify? "The title is the title of the text," Derrida says of Poe's "The Purloined Letter": "It names the text, it names itself, and thus includes itself by pretending to name an object described in the text" (204). Just as "The Purloined Letter" names itself while pretending to name an object within its parameters (another text: the titular letter), *Billy Summers* names itself as well: its title (*Billy Summers*) doubles as the title that Alice has chosen for Billy's so-called autobiography as well as the object of the study (Billy Summers the character). To reclaim Derrida's famous phrase, there is seemingly nothing outside of the text in *Billy Summers* because the text has no stable signified, only a plethora of additional signifiers—the book-within-a-book called *Billy Summers*, or the name "Billy Summers," which endures as one of countless *nom de plumes*. King's reader cannot easily locate a perch upon which to overlook the proceedings, but instead she must float from one (con)text to another, without the comfort of an ur-text to explain it all. As King's archvillain Pennywise from *IT* intones, "Everything floats." What can an earnest detective hope to accomplish in such a postmodern malaise?

We should note that the target of King's mockery in *Billy Summers* is not exclusively the elitist reader, which is to say, the academic reader with presumed mastery over the text. In the novel, King sets his sights on another reader with "assumptions of superiority": the reader with "Trumpian prejudice" (404). King populates his novel with avid Trump supporters, each of whom fails to "read" Billy correctly. As Trump himself has always moved easily between lawful business ventures and illegal transgressions, the characters in this novel merge supposedly legitimate business fronts with mobster behavior, creating a fusion between criminal and businessman to the point where it is nearly impossible to distinguish the difference. Unable, or unwilling, to conclude that a member of their tribe would ever be a subtle reader or writer, everyone assumes that Billy is dumb. The patsy Ken Hoff, for instance, "has seen too many movies," so he—a "Donald Trump Mini-Me"—completely botches his role, turning it into a ham-fisted effort that leads to his death (45). Unlike Billy, Hoff relies upon the simplistic plotlines of crime fiction to understand his own place in the universe, and his overly literal take on things destroys him. "Straight to the meat of the thing, that's me," Hoff boasts ironically to Billy, "Cut through the bullshit" (66–67). King's reader ought to consider carefully this invitation to "cut through the bullshit." Is this truly the goal of literature as an exercise? Hasn't metacommentary on the genre of crime fiction prepared King's audience to recognize the folly of such naïve incision?

Put differently, *Billy Summers* challenges the facile sort of detective work that characters like Hoff presume as part of their calculated crime persona. Hoff does not recognize the *complexity* of the detective's task in reading a given text; like many of the mobster businessmen with whom he associates, he assumes a Trumpian position of ignorant superiority, and he lacks the critical skill to understand what is truly happening all around him, especially regarding Billy. A well-known critic of Trump and his more vocal supporters, King wants to inculcate a different sort of reading (and writing, as we will see), one that does not presumptively "cut through the bullshit" to claim the ultimate prize of total comprehension. Harkening back to Dostoevsky and Chandler, King seems to recognize the value of ambiguity in *Billy Summers*. Reading is never easy, King warns his audience. To put a finer point on it: Billy's initials—"B.S."—ought to chasten the excessively confident reader. As if in a Russian nesting doll, "Billy" (the content and the form; the name and the thing-itself) cannot be captured by the reader's incisive gaze. The reader will not be able to "cut through" to the imagined core of Billy. Although Billy himself promises to guide the reader to the heart of his story "with a minimum of bullshit" (217), this promise should raise red flags for the careful reader. A story with minimal bullshit, after all, would be a story with minimal B.S. (the very object—Billy Summers; B.S.—that readers are waiting to uncover). King thus leaves his reader with a web of textual references without a deeper meaning, in a world in which perhaps nothing really exists outside of the text. With this approach to reading the text in mind, the following line from King's novel gains a good deal of resonance: "I don't know if there's really an underworld anymore. I think the Computer Age pretty much killed it" (333). Readers who plumb the depths of *Billy Summers* in search of a literal or figurative underworld, or an allegorical undercarriage, will eventually return to the surface empty-handed.

Which brings us full circle back to *The Shining*. If an ur-text does exist in *Billy Summers*, other than Zola's *Thérèse Raquin*, it is surely King's initial masterpiece. Like the writer himself, the reader is willingly drawn back to the Overlook for more unfinished business. The passage of time—nearly fifty years—has transformed the place into one of the great touchstones of evil in the American haunted house tradition, assuming a status alongside dark loci such as Poe's Usher Mansion and Shirley Jackson's Hill House. Yet subsequent visits to its site turn out to be pale reflections of the original source. In *Doctor Sleep*, his sequel to *The Shining*, King elects to focus on lesbian vampirism, a subject with great cultural cache in 2013, instead of engaging in a meaningful return to the location of the first bestseller. Although the vampiric Rose the Hat and her True Knot compatriots maintain a campsite on the former grounds of the Overlook Hotel, the burnt-out place has lost much if not all its supernatural power; it is neither capable of supporting the True Knot in their puerile quest for greater levels of "steam" nor does it rise to thwart an adult Dan Torrance's battle against the Knot. What is left of the Overlook's potent supernaturalism appears smoldering in the husk of its blackened detritus, relegated to the spirit of Jack Torrance, who has somehow managed to reject the evil that entraps him in *The Shining* and reprise himself back into the status of a good father who aids his son in moving toward *Doctor Sleep*'s happy ending. What father Torrance could not manage in *The Shining*, son Dan Torrance pulls off in *Doctor Sleep*: namely, to triumph over his alcoholism and save from the True Knot an imperiled child, Abra Stone, in possession of her own version of "the shining." This maudlin, and arguably derivative, sequel leaves much to be desired.

We contend that *Billy Summers* takes King's audience back to the Overlook in a more subtle and engaging manner. King achieves this nuance by returning to the crucial impasse of *The Shining*: the tension between fate or structural determinism and the potential of individual choice or autonomy—a tension that defines crime fiction even more than it defines its cousin horror. Without a doubt, one could conclude that this third iteration of an Overlook-haunted text comes down on the side of individual autonomy: "[Billy] can't change his past but he means to change his future" (333). Indeed, the novel's opening line, taken from the hymn "Amazing Grace," foreshadows the final line regarding Alice: "She was found" (414). In the novel's elaborate game of hide-and-seek, Alice joins Billy in using the power of the written word to establish and assert their ostensibly authentic identities, that is, to unearth who they truly wish to be. Drawn to the Overlook's transportable hedge animals featured in the painting in the room where he is working on his book in Bucky's cabin, and again, when he and Alice gaze separately across a Colorado mountain range to the hotel's original site, neither Billy nor Alice feels constrained to visit the place, much less assume a sympatico residency within its smoldering ruins. Whatever supernatural compulsion that once drew others to the location (and Billy's history of murdering would seemingly provide the necessary gilded invite to join the hotel's guest registry) barely emerges as more than a distraction. The Overlook's lethal potency is no more viable in *Billy Summers* than it is in *Doctor Sleep*, and both Alice and Billy maintain their distance from it without much effort. Their respective abilities to do so serve as an appropriate indication of their success at avoiding the deterministic trap that once reduced Jack Torrance to a faceless appendage.

Unlike Jack Torrance, who seeks authorship of the hotel's colorful history (instead of his own), Alice takes her cue from Billy by turning to the art of writing to redeem herself, to take charge of her own narrative: "Did you know that you could sit in front of a screen or a pad of paper and change the world?" (513).[8] Billy has already had this revelation, of course: his life with Alice follows the trajectory of his fiction, as he dresses up in various costumes and adopts various identities to advance his own redemption tale. "You're free. You can do whatever you want," he comes to realize (211).

It gradually dawns on Billy what it is he has chosen to write: "He is now starring in his own last job story" (26). Yet this apparently optimistic conclusion—that the act of writing invokes what King has often called a portable magic[9]—deliberately does not offer a resolution. Rather, it remains quite plausible that Billy as well as Alice may have been coopted within the historical palimpsest of the long-demolished Overlook. In fact, with this late-career entry, King sounds a bit like his old nemesis Stanley Kubrick, the film director who famously adapted *The Shining* but removed King's redemptive ending in which the Torrance surrogate family regroups (minus Jack) while fishing somewhere in Florida. Kubrick chose to end his adaptation of *The Shining* with a shot of the static Jack Torrance (Jack Nicholson), twice frozen in the Overlook's hedge maze as well as in its black and white photograph from 1921. Kubrick's film provides King's tortured writer with no redemptive quarter, no triumphant return into Danny Torrance's life similar to what takes place in *Doctor Sleep* or King's ABC miniseries adaptation of *The Shining*. Importantly, though, Kubrick's more pessimistic ending ghosts King's novelistic version of *The Shining*, since it carries with it the trepidation that young Danny and Wendy are in danger of being tracked by the generic as well as genetic pathways prescribed for them—even if King ultimately backs away from this brink.[10] Powerful forces of personal enclosure prove still relevant fifty years later, as *Billy Summers* notes: "[Billy] is in a box. And all he can do is shoot his way out" (166). What chance did Billy's single mother have in a society indifferent to her welfare? What hope does Alice have in a legal system that will blame her, the victim of sexual assault, for not doing enough to defend herself? Billy himself gets stuck inside his own archetype, becoming at times a mere "spectator" of his own life story (250). He feels tremendous paranoia that his life has been scripted for him and that his dream of freedom through writing may be nothing more than an illusion: "He could tell himself everything happens for a reason, but that's goofy bullshit for people who can't face plain unpainted truth" (265). Goofy "B.S.": a version of his story that covers up the truth and replaces it with a fairytale, simply swapping one B.S. for another. Billy's paranoia is well-founded because Alice does eventually rewrite Billy's ending through the lens of pure fantasy, thus imprisoning him within a conventional framework for narrative redemption: a "last job story" that erases any trace of the "real Billy" and replaces him with a generic set of problems as well as resolutions.

The lineage of *Billy Summers* remains highly significant: Zola's *Thérèse Raquin* has been pegged by literary historians as one of the first naturalist novels, and as we detailed in the earlier Bachman chapter, King has long held a fascination with naturalism, especially its emphasis on the forces that determine behavior. One of King's favorite writers, James M. Cain, also looked to *Thérèse Raquin* for inspiration when he penned his masterpiece,

The Postman Always Rings Twice (a *roman noir* that has been remade a number of times as successful Hollywood films).[11] One thing that joins Cain to Zola is their fascination with the story of a pair of star-crossed lovers trying to free themselves from the oppressive and claustrophobic confines of their quotidian existence. Tragically, both characters find themselves haunted by their own traumatic pasts; they wind up trapped in a fatal embrace, racked with guilt and tormented by phantoms. *The Shining* recycles this evergreen plot, since it too is a novel about a tragic couple, each of whom cannot extricate him- or herself from the doomed delusions of their romantic union. From naturalism to noir, King's obsessive return to Billy's paperback copy of *Thérèse Raquin* conjures the ghosts of entangled literary pasts, revealing the degree to which King remains conscious of his own debts as well as his proclivities as a writer of genre fiction. Yet why does King choose this particular text, which has already been carbon-copied by Cain in the production of one of the best-known hard-boiled stories of the twentieth century? Why re-create yet another copy of a copy (of a copy, etc.)?

King's long-standing fascination with fatalism connects him to naturalism as well as noir. He frequently takes as his muse the tragic figure that must try to assert her free will against uncontrollable forces, be they cosmic (King's fantasy and horror stories) or naturalistic (King noir). When at its close *Billy Summers* symbolically buries the Zola text, it can be argued that King's readers witness yet another vote being cast in favor of individual agency. *Billy Summers* further cements King's status as a dutiful keeper of the liberal tradition, one that relentlessly privileges personal autonomy over the impositions of the collective. "Unlike the strictest literary naturalists like Zola," Heidi Strengell argues, "King only seldom leaves his characters completely at the mercy of indifferent forces, but allows them to discover humanity, even morality, in their fellow human beings" (223). But when it comes to *Billy Summers*, readers cannot be so sure. And this uncertainty may be the novel's greatest asset.

King is at his most intellectually interesting when he keeps alive the fatalistic streak that first connected him to Zola and Cain via his pseudonym Richard Bachman. Even though it might be intriguing to read Alice as a resurrected Wendy Torrance—this time, she takes the typewriter for herself and writes her way out of both work proverbs and patriarchal oppression—such a fantasy offers only one possible interpretation of *Billy Summers*, and it proves to be one of the less interesting options available. Consider the novel's closing pages, in which Alice looks out at "where the old hotel used to stand" (514). Seemingly empowered in this moment, she thinks to herself: "I could make it be there. I could even fill it with ghosts, if I wanted to" (514). In truth, this bookend encloses Alice as well as the reader within a larger narrative prison because *The Shining* at last reveals itself to be both the past and potential future of *Billy Summers*. Alice, now a stand-in for Billy as well as King the author (in a gender-bending twist), asserts herself as the aspiring creator of yet another rendition of *The Shining*—or she can be, if she chooses to reanimate the hotel fictionally. The cyclical design of *The Shining* coils like a sidewinder as the plot of King's ur-text, nearly fifty years after its original appearance, continues to haunt both the author himself and many of his subsequent characters. It is not just that *The Shining* remains one of the great horror novels of the twentieth century; it is something more—the book carries a surreptitious charge that refuses to be extinguished over time and events, and it is, like the archaic Micmac burial ground in *Pet Sematary*, always restless and searching for its next opportunity for reanimation. That high voltage charge undermines the sentimental gloss of matrimonial ideals as well as the ties that ought to be deathless between a father and son. This charge kept the Overlook lit and it stayed alive in the forces that paid Billy handsomely for carrying out assassinations. The ratiocinative reader once more cannot be sure of what exactly she has been pursuing, then, as King's text references other texts in a free-floating, ever-circulating postmodern maze. *Billy Summers* offers another *mise-en-abyme*, story within a story, that forces readers to reflect upon the many interpretive traps into which they could fall.

Let us return in closing to that picture of the Overlook hedge animals hanging in Bucky's cabin. The picture, like the animals themselves, is constantly in motion. A series of frames grow increasingly visible as the novel progresses: "This haunted room with its haunted picture" (448). The "pictures in a book" that young Danny Torrance confronts in the early pages of *The Shining*, as he struggles to learn to read, reformulate on the cabin wall of *Billy Summers*. Texts within texts within texts. . . . In turn, we uncover a far-reaching fatalism in *Billy Summers* that stretches back past the Overlook, at least as far back as the gloomy crime fiction penned by Bachman. The delusion of finding oneself—let alone finding one another—could be nothing more than the sort of fluff that King suggests is peddled by US forces in Iraq: "Candy and toys and Superman comic books" (*Billy Summers* 270). The falcon loses the falconer as the psychical positions of detective and criminal, reader and writer, no longer correspond to one another to a meaningful degree.

Nevertheless, there may still be redemption available to King's reader, even as it eludes Billy (although it will not be easy to find). In *Billy Summers*, redemption requires that the detective-reader reconnect with the criminal-writer: Alice specifically asks for a detective story, and Billy obliges by giving her his own memoir. For Billy and Alice, textual playfulness involves a sophisticated, albeit macabre, dance that the novel likens to unwitting collaborations between criminal and detective.[12] To survive in the hyper-mediated twenty-first century, an individual must be able to recover the self (to be a detective) as well as hide it from others (to be a criminal). Billy cites an interview that he heard on the radio: "I always keep two people in mind when I sit down to write: myself, and the stranger" (228). A dense patch of cross-connections, *Billy Summers* complicates a seemingly effortless relationship between reader and writer through its nuanced reassessment of the bond between detective and criminal. Billy "thinks writing is also a kind of war, one you fight with yourself" (211).

Whereas the reader may presume to "cut through" to reality, thus outwitting the writer, the enlightened reader of *Billy Summers* knows that things are never quite so simple. As Poe formulated a century and a half ago, criminals need to challenge themselves to think like detectives and detectives need to challenge themselves to think like criminals. In the final tally, every life must be lived *relationally*, in part through the eyes of the Other, and this duet—to gesture at the recitation that Billy and Alice perform together as a mantra on several occasions to calm her during anxiety attacks—can be reduced neither to an omniscient reader who surveys his surroundings with supreme confidence nor to an omniscient writer who eternally evades the reader's penetrative gaze. A confession must be heard by an empathetic ear; a missive that declares love must be received, read, and eventually returned. Billy "expects, or just hopes, that someday someone will read what he's writing. If he doesn't, it means he has given up that expectation" (228). King recycles the words of author Tim O'Brien to convey the broader significance of *Billy Summers*: "Fiction wasn't the truth, it was the way to the truth" (*Billy Summers* 140). King attempts, with this signature in quotation marks, to redeem the work of fiction in a world wearied by ceaseless fabrications spouted by the likes of Trump or Roger Ailes or countless others. While it is true that fiction can prop up bumptious charlatans, and it is true that fiction can obscure reality in dangerous ways, such as convincing listeners to keep smoking cigarettes or accept that climate change is "fake news" (a popular saying of the day), fiction can also cultivate an empathetic bond between reader and writer—or, in a related register, between detective and criminal. Truth can still be found, King contends. But it can only be found if we keep the channels open and avoid locking ourselves into claustrophobic echo chambers of our own design. The compensatory correspondence between Alice and Billy illuminates a pathway that Jack failed to recognize in his own doomed relationship with Wendy.

Maybe King's reader can hold two oppositional truths in tension with one another to achieve a higher truth. Perhaps King's reader can recognize the generic prison of *Billy Summers* and admit the impossibility of a secure place from which to pass judgment, even as she clings to a belief in the power of language to free individuals from their existential confinement. Healing without blindly erasing the bifurcation of "good" and "bad"—an invisible cut between detective and criminal—King at last returns to Jack Torrance with something new to say, thanks in part to the generic possibilities of criminal fiction, and he gives his best-known character something like a proper burial. Furthermore, as a meta-commentary upon crime fiction, *Billy Summers* remains one of Stephen King's most redemptive tales to date.

Conclusions

A NEED FOR THE UNKNOWN

ARTHUR CONAN DOYLE'S NOVEL *THE HOUND OF THE BASKERVILLES* (1902) begins with a declaration by Sherlock Holmes that if "we are dealing with forces outside the ordinary laws of Nature, there is an end of our investigation. But we are bound to exhaust all other hypotheses before falling back on this one" (358). In this statement, Holmes does not deny the possible existence of the supernatural, just our abilities to deal with it. And before we accept the presence of such phenomenon, we must first confront and exhaust all other hypotheses within the empirical realm. In fact, Holmes is willing to—indeed, asserts that he *must*—abandon the case if it proves to contain a supernatural source. Even more than the world of Edgar Allan Poe's Dupin, who at least remains open to the importance of intuition and imagination as crucial aids to crime-solving, Holmes's world is one of strict probability and rationality. He is reluctant to admit to the existence of paranormal causation, even though in the Baskerville case there seems to be a weight of supernatural evidence present. Many ghost tales would have found the Baskerville hound triumphant in destroying the remnants of the family. But Holmes's point of view signals the primary existence of a detective, not a ghost, and in his world, nothing is allowed to exist that cannot be scientifically explained. As this book has shown, Stephen King's detectives operate in a very different register.

In addition to the many examples of King characters traced throughout this book who act as unofficial detectives, there are certainly those individuals who operate as actual detectives, most notably Bill Hodges and Holly Gibney, who are located at the epicenters of their own ratiocinative tales. As we have seen, both of these characters rely on a combination of police procedural techniques and personal intuition as aids in their crime-solving. In addition, King writes frequently about another lawman, Alan Pangborn, the Castle County sheriff in *Needful Things, Sun Dog*, and *The Dark Half*, who appears, at least initially, as a more conventional officer of the law than either Holly or Hodges.[1] Along with Hodges in *Mr. Mercedes* and Buster in the film version of *Misery*, Sheriff Pangborn is one of the few "legitimate" lawmen who operate in an official capacity as a detective in King's canon. Convinced that Thad Beaumont's fingerprints are evidence enough that the novelist has committed the brutal murder of Homer Gamache in *The Dark Half*—"We have you cold" (81), he announces to Beaumont at their introduction—the sheriff begins to question his effort at solving cases through accepted police procedural behavior and opens himself to the possibility of the supernatural only after Beaumont provides a substantial alibi. Each narrative in which Pangborn appears follows an identical arc: he begins investigating a mystery that challenges his belief in "all the natural laws" (*Dark Half* 224); as evidence accumulates, he comes to accept the necessity of what cannot be known. Like Holmes, Pangborn is initially resistant to phenomena that occur without a rational basis in fact and outside the realm of standard police practice. As Beaumont posits early in the novel: "Our practical Sheriff from Maine's smallest county, who puts his faith in computer print-outs from A.S.R. and I. and eyewitness testimony"—he "would be more likely to believe insanity than to accept an occurrence which seems to have no explanation outside the paranormal" (121). What separates Pangborn from Holmes and the police in Poe's detective stories, however, is that King's sheriff is seduced and ultimately convinced by the reality of the paranormal. Its empirical presence proves so overwhelming that the sheriff must acquiesce. And this is where King's detectives typically distinguish themselves from Dupin and Holmes and, for that matter, the majority of other detectives populating the genre.

Needful Things, the novel most extensively dedicated to Pangborn, follows a similar trajectory. An inexplicable crime spree erupts in Castle Rock. Pangborn realizes—albeit a bit too late—that a fiendish business owner, Leland Gaunt, has recently moved into town and started to sow seeds of chaos through his unorthodox series of commercial exchanges. Pangborn never directly confronts Gaunt; he is perpetually led astray by other pressing concerns, and he appears to discount (for most of the novel) the possibility that the crime spree could have been triggered by supernatural events. That is, the detective follows the same path that nearly leads him astray in *The Dark Half*: the very thing that makes Pangborn a "tough sell" for Gaunt is also what prevents Pangborn from solving the case until it is almost too late (*Needful* 184), namely, his staunch reliance upon a rigid rationalism. Like Holmes, the sheriff of Castle Rock feels compelled to hound the truth until it becomes visible to him, through a process of "agonized comprehension" (764). Even Pangborn's love interest, Polly, recognizes this near-fatal flaw in her beau: "It was that very reasonableness, that stubborn rationality in the face of what seemed to her to be an authentic miracle cure, that was now driving her anger" (517). At the crux of *Needful Things*, King injects into his skeptical sleuth a truth that Pangborn must learn in every book in which he appears—the need, like so many of King's hard-boiled heroes, to acknowledge the primacy of the unknowable: "Something totally beyond his ability to understand what was happening in Castle Rock" (560).

Midway through *The Dark Half*, after Pangborn dismisses Thad Beaumont as the possible murderer, he begins to look for someone, perhaps a fan, connected to the writer's work; but at this point his investigation centers on searching for merely a man: a psychologically disturbed individual who has assumed the identity of Beaumont's pseudonym, "the guy we want actually thinks he *is* George Stark" (136; emphasis in the original). At this point, Pangborn is still operating at his most rational, believing that a psychotic killer is responsible for the grisly murders performed as an homage to Beaumont's pseudonym. Pangborn clings to psychology and police work to discredit the supernatural and desperately seeks to uncover in the narrative of this crime a natural cause, or a belief system that stands in opposition to the supernatural transformation that has rendered Stark a reality: "I could have come closer to believing a ghost story than this. We're not talking about a ghost, we're talking about a man who never was" (188). Early on, Pangborn strives to assemble data to reach logical conclusions, searching for explanations that fit into acceptable frames of reference. But this side of Pangborn represents only part of the process in which a King detective must engage to move forward. Actually, his logical thinking through most of the book is a *hindrance*, resulting in red herrings, and Pangborn must move beyond Holmesian explanations of Stark-produced violence and accept that his own rational thinking as an officer of the law is holding him back from solving the case. As George Stark proves himself to be a viable physical entity, and not just a "fiction by a fiction" (112), the sheriff comes to realize that in King's world *doppelgänger*s are not merely literary tropes or psychopathic copycats; instead, they are capable of emerging as independently animated ghosts/spirits, proficient at exercising their own will. Unlike so many of the nineteenth century's profusion of doubles whose symbiotic relationships to their main avatars are left deliberately cryptic, such as Poe's William Wilson (alluded to by Beaumont after a dream) or Dostoevsky's Golyadkin in the novella *The Double*, who are invisible to everyone except their euphonious alter egos, Stark proves to be an independent agent, perhaps more akin to Stevenson's Mr. Hyde, who gradually evolves into a being operating outside the purview of Dr. Jekyll. It is Pangborn's job in *The Dark Half* to accept what Beaumont understands immediately: he must move beyond the Holmesian, ratiocinative limitations described above to embrace the irrational plausibility of Stark's existence as another one of King's supernatural creations.

Needful Things, like *The Dark Half*, tarries around a lacuna, a black hole, be it embodied in unknown supernatural agents like Stark or Gaunt, or be it articulated as a traumatic event that exists outside the detective's hyper-rational worldview. The real case that Pangborn unconsciously sets out to solve in *Needful Things* is the reason why his wife and son died in a car crash; as a result, he spends much of the novel in pursuit of "answers which were almost certainly not there" (213). Although Pangborn displays a keen ability to shed light on clues that his contemporaries would never see—a fact that alarms Gaunt greatly—King chastens his sheriff by forcing him *to recognize what can never be fully resolved*. At the start of the novel, Pangborn's "mind went back to work on [the case], like a puppy working an old and ragged strip of rawhide" (208); by the close of the narrative, the sheriff has learned that not all cases can be solved, and sometimes an inherent need to reach firm conclusions is, in fact, the deadliest disease of all. And it is not just his own traumatic past that pushes Pangborn to this revelation—he also realizes that no detective can ever know the totality of a town's secrets, regardless of its provincial façade. What sets Pangborn apart from detectives like Holmes, then, is his reluctant toleration of what he cannot know: he allows himself to be only "provisionally" satisfied (193); at the terminus of the text he informs Polly: "I never *want* to know"; "let the darkness bear it away" (797–98; emphasis in the original). Pangborn, unlike most other conventional heroes in the detective genre (broadly defined), admits that he has been harboring "an illusion of control" and this illusion has hindered his pursuit of the truth (726).

Whenever King's heroes encounter violence produced by nonhuman monsters, the skeptical disbelief that is their initial response turns into a gradual integration of the irrational into their perspective. Empirical evidence of the paranormal reshapes rational thinking. Solving mysteries in the King universe requires that the hero-detective possess an imagination open enough to deal with whatever version of reality—no matter how far-fetched—is presented to him or her. Before Wendy Torrance can comprehend what is happening to her husband and rescue herself and her son, she must accept that Jack is under the influence of ghosts in residence at the Overlook; similarly, Dennis Guilder must first identify and then accede to the fact that Arnie Cunningham's Christine (in the novel of that name) is no mere Plymouth Fury, but a demonically possessed machine. After speaking with Beaumont's childhood surgeon and discovering that the writer had a twin in utero, Pangborn joins these other King characters in relinquishing, however reluctantly, his disbelief in nonrational thinking and buying into Beaumont's theory that Stark is a real projection of a monstrous revenant brought to life: "Alan decided he didn't have time for protocol. Not in any of its forms. He was simply going to keep all possible circuits open and proceed"; "It drew an ugly scratch not just across everything he believed but across the way he had been taught to *think*" (359, 362). It is the rational side of the sheriff, what he has been "taught to *think*," that gets challenged and surmounted in the course of enacting his duties as a detective.

When Pangborn comes to accept Stark as a supernatural agent, making Pangborn into the kind of detective appropriate to the fiction of Stephen King, he also understands that Beaumont "had made Stark; he would have to unmake him" (398). Pangborn has come full circle in accepting that "*The monster is gone now, but you still don't like to be too close to where it came from. Because there might be another*" (428; emphasis in the original). Although Sheriff Pangborn begins both this novel and *Needful Things* as a Holmesian skeptic, he ends each text like a member of the Crew of Light in *'Salem's Lot* or the Losers' Club in *IT*: convinced that there are things in the universe that are neither scientifically organized nor rationally comprehensible; to do battle against the supernatural, he first must embrace its actuality. In *The Dark Half*, Stark becomes as real as one of King's vampires—in fact, Liz Beaumont even identifies Stark correctly as "a goddamn vampire" (313)—but before you can kill a vampire, as the Crew of Light discovers in *'Salem's Lot*, it is first necessary to believe it exists. Alan Pangborn thus belongs to an identifiable grouping like Roland and his *ka-tet* in *The Dark Tower*, the Losers' Club in *IT,* James Gardener in *The Tommyknockers*, the Free Zone core in *The Stand*, and Dr. Louis Creed in *Pet Sematary*, as well as many of the other character alliances in King's multiverse. In the end, the importance of these quasi-detective characters and their alliances is a reminder that, unlike Dupin, Sherlock Holmes, or Raymond Chandler's hard-boiled sleuth Philip Marlowe, the detective is seldom the lone hero in a King's narrative. He contributes to resolving the mystery but does so as a functioning member of a *ka-tet*—that singular collective present in so many King novels, forged more by magic than the forces of ratiocination. This *ka-tet* forms in response to the unknowns that it must confront daily, and it endures when the characters accept that they cannot even fully know one another. Strong relationships are therefore built on an embrace of mystery rather than its resolution, as we see with Polly and Pangborn in *Needful Things*.

As such, King's detectives are always relational, and in much more vulnerable ways than, say, Holmes and his sidekick, Watson. The romance between Polly and Pangborn unfolds like a cat-and-mouse game, or "cross-examinations" choreographed by artful detectives and evasive criminals (*Needful Things* 211). A stereotypical New Englander, Polly does not "want to spread her business around" (560)—she remains "afraid to let [Alan] know too much" (188). Gaunt nearly defeats his detective nemesis by convincing Polly that Pangborn has been snooping around in her personal affairs, invasively investigating the quiet corners of her past. Pangborn and Polly thrust and parry, acting like a star-crossed detective and his prey as they evade one another's critical gaze. In the end, though, they desperately need one another as sounding boards, as partners with whom to process their private griefs. Pangborn allows himself to be open with Polly in a way that the Victorian Holmes never could with Watson. The most needful thing of all is the unknowable traumas that blend human beings into concert with one another.

So why doesn't Pangborn feel a good deal more interesting than Doyle's archetype? Because in King fashion, his protagonist has already learned his lesson from the start, and so his transformation is a *fait accompli*: Pangborn confesses in the early pages of the novel that he cannot know what people "really want" because it remains "too damn hard" (137). The unknowable, the secret, of *Needful Things* is already out in the open, and King's reader can solve the text without too much strain. Pangborn exposes himself as another of King's blue-collared savants: a chastened detective who is already "in the know." Mirroring Holmes, Pangborn improbably solves the (existential) case from the beginning, arriving at the novel's thesis statement before any major obstacles arise to throw him off the scent: "One of the great truths of small towns: many secrets—in fact, all the really *important* secrets—cannot be shared" (95; emphasis in the original). If King's detective already grasps the secret at the heart of the text, and he immediately shares it with King's Constant Reader, why bother reading the story that follows?

Despite this shortcoming, King's alterations to the genre do bear fruit. Through his respective engagements with Polly and Gaunt, Pangborn comes to terms with his own status as a traumatized subject. Far removed from the cool, calculating, and rational Holmes, King's detectives almost always are forced to accept their existential incompleteness as well as the existence of what is never fully comprehensible. This sense of traumatic subjectivity is a quintessential element found in the works of King noir, a point further underscored by Pangborn's name—"Pang-born," or birth pangs—the trauma of something new, the rupture of modernity, *of change*. Echoing countless hard-boiled heroes from the likes of Chandler and Mickey Spillane, the character of Pangborn is defined by painful losses that cast a shadow over his subsequent missions.

This thesis perhaps finds its fullest expression in King's *Billy Summers*, discussed in the previous chapter: the detective needs the criminal; the criminal needs the detective. Sometimes secrets are the things we need most, to keep us going in pursuit of truths. "Desire was a little too coy," Pangborn admits in *Needful Things* (197). Yet King's Yankee philosopher comprehends a detective's innate need for secrets—in truth, undisclosed secrets may be his greatest inspiration: "That was both the curse and the blessing of police work; something always came up" (335). At first, readers might interpret Pangborn's relational maneuvers with Polly and Gaunt as transactional in a way that seems entirely too rational and devoid of romance. *Needful Things* describes marriage as "a lifetime in aggression," in which a partner holds "many secrets" because "in a war, you held onto every advantage" (151). Nevertheless, Pangborn also preaches the value of honesty, and he embraces the fact that his temporary satisfactions can only ever be "provisional" (193). As a result, there is something almost paternalistic about Pangborn—somehow, his libido comes across as too clinical, too rational, too philosophical (by half, however dark the half). The looming issue at hand is one of desire and the detective.

DESIRE AND THE DETECTIVE

While this book has stressed the connections between King's fiction and the behavior of the detective in conventional crime cinema and novels, there remains an area of discussion where this tradition has failed to exert a pronounced influence over King's canon. The noir detective possesses a sexual charge that finds its companion echo in the presence of the *femme fatale*.

A major characteristic that attends noir is the presence of the ubiquitous "fatal woman" responsible for "the extremely destructive effects [she has] on the male protagonist," her dangerous and unknowable connection to the hero's ultimate destiny (Kaplan 5). While she is demarcated by her independence, changeability, and treachery, her nature is fundamentally and irredeemably sexual, from her choice of attire (e.g., fetishized stiletto heels, long elegant legs, tight sheath dresses and skirts) to her layers of makeup and suggestive mannerisms and behavior: "Classic film noir sexualized its heroines through highly coded glamour, and an armory of visual iconography arranged to signal sex and define her as a sexual presence" (Stables 172). One might call to mind here the ankle bracelet worn by famed *femme fatale* Phyllis Dietrichson (Barbara Stanwyck) in Billy Wilder's 1944 noir film *Double Indemnity*, heavily coded as sexual like many of the objects found within these kinds of works. Innuendo and fetishes abound. The detective is magnetically drawn to the *femme fatale* not only because of her provocative visual and heterosexual presentation, but also because she is simultaneously a threat and a challenge to his sense of manhood. As Richard Dyer argues, "It is femininity, sexualized, excessive femininity, that disturbs the masculine sense of security, selfhood and knowledge of the world in film noir" (127).

King has provided the occasional nod to this archetype in such characters as Nadine Cross (*The Stand*) and perhaps Janey Patterson (*Mr. Mercedes*), but these archetypes do not appear with any frequency throughout his canon, nor are they ever associated for long with any of the author's world-weary detective types who might seek at least momentary relief from their weariness in these women's company. Janey skirts the edges of *fatale*-ism in her seductive pursuit of Hodges, but that's as intimate as any woman gets to the retired cop, and even then, she is allowed only a couple of sexual encounters with him before she forcibly exits the novel. It is important to note that once she dies, Hodges is literally and figuratively impotent for the remainder of the book. The quest for revenge displaces his libido as he not only elects not to pursue sex again; he appears to never really want it in the first place. Nadine in *The Stand* is as close to the noir *femme* as King ever gets: her "one little thing" of sexual intercourse (793) is forever denied to Harold Lauder. The fact that he technically dies a virgin, never having participated in coitus, duped by Nadine's fatal charms and duplicitousness, serves to highlight his failure to view sex as anything other than a self-enclosed act—its sole purpose his own physical release. Since Nadine is willing to inspire and accommodate his array of sexual fantasies primarily with her mouth, she becomes nothing more than an extension of Harold's chronic urge to masturbate (as he does even on the most inappropriate occasions—such as after reading Fran's diary, or as his sister confides to Fran, "Whacks off in his pants and wear the same pair of undershorts until they'll just about stand up by themselves" [249]). As such, their relationship serves Randall Flagg's design perfectly, as the dark man thrives on human isolation and the pursuit of selfish desire. The threat of sexual desire turns King's detective away from the brink—back into the status of Holmesian prude. Illicit secrets and titillating mysteries are transformed through King's seemingly unshakeable faith in pastoral didacticism.

The absence of sexuality as a topic of note in King's fiction, especially his crime fiction, is worthy of commentary on its own, since how an individual character responds to sex is treated as a measurement of his or her place on the writer's moral continuum. Typically, King's characters are sexually unresponsive, and those who aren't run the risk of becoming ensnared by it. To make the point emphatically, the potential for King's characters to produce acts of good or evil is always dependent on their ability to repress and direct their sexual impulses. Those in King's world unable to resist sexual entrapment sever their connection to humanity.[2] One might raise the argument that self-control can be viewed as a mark of the noir male, but King's noir protagonists—such as Billy Summers, Barton Dawes, or Hodges after the demise of Janey—are never all that tempted by sexual advances. In contrast, King marks the characters most drawn to the sexually forbidden, like Lauder or Gerald in *Gerald's Game*, as doomed. Nadine Cross's soullessness is an extreme manifestation of what happens to every King character whose life is shaped by lust. As "deviant" sexual practices become more frequent and intense in each King book, its participants' affiliation with evil becomes correspondingly stronger. In his interview with *Playboy* magazine, King was remarkably candid about sex, famously acknowledging his own personal conservatism which, in turn, translates into his fiction: "There's a range of sexual variations that turn me on, but I'm afraid they're all boringly unkinky" (Underwood and Miller 45). Although Alan Pangborn realizes the necessity of the unknown, his pangs are always born of an intrinsic sense of guilt or trauma; they are pangs born of heartache, certainly, but never pangs born of arousal.

There is a level of sexual purity in King's world that is antithetical to the noir tradition, both in terms of the detective's response to women and his attitude in general. Unlike Chandler and his film noir brethren,

King's crime fiction is never primarily a site of gender fluidity or gender turbulence within patterns of submission and dominance. King remains a typical New England moralist when dealing with sexual matters, and he has always believed that the human world is involved in a deathless struggle to distinguish a human being's basest impulses from her most noble virtues. Perhaps this orientation explains why King borrows so readily from certain elements of noir fiction and film, while still managing to circumvent the sexual entanglements that complicate the lives of classic noir males. In the end, King noir decentralizes the role of sexuality in the fantasy work of the genre.

In sum, King's narrative asexuality rarely attends to the messiness of sexual desire: a major pillar in the structure of hard-boiled fantasies. He circumvents the lacunae that necessitate living, pulsating desire. What case could be worth pursuing, after all, *without* a genuine mystery, a gaping hole in the detective's knowledge? It's not just that King's detectives repress their sexuality—it's that they are hardly sexual beings in the first place. Instead, they appear as parental figures that know, from the very start, the difference between right and wrong, and they do not truly grapple with the temptations that leave Chandler's Marlowe racked, interminably, with self-doubt. In the absence of sex, many of these works can be said to lack a real bite. To circle back to the argument advanced in chapter 3, King once more resembles Poe, since in most of Poe's tales, sexuality operates more as a threat or curse than an actuality, where desire "takes place very much under the pressure of constriction" and "seems unable to realize itself, to make itself fully coherent as sexuality" (Stadler 19–22).[3]

King's forays into the classical as well as hard-boiled detective modes are lacking another essential ingredient as well as a realistic sexual component: cities. Dupin and Holmes feed upon the anarchical elements of Paris and London, respectively. King's fiction features the occasional broad snapshot of urban life, places such as Lud in *The Dark Tower* or Las Vegas in *The Stand*, but these environments are more thin sketches than vivid portraits. Crucially, King's cities are devoid of the *femme fatale* who prowls the mean streets of the noir metropolis, offering her wares. The *femme fatale* is "the sleek sophisticate of the city" and one of the city's darkest embodiments (Spillane, *Kiss* 30). Places like Derry in King's *IT* seem to us on the cusp of qualifying as a noir city, with all its attendant problems of anonymity, violence, and decay; but they remain entirely too parochial, too incestuous, to serve as a satisfying surrogate for the ominous sprawl of San Francisco or, better still, Los Angeles. The atmospherics of noir demand a city: "The city is a setting in which money links a variety of social groups—the old rich, businessmen, gangsters, hustlers and con men. Money—and its flows—is seen to bind these people together in symbiotic and unstable patterns of relationships. The city is ripe with the possibility and reality of corruption and moral decay: it is represented as a tangled web of strands connecting apparently separate individuals in a network of power, corruption and crime" (Clarke 82). In Mickey Spillane's seminal *Kiss Me, Deadly* (1952), private dick Mike Hammer describes the vast "spiderweb" of the city as "a living, moving kaleidoscope"; as he sits, stewing in his indignation, he hears it: "The voice of the monster outside the glass was a constant drone," brewing a "decisive laugh that thought blood running from an open wound was funny" (37). While the city plays an absolutely pivotal role in the noir tradition, including the space where the detective lives and conducts his business, King's canon is remarkably devoid of such cities. As a college student, King penned a novel about a race riot in a major city and he eventually recognized his mistake—which went unrecognized by his younger self: "It didn't strike me as either particularly presumptuous or particularly comic that a fellow who had grown up in a Maine town of 900 souls should take a city of millions for his setting" (17). When his characters do venture into urban sites, they tend to be postapocalyptic shells, as in the *Dark Tower* series, *The Stand*, or *Fairy Tale*. It seems likely that King (after his aborted race riot novel) only engages with cities allegorically, turning them into the stuff of myths and fables, because he so strongly identifies with the rural climate of his home state of Maine. To our knowledge, King has never actually lived in a big city for any protracted period, and he tends to view cities skeptically, as a rural outsider, in contrast to streetwise urbanites like Marlowe or Dupin (the latter so comfortable in the bowels of Paris that he and his narrator-friend willingly venture out without fear to wander the streets alone in the early morning hours). Even a work such as *Mr. Mercedes*, which is about as hard-boiled as a reader is apt to find in King, is primarily set in the suburbs. Hodges ventures into the Lowtown section of his city to visit his favorite restaurant or in pursuit of Brady Hartsfield, but the real action of the novel takes place in some midwestern suburb. Meanwhile, at the start of *Needful Things*, Pangborn has left the big city to patrol the intimate corners of Castle Rock. Although it is true that some hard-boiled heroes did migrate into the suburbs in the 1970s—Paul Schrader famously remarks that, after World War II, "crime had to move to the suburbs" (589)—the real staples of the genre are inextricably linked to the American cityscape. One could argue that, without the pulsating presence of cities, King's detective tales do not critique the flow of money that binds broken people in their tangled webs; in turn, King's reader cannot satisfactorily interrogate the fraught relationship between modernity and criminality—a crucial element of crime fiction, indeed, its very *raison d'être*. It is the unknowable engine of his corrupt urban environment that first goads the chivalrous detective into action. With neither cities nor sex, what unknowable element remains to enflame the desire of American sleuths in King's multiverse?

Of course, as this book has shown, King tries to adopt the raw pathos of noir, as he does in the gritty realism of the Bachman books, and he certainly approaches Marlowe's brand of existential vulnerability in works such as *Mr. Mercedes* and *Joyland*. His female detectives, be they literal sleuths (Holly Gibney) or figures occupying a similar psychical position (Dolores Claiborne), regularly speak back to the patriarchal underpinnings of the genre in an attempt to correct the misogynistic sins of the mid-century private dicks—and even if these attempts fall short of their goal, the fact that King continues to make the attempt anew speaks to the power of his convictions. And King's uses of crime fiction have undoubtedly helped him to sharpen what he wants to say about the proper role of mystery and doubt in his reader's everyday life. Fifty years after he launched his career, crime fiction continues to challenge King to explore new territory. By venturing into the darkened alleyways of King noir, readers move closer to understanding King's limitations as a writer as well as his stirring triumphs as one of America's primary storytellers.

NOTES

INTRODUCTION

1. The Hopper painting resides in the Sheldon Museum of Art, University of Nebraska–Lincoln.

2. King's longtime friend David Morrell has discussed this reading assignment in several interviews.

3. As Rick Altman observes, "The initial generic attribution tends to subordinate all else to a single genre identity" (126).

4. On his shift into establishing a hard-boiled personal library, King says: "Up until then what I had been reading was Nancy Drew, the Hardy Boys, and things like that. The first books I picked out were these Ed McBain 87th Precinct novels. In the one I read first, the cops go up to question a woman in this tenement apartment and she is standing there in her slip. The cops tell her to put some clothes on, and she grabs her breast through her slip and squeezes it at them and says, 'In your eye, cop!' And I went, Shit! Immediately something clicked in my head. I thought, That's real, that could really happen. That was the end of the Hardy Boys. That was the end of all juvenile fiction for me. It was like, See ya!" (King interviewed by Nathaniel Rich and Christopher Lehmann-Haupt).

5. We do not intend to treat the terms "crime fiction," "hard-boiled fiction," "detective fiction," and "noir" as synonyms; we are aware that these subgenres are distinctive, and we attend to these differences when the situation calls for it. Even though crime fiction serves as an umbrella term throughout the book for these various subgenres, we are not suggesting that they can be distilled to a singular essence.

6. Of note, King heaps praise on Henry James throughout the pages of *Danse Macabre*.

7. It may be worth noting: the companion who accompanies Jack through his initial investigation of the hotel is named Watson—perhaps a nod to Sherlock Holmes's right-hand man in the Arthur Conan Doyle series.

8. In his seminal book on the American Gothic, Charles L. Crowe writes, "We would now include *Noir* cinema within our definition of Gothic (as well as) crime fiction (for example that of Ross Macdonald and James Ellroy)" (1).

9. Although, as Peter Hutchings and Blair Davis argue, the influence of horror on noir has largely "gone unnoticed" (193).

10. Raymond Borde and Etienne Chaumeton insist that the horror film, for audiences, "undoubtedly played an emotional role akin to film noir's": "the same need to experience shudders of fear" (25).

11. King writes, of his college years, "I was also taken by [Ross] Macdonald's main character, Lew Archer, who was profoundly alienated from—and critical of—the society he investigated"; "I moved on to Raymond Chandler, Macdonald's literary father, and in Philip Marlowe I found the ultimate outsider, moral but profoundly lonely" ("Five" 57).

12. See Corber (1997).

13. An exception would be King's "The Wedding Gig," a short story in which King played with the ethnic stereotypes of crime fiction to amend some of the genre's liabilities on this front.

14. Sold in drugstores, popular detective magazines with names such as *Real Detective* and *Master Detective* emerged during the early decades of the twentieth century, arguably fueled by the increase in violence and suicide caused by the Depression and Prohibition. The genre provided its audience with crime scene photographs, interviews, and detailed accounts of criminal activities. These magazines, although salacious and exploitative, were the next generation from British crime broadsides published in the prior century, and they established a bridge to the emerging genre of crime novels and noir cinema popularized in the 1930s and '40s.

15. For related discussions of King's indebtedness to Twain, see Indick (1986), Magistrale (2011), and Wiater et al. (2006).

CHAPTER 3: EDGAR ALLAN POE, STEPHEN KING, AND THE AMERICAN DETECTIVE

1. At a press conference held shortly before the ABC telecast of *The Shining* as a miniseries, Rebecca De Mornay, who played Wendy, was asked about her perspective on the character. She said, "The [domestic abuse] subtext of the movie can and does happen to smart women, and not just to women who look and act like victims. I thought it was important to play her and give her the integrity and the intelligence that she deserves" ("At *The Shining*" 25). Of the three Wendys—from King's novel, Kubrick's film, and the ABC miniseries—De Mornay's portrayal emerges as the strongest, enough to almost redeem the maudlin and overwritten televised series. Whenever De Mornay is on the screen, she captures our attention, and not just because of her resplendent hair and other physical attributes. Her version of Wendy is a serious painter, a wife still connected to an active sexuality, and a woman who doesn't hesitate to fight back. She is a radiant contrast to her husband's mental and hygienic dissolution and to Kubrick's "endangered woman" stereotype. She ultimately challenges Kubrick's interpretation of Wendy as a hapless victim; King's Wendy, first in the novel and even more so twenty years later in the miniseries' teleplay, emerges as the clear heroine of the story.

2. David Van Leer writes, "Even as he 'invents' the genre of detective fiction, Poe questions its epistemological limitations, the processes by which detection constructs truth, suppressing realities as fully as illuminating them" (88).

3. For more on King's connection to the neoliberal moment, see Michael Blouin's *Stephen King and American Politics*.

4. The *Fantômas* series, published in France between 1911 and 1913 by Pierre Souvestre and Marcel Allain, consisted of thirty-two volumes and serves as a good example of the suturing of Gothic and crime fictions. It was Gothic in its glorification of death, the grotesque, and violence mostly perpetrated by the main character, Fantômas, himself. Set in the bowels of Paris, the narratives also transformed the Gothic villain into a modern figure of criminality and anarchy. Embattled by the police and the penal system, Fantômas gave vent to fantasies of crime and violence drawn from popular sources, especially crime novels and cinema. The Surrealists of the era were deeply attracted to these texts because of the antisocial acts of Fantômas, such as blowing up bridges and assaults against the bourgeois "foundations of society." For more on the series and its cultural relevance, see Matheson 44–79.

5. As Kenneth Burke would tell us, we need not choose between the extremes, but only comprehend where—and how—the extremes meet. Detective fiction and the American Gothic are perhaps best differentiated by distinctions of degree instead of kind: "The choice here is not a choice between magic and no magic, but a choice between magics that vary in their degree of approximation to the truth" (6).

6. On this front, we might read Poe as a product of his age, since early American newspapers were rife with parodies and hoaxes: "Almost nothing was believed solely on the strength of its appearance in print" (Walsh 16).

7. Although this is no longer the case, King's early novels received scurrilous reviews in the *New York Times Book Review* and elsewhere. Bloom remained one of the last elitist holdouts in refusing to recognize the significance of King's storytelling skills and their resonant cultural impact, pointing out that "the genial King is a large emblem of the failures of American education" (2).

8. Part of this engagement would perhaps involve a willingness to submit to greater editorial oversight. As Magistrale remarks, "In all honesty, much of King's oeuvre would benefit from the tough advice of a good editor" (*Landscape* 12).

CHAPTER 4: THE MULTIPLE DEATHS OF RICHARD BACHMAN

1. For an extended discussion of this generic hybridization, see Peter Hutchings, "Film Noir and Horror" (2013), Eric Somer, "The Noir-Horror of *Cat People*" (2004), and Michael J. Blouin, "The Loomis Look: Re-watching John Carpenter's *Halloween* as Film Noir" (2022).

2. From 1977 to 1984, Stephen King published five novels under the Richard Bachman pseudonym: *Rage* (1977), *The Long Walk* (1979), *Roadwork* (1981), *The Running Man* (1982), and *Thinner* (1984). The writing in at least two of these books predates *Carrie*; King began composing *Rage* and *The Long Walk* when he was in high school. The other Bachman books were written at various points during the first decade of King's career as a published author. But each novel was subsequently revised prior to its release, and the publication dates of at least the last two, *The Running Man* and *Thinner*, extend the Bachman canon solidly into the 1980s.

3. See King's 1980 interview with Paul Janeczko: "The books that influenced me most when I was growing up were by people like Thomas Hardy, Frank Norris, and Theodore Dreiser. All those people of the naturalistic school believed once you pull out one rock, it's sort of a

relentless slide into the pit. I don't think that any thinking person can look at the world and our society and see anything very secure. I don't think the future looks very bright" (qtd. in Underwood and Miller, *Bare Bones* 79).

4. Elsewhere, we have addressed the issue of King's response to the 1960s—his perspective on the counterculture and the political-social events taking place during the period. The reader should consult "Chapter 4: The Vietnamization of Stephen King" in Magistrale and Blouin's *Stephen King and American History*, 89–109, as well as King's own bitter voice found in "Five to One, One in Five: UMO in the '60s" in the collection *Hearts in Suspension*, 23–76.

5. As he revealed to Eric Norden in his *Playboy* interview, after graduation from UMO, "I'd lie awake at night seeing myself at fifty, my hair graying, my jowls thickening, a network of whiskey-ruptured capillaries spiderwebbing across my nose with a dusty trunkful of unpublished novels rotting in the basement, teaching high school English for the rest of my life and getting off what few literary rocks I had left by advising the student newspaper or maybe teaching a creative writing course" (qtd. in Underwood and Miller, *Bare Bones* 32).

6. See Susan Sontag, *Illness as Metaphor* (1978).

7. For a discussion of King's caricatures of Italian Americans, see Tony Magistrale's "Reading Stephen King Through the Years: Theoretical Permutations" in *Theorizing Stephen King*, edited by Michael J. Blouin, University of Amsterdam Press, forthcoming.

8. Barton's unwillingness to become "a cop" stems from his antigovernment position, and particularly the general distrust of police themselves, a sentiment that had its origins, ironically, in the counterculture throughout the 1960s and '70s. King recalls his mental state as a writer in the late 1970s in a 2022 interview with *Vanity Fair*: "I was also in full don't-trust-the-government mode when I wrote that book (in this case, *Firestarter*). We were still talking about Vietnam at that time. There was a hangover from that in the late '70s. And there were all kinds of stuff going on where you just could not trust the government."

CHAPTER 5: THE OPEN-AND-SHUT CASES OF *MR. MERCEDES* AND *HOLLY*

1. On multiple occasions, King has publicly praised the achievement of Thomas Harris. When *Red Dragon* was released in paperback, King supplied a blurb on its back cover, which tremendously increased the novel's sales. King was also keen to write the *New York Times* review of *Hannibal* in 1999, naming the book "one of the two most frightening novels of our time, the other being *The Exorcist*": "*Hannibal* is not really a sequel at all, but rather the third and most satisfying part of one very long and scary ride through the haunted palace of abnormal psychiatry." King's review reminds us of his own attraction to the genre of suspense, commending Harris on his similar ability to compose such tomes: "What is true of gourmet meals and cannibal feasts is equally true of the suspense novel: knowing too much beforehand spoils the surprise" ("Review").

2. In their seminal study, Raymond Borde and Etienne Chaumeton illuminate how early horror films "undoubtedly played an emotional role akin to film noir's": "the same need to experience shudders of fear" (25).

3. Brady is also related to the anarchic Crimson King in King's *Dark Tower*, as he, too, wishes to destroy the Beams of History—inspired by a vision of mass chaos and destruction that is located at the extreme of the white supremacy movement.

4. Jerome Robinson, Hodges's African American neighbor, emerges as Brady Hartsfield's subtle foil, as well as a version of Watson to Hodges's Sherlock. Although separated by no more than a decade chronologically, Jerome appears far more emotionally mature and sophisticated than the older Hartsfield; he maintains a positive perspective on life in contrast to Hartsfield's cynical nihilism. Jerome is future-orientated, as he looks forward to attending Harvard, and his impressive computer skills are used to help people in contrast to the six computers brimming with chaos in Hartsfield's basement. Jerome is what Hartsfield could have been with a better home life, more positive attitude, and serious medication. Most of all, Jerome possesses a sense of humor that is sorely absent from Hartsfield's personality. Although his Stepin Fetchit routine with Hodges is overdone, King employs it out of a lame effort to suggest the ease with which the two males of different races interact and their level of friendship. Scott Woods disagrees with this assessment, arguing that the levity of the "Amos and Andy dialect" that Jerome blatantly mocks "is an eye-rolling characterization that no actual 17-year-old Black child would likely be aware of, an example of King's Romantic nostalgia smashing headlong into his [King's] ignorance of Black culture in general." It is regrettable, however, that Woods has so restricted his racial reading of King that he has nothing to say about the fact that Jerome's bravery shines throughout the novel as he willingly risks his own life by becoming enmeshed in the detective's case and joins Holly as one of the heroes of the book when Hodges is incapacitated physically.

5. King's novel was published in 2014, less than two years after the Sandy Hook massacre (December 14, 2012). *Mr. Mercedes* also references the recession of 2008 and the Deepwater Horizon oil spill, which occurred in April–October 2010, approximating the time frame for this fiction between 2010 and 2014.

6. *Mr. Mercedes* is not the first novel in which King connects the act of creating art to literal and figurative rehabilitation. In *Duma Key* (2008), for instance, a badly injured Edgar Freemantle retreats to Florida and finds that he has a hidden talent for painting, a skill set that restores him to life.

7. King describes the truthfulness as follows: "The job of fiction is to find the truth inside the story's web of lies" (*On Writing* 159).

8. Good writing, King continues, "has more to do with instinct than with anything resembling 'higher thought'" (248).

9. See Scott Woods (2020).

10. Early in *On Writing*, King writes: "Don't bother trying to read between the lines, and don't look for a through-line. There are *no* lines—only snapshots, most out of focus" (18; emphasis in the original).

CHAPTER 6: FEMME NOIR: *MISERY* AND *DOLORES CLAIBORNE*

1. When *Playboy* magazine in 1983 cited Chelsea Quinn Yarbro's lament that "it is disheartening when a writer with so much talent and strength of vision is not able to develop a believable woman character between the ages of seventeen and sixty," King agreed with the charge and called it "the most justifiable of all those leveled at me" (Underwood and Miller 47). In 1998, Kathleen Lant and Theresa Thompson published their regrettably titled

study, *Imagining the Worst: Stephen King and the Representation of Women*, a collection of eleven essays in which only Carol Senf's treatment of *Dolores Claiborne* and *Gerald's Game* recognized and applauded King's efforts to create memorable fictional females. In their Introduction, Lant and Thompson concluded begrudgingly that, in analyses of King's depiction of women, "it is tempting to relegate him to the category of unregenerate misogynist or conversely to elevate him to the status of newly sensitive male" (4).

2. For a thorough examination of these masculinist fantasies, see Krutnick (1991).

3. This chapter is, in a sense, a response to Sally Munt's call for a complementary study to analyze the influence of feminist discourse on male writers working within the tradition of the detective story (28).

4. When asked about the connection, King told us that he was not familiar with Braddon's novel (King, "Quick Question"). Still, whether the connection was conscious or not, it speaks to the interesting ways that King continues to interact with generic expectations. The connection also strengthens our thesis that *Claiborne* is, at its core, a detective story.

5. In *The Stand*, King writes: "There are all sorts of dream interpretations, Freud's being the most notorious, but I have always believed they served a simple eliminatory function, and not much more—that dreams are the psyche's way of taking a good dump every now and then" (346). King ridicules Freud's "notorious" theory of dream interpretation and reduces the complexities of psychoanalysis to intellectual defecation.

6. See Felman, "Turning the Screw of Interpretation," 94–207.

7. Perhaps this is why King chose to tell the narrative through a recorded monologue: we step inside Dolores's head in pursuit of clarity. It is tiring but exhilarating, as in a convoluted conversation when the subject matter is important but murky, and, like a good detective, the reader has to be patient and work to figure things out.

8. As Theodor Adorno puts it, "Knowledge comes to us through a network of prejudices, opinions, innervations, self-corrections, presuppositions and exaggerations, in short through the dense, firmly founded but by no means uniformly transparent medium of experience" (86).

CHAPTER 7: THE INCESTUOUS *LATER*

1. See Alioto (2012).

2. In a related sense, Laura Mulvey argues that the desire for a detective exemplified by Oedipus thinly disguises a drive to repress (and return) a pre-Oedipal father—specifically, Laius—a figure who "exists in a sphere of pure action, outside self-consciousness" (198). While Jamie, like Oedipus, constantly wrestles with his own psychoanalytical concerns, he must ultimately face the brutal, violent, and nonreflexive deeds of a primal, pre-Oedipal father (Uncle Harry). Said another way, Mulvey helps us to recognize the line being drawn between what the detective can know—for example, his own guilt—and what the detective cannot know—the Otherness that precedes and threatens the symbolic orderliness of Jamie's world.

3. David Lehman remarks on "the enabling irony of the detective": the fact that the detective story "transmutes the cruelty and brutality of human nature into a species of entertainment, presenting homicide not as an ethical violation or tort but as an aesthetic

spectacle, a parlor game with rules" (16). The deductive model of the orthodox detective, in other words, suppresses the real and replaces it with a sleek yet phony symbolic chain of events.

4. For more on King's problematic equation of homosexuality and perversity, see Blouin and Magistrale's *Stephen King and American History*, particularly the chapter entitled "Outing Stephen King," 110–32.

5. Nor, for that matter, does *Later* begin to approach the sort of Oedipal disorientation on display in Alain Robbe-Grillet's 1964 novel, *The Erasers* (*Les Gommes*), a text that literally and figuratively moves in repetitive circles around an existential chasm.

6. As Page Dubois writes, in this generic turn, "The reader is detective and murderer, a new Oedipus" (103).

CHAPTER 8: STEPHEN KING AT THE BRINK: THE COMPLICATED INFLUENCE OF RAYMOND CHANDLER

1. King credits hard-boiled writers for inspiring him in the development of his own style. He first learned how compact language conveys powerful emotions by emulating popular heavyweights such as Chandler, Dashiell Hammett, and Ross Macdonald (*On Writing* 180).

2. Doug Cowan argues that King's story worlds "consistently call into question the incomplete, insular, and self-congratulatory ways we do often imagine the unseen order and our place in it" (9).

3. Perhaps this is the main reason the televised version of the novel drew the attention of James Franco—a character actor who has often appeared in action narratives, such as *Spider-Man* and *Rise of the Planet of the Apes*—for the role of Jake. Franco was so attracted to King's primary text that he tried to purchase the screen rights to it. When he was denied them, his vocal disappointment attracted the attention of the director and company that had acquired the rights, J. J. Abrams and Bad Robot Productions, and they ended up casting Franco in the central role.

4. See Jameson's seminal *Postmodernism; or, The Cultural Logic of Late Capitalism*.

5. In his well-known essay "Historicism in *The Shining*," Jameson openly displays a distaste for King's fiction, arguing that King's "mediocre original" fails to "transmit a coherent ideological message," unlike Kubrick's film (123–24). Consequently, Jameson deals nearly exclusively with Kubrick's film adaptation, centering on the era of the American 1920s, which is essential to his reading of the Kubrick movie in the context of a socioeconomic ghost story. Meanwhile, he fails to reference, much less address, the chronological distance that distinguishes the two texts as historical signifiers, since King's novel deliberately eschews the 1920s, choosing instead to employ a post-World War II timeframe linked to the Overlook Hotel. This time warp would appear to be worthy of further consideration as the two eras provide different portraits of America, both historically and economically.

6. Chandler's fiction similarly stresses its own generic futility. *The Little Sister* especially undermines its own "tired cliched mannerisms" (63) by exposing the abject superficiality of Hollywood. Marlowe finds himself surrounded by men in toupees and actresses who languish in "a mail-order city" (184). On his client/love interest, Mavis Weld (a stage name), he laments: "She won't be a real person anymore. Just a voice from a soundtrack, a face on

a screen" (248). Marlowe begins to hate his own hard-boiled persona, echoing the sentiments of Mavis: "I guess I don't like the script. I don't like the lines. It just isn't me" (203). Chandler often seems to be ramming up against the rigid confines of a genre that he helped to popularize. Satirizing itself, *Little Sister* undercuts cops who have been reading too many pulp magazines and rely too heavily on "nineteen-thirty dialogue" (170). Genre expectations pale in comparison to the vast mystery that surrounds them: death as well as the existential meaning of life that forever eludes Marlowe's grasp (and the reader's).

    7. For a fleshed-out analysis of this cross-hybridization, see Blouin's "The Loomis Look: Re-watching John Carpenter's *Halloween* as Film Noir."

    8. King writes, "When I read James M. Cain, everything I wrote came out clipped and stripped and hard-boiled. [...] This sort of stylistic blending is a necessary part of developing one's own style" (*On Writing* 147).

    9. It is important to note that Erin's black and white photographs assembled from combing the archives of Joyland's roving Hollywood Girls prove instrumental to solving Linda Gray's murder. Erin recognizes the presence of the killer in the company of his victim in multiple shots and passes this information on to Devin. She serves in the role of the detective's "Girl Friday," providing the research and subsequent evidence that directs and aids the young male detective in his pursuit of the case. Erin's photographic evidence of Lane Hardy provides Devin with images that he studies and pursues with relentless imagination. Devin notes the way Lane Hardy wears and keeps adjusting the baseball cap that he has pulled down to hide his face. Ironically, instead of "'fading into the background'" (207), the omnipresent cap and sunglasses stand out in Erin's photos. Using the deductive reasoning of a detective, Devin uncovers a similarity between how Hardy tilts his bowler hat when working at Joyland and how he keeps rearranging his baseball cap on his head when attempting to disguise himself on his last date in the amusement park with Linda. As in his obsession with the Horror House ride, Devin once more both tracks and identifies with Hardy's history—the detective inserting himself into the criminal's personal orbit.

CHAPTER 9: *BILLY SUMMERS* AND THE CRIMINAL'S REDEMPTION

    1. In a particularly hard-boiled moment, Billy notes that Lady Justice was "more or less invented by the emperor Augustus," which implies that the very concept of justice is inherently tainted by the corrosive influence of political and economic power (15).

    2. If we continue the parallel with Dostoevsky's fiction, Billy's relationship with Alice Maxwell is highly suggestive of how Raskolnikov in *Crime and Punishment* views both the prostitute Sonia and his sister Dounia as abused and degraded women, symbols for all the suffering, innocent, and chagrined people in the world. It is Sonia's love for him that helps produce in the young student an awareness of his Hegelian limits while also inspiring his efforts at moral regeneration. Alice likewise operates as a symbol of victimization that arouses Billy's compassion while, at the same time, forcing him to question his own involvement in perpetuating acts of cruelty. As a result of his kindness and commitment to her, Alice gains "a start in life as a fine independent woman" (489). *Crime and Punishment* also ends much like King's novel: although the paths of their main characters toward moral regeneration are

left open and ultimately unfinished, Raskolnikov and Billy both acknowledge their alacrity to undertake similar journeys of reform via atonement.

3. It's another example of the way in which, over time, the art of horror has forged hybrid bonds with multiple genres, including the gangster story, fairy tale, science fiction, and especially the detective genre, as Poe was first to recognize fully. For a more thorough consideration of the imbricated relationship between crime fiction and horror, see Michael Blouin's "The Loomis Look" and Magistrale and Poger's *Poe's Children*.

4. Neo-noirs are propelled by repetitive trauma: "A repetition [that] suggests an inevitable, inexorable fate, an unevadable [*sic*] fatality" (Gilmore 51).

5. For more on the antagonism between Poe and his critics and how that informed Poe's seminal detective tales, see Walsh.

6. These multiple references to the Bills in *Billy Summers* remind us of another famous Bill in the King canon, Bill Denbrough from *IT*; like Summers, Denbrough struggles with writer's block and the various structures, textual, verbal, historical, and otherwise, that confine and define him.

7. King obsesses over the theme of aesthetics and selfhood in many texts including *The Dark Half*, *Rose Madder*, and *Duma Key* (to name but a few).

8. Billy acknowledges, "It's about power. He's finally tapped into power that doesn't come from the barrel of a gun" (92).

9. As King informed Magistrale in a 1989 interview, writers "have powers. The guy in *The Dark Half* says that writers, actors, and actresses are the only recognized mediums of our society. Our job [as writers], basically, is to create the possibility of making people believe the unbelievable—the suspension of disbelief" (Magistrale, *Stephen King: The Second Decade* 11).

10. The Torrance family members are doomed by their family histories—alcoholism, violence, and psychological abuse are their inheritances. Throughout *The Shining*, whenever a familial ghost from the past appears to affect the present, a tear in the current family's fabric occurs. The novel is thus a relentlessly negative history of parenting and families—haunted, torn apart, and threatened by the recollected ghosts of the past; and the destruction of the Overlook and the Torrance family occurs, at least in part, because of the deterministic track of these dysfunctional family patterns. Perhaps this is why Dick Hallorann, alert to the links that connect fathers and sons, feels compelled to remind Danny at the end of the book to "'grieve for your daddy . . . But see that you get on'" (449).

11. Heidi Strengell, writing about King's debt to naturalism, argues that his novels feature "protagonists who are sociologically so tightly determined and whose free will is so limited that they find violence and self-destruction as their only means to take a stand and defy the prevailing circumstances" (218).

12. Alice slowly learns "to play" Billy by continuing the authorship of his book, and Billy views that as "a change for the better" (308).

CONCLUSIONS: A NEED FOR THE UNKNOWN

1. Pangborn also surfaces in *Gerald's Game*, as an absent mentor to the novel's lead detective, Ridgewick, who "learned from Alan Pangborn, the guy who had the job before him, and that means he learned from the best" (422).

2. This remains a strict maxim throughout the novels, but it is especially pronounced in *The Stand*. At the opposite extreme of the sexually purified—Glen Bateman, Nick Andros, Larry Underwood, Fran Goldsmith, Stu Redman—King provides a group of immoral men who have used the collapse of civilization to indulge their hostility toward women. The four men who are responsible for the traveling concubine called "the zoo" have kidnapped eight women and hold them as sexual slaves. The sole purpose of their enterprise is the carnal satisfaction of the men involved; their captives are stripped of their humanity, reduced to orifices that are filled or tortured according to the daily whims of the men in charge. While they refer to their enterprise as "the zoo," the real beasts are the men who maintain it and are appropriately moving west, their destination to join Flagg in Las Vegas, where no doubt they will be placed in charge of nightly entertainment at the MGM Grand.

3. In many of Poe's tales, such as "Ligeia," "The Black Cat," "Berenice," "The Fall of the House of Usher," and "Morella," to name only the best examples, sexual desire is linked with repulsion and denial, the need on the part of the Poe male protagonist to murder desire. In King's case, it appears to be less about the need to murder sexual desire than about repressing it, making sure that it conforms to a highly conventional monogamous heterosexuality.

WORKS CITED

Adorno, Theodor. *Minima Moralia: Reflections from Damaged Life*. Verso, 2020.
Alioto, Daisy. "Stephen King's 10 Favorite Books." *The Christian Science Monitor*, 20 Jan. 2012, www.csmonitor.com/Books/2012/0120/Stephen-King-s-10-favorite-books/Bleak-House-by-Charles-Dickens.
Altman, Robert. *Film/Genre*. British Film Institute, 1999.
Ardai, Charles. "The Birth (and Rebirth) of *The Colorado Kid*." Stephen King's "*The Colorado Kid*," illustrated ed., Hard Case Crime, 2019, pp. 15–23.
Arnold, Sarah. *Maternal Horror Film: Melodrama and Motherhood*. Palgrave Macmillan, 2013.
Ascari, Maurizio. *A Counter-History of Crime Fiction: Supernatural, Gothic, Sensational*. Palgrave Macmillan, 2007.
Athanasourelis, John Paul. *Raymond Chandler's Philip Marlowe: The Hard-Boiled Detective Transformed*. McFarland & Company, 2012.
"At *The Shining* Press Conference." ABC Television Network, 9 Jan. 1997. Cited in *Phantasmagoria*, vol. 5, 1997, pp. 24–32.
Auden, W. H. "The Guilty Vicarage." *Harper's Magazine*, May 1948, harpers.org/archive/1948/05/the-guilty-vicarage/.
Barzun, Jacques. "The Place and Point of 'True Crime.'" *A Jacques Barzun Reader,* reprint ed., edited by Michael Murray, Harper Modern Perennial Classics, 2003, pp. 578–81.
Baudelaire, Charles. *The Painter of Modern Life and Other Essays*. 1863. Translated and edited by Jonathan Mayne, Phaidon Press, 1964.
Beahm, George. *Stephen King from A to Z: An Encyclopedia of His Work*. Andrews McMeel Publishing, 1998.
Belton, John. "Language, Oedipus, and *Chinatown*." *Modern Language Notes*, vol. 106, 1991, pp. 933–50.
Bishop, Bart. "Academia vs. Imagination: The Problem of Intellectualism in the Works of Stephen King." *litreactor*, 17 July 2015, litreactor.com/columns/academia-vs-imagination-the-problem-of-intellectualism-in-works-of-stephen-king.
Bloom, Harold. Introduction. *Stephen King: Bloom's Modern Critical Views*. Chelsea House, 2007.
Blouin, Michael J. "The Loomis Look: Re-watching John Carpenter's *Halloween* as Film Noir." *The Journal of American Culture*, vol. 45, no. 4, 2022, pp. 386–402, onlinelibrary.wiley.com/doi/abs/10.1111/jacc.13412.
Blouin, Michael J. *Stephen King and American Politics*. UP of Wales, 2021.

Borges, Jorge Luis. "Death and the Compass." *New Mexico Quarterly*, vol. 24, no. 3, 1954.
Braddon, Mary Elizabeth. *Lady Audley's Secret*. Oxford UP, 2012.
Bradford, Richard. *Crime Fiction: A Very Short Introduction*. Oxford UP, 2015.
Breu, Christopher. *Hard-Boiled Masculinities*. U of Minnesota P, 2005.
Brooks, Peter. *Reading for the Plot: Design and Intention in Narrative*. Knopf, 1984.
Brown, David. "Future Fears: How a 19th-Century Writer and Polymath Anticipated the Modern World." *The American Scholar*, 6 July 2021, theamericanscholar.org/future-fears/?fbclid=IwARodgugo6L6QLjVsg35rWdHNnhxkKzgYzzP2vp_liApp6sNMEtpVlV_AxfA.
Brown, Jeff. "Stephen King Wants to Reach Out and Grab You—with His Writing." *PBS NewsHour*, 6 Oct. 2016, www.pbs.org/newshour/show/stephen-king-wants-reach-grab-writing.
Bullough, Edward. "'Psychical Distances' as a Factor in Art and Aesthetic Principles." *British Journal of Psychology*, vol. 5, 1912, pp. 87–117, home.csulb.edu/~jvancamp/361_r9.html.
Burke, Edmund. *Philosophical Inquiry into the Origins of the Sublime and the Beautiful*. 1779. Google Books, www.google.com/books/edition/A_Philosophical_Enquiry_Into_the_Origin/G_28Q73B2GcC?hl=en&gbpv=1&printsec=frontcover.
Burke, Kenneth. *The Philosophy of Literary Form: Studies in Symbolic Action*. 3rd ed., U of California P, 1973.
Byrd, Max. "The Detective Detected: From Sophocles to Ross Macdonald." *The Yale Review*, vol. 64, 1974, pp. 72–84.
Cain, James. *Double Indemnity*. *Three Novels*, Bantam, 1973, pp. 103–209.
Cassuto, Leonard. *Hard-Boiled Sentimentalities: The Secret History of American Crime Stories*. Columbia UP, 2009.
Chandler, Raymond. *The Big Sleep*. Vintage Crime, 1988.
Chandler, Raymond. *Farewell, My Lovely*. Vintage Crime, 1992.
Chandler, Raymond. *The Little Sister*. Vintage Crime, 1988.
Chandler, Raymond. *The Long Goodbye*. Ballantine Books, 1973.
Chandler, Raymond. *The Simple Art of Murder*. Vintage Crime, 1988.
Chinatown. Directed by Roman Polanski, Long Road Productions, 1974.
Clarke, John. "The Pleasures of Crime: Interrogating the Detective Story." *The Problem of Crime*, edited by John Muncie and Eugene McLaughlin, Sage, 2001, pp. 72–104.
Corber, Robert. *Homosexuality in Cold War America: Resistance and the Crisis of Masculinity*. Duke UP, 1997.
Cowan, Douglas. *America's Dark Theologian: The Religious Imagination of Stephen King*. New York UP, 2018.
Crow, Charles. *American Gothic*. U of Wales P, 2009.
Davis, Blair. "Horror Meets Noir: The Evolution of Cinematic Style, 1931–1958." *Horror Film: Creating and Marketing Fear*, edited by Steffen Hantke, UP of Mississippi, 2004, pp. 191–212.
Derrida, Jacques. "The Purveyor of Truth." *The Purloined Poe: Lacan, Derrida, and Psychoanalytic Reading*, edited by John Muller and William Richardson, Johns Hopkins UP, 1987, pp. 173–213.
Dolan, Colleen. "The Feminist King: *Dolores Claiborne*." *The Films of Stephen King*, edited by Tony Magistrale, Palgrave-Macmillan-Springer, 2008, pp. 155–65.
Dolores Claiborne. Directed by Taylor Hackford, Castle Rock Entertainment, 1995.

Dostoevsky, Fyodor. *Crime and Punishment*. Translated by Constance Garnett, 1864. Project Gutenberg, www.gutenberg.org/cache/epub/2554/pg2554-images.html.

Dostoevsky, Fyodor. *"The Double" and "The Gambler."* 1866. Translated by Richard Pevear and Larissa Volokhonsky, Everyman's Library, 2005.

Double Indemnity. Directed by Billy Wilder, Paramount Pictures, 1944.

Downey, Dara, and Darryl Jones. "King of the Castle: Shirley Jackson and Stephen King." *Shirley Jackson: Essays on the Literary Legacy*, edited by Bernice M. Murphy, McFarland & Company, pp. 214–36.

Doyle, Arthur Conan. *The Hound of the Baskervilles. The Original Sherlock Holmes*, Castle, 1902.

Dubois, Page. "Oedipus as Detective: Sophocles, Simenon, Robbe-Grillet." *Yale French Studies*, vol. 108, 2005, pp. 102–15.

Dyer, Richard. "Postscript: Queers and Women in Film Noir." *Women in Film Noir*, edited by E. Ann Kaplan, British Film Institute, 2005, pp. 123–29.

Felman, Shoshana. *What Does a Woman Want?: Reading and Sexual Difference*. Johns Hopkins UP, 1993.

Friedlander, Jennifer. *Feminine Look: Sexuation, Spectatorship, Subversion*. State U of New York P, 2008.

Genette, Gérard, and Marie Maclean. "Introduction to the Paratext." *New Literary History*, vol. 22, 1991, pp. 261–72.

Gilbert, Sandra, and Susan Gubar. *The Madwoman in the Attic: The Woman-Writer and the Nineteenth-century Literary Imagination*. Yale UP, 2020.

Gilmore, Richard. *Postmodern Movies: Neo-Comic Tragedies, Neo-Noirs, Neo-Westerns*. Silver Goat Media, 2016.

Gruesser, John. "Dupin's Descendants in Print and on Screen." *The Oxford Handbook of Edgar Allan Poe*, edited by J. Gerald Kennedy and Scott Peeples, Oxford UP, 2019, pp. 659–75.

Hammett, Dashiell. *The Glass Key*. Vintage Crime, 1931.

Hartman, Geoffrey. "Literature High and Low: The Case of the Mystery Story." *The Geoffrey Hartman Reader*, edited by Daniel T. O'Hara, Edinburgh UP, 2004, pp. 164–79.

Harris, Thomas. *Hannibal*. Delacorte Press, 1999.

Harris, Thomas. *Red Dragon*. Dell, 1981.

Harris, Thomas. *The Silence of the Lambs*. St. Martin's Press, 1988.

Hull, Richard. "'The Purloined Letter': Poe's Detective Story vs. Panoptic Foucauldian Theory." *Style*, vol. 24, 1990, pp. 201–14. *JSTOR*, www.jstor.org/stable/42945851.

Hutchings, Peter. "Film Noir and Horror." *A Companion to Film Noir*, edited by Andre Spicer and Helen Hanson, Wiley, 2013, pp. 111–24.

Indick, Ben P. "King as a Writer for Children." *Kingdom of Fear: The World of Stephen King*, edited by Tim Underwood and Chuck Miller, NAL Penguin, 1986, pp. 219–38.

Irwin, John. *Unless the Threat of Death Is Behind Them: Hard-Boiled Fiction and Film Noir*. Johns Hopkins UP, 2006.

James, Henry. "The Figure in the Carpet." *"The Aspern Papers" and Other Tales*, edited by Michael Gora, Penguin, 2014, pp. 277–317.

Jameson, Fredric. "Historicism in *The Shining*." *Signatures of the Visible*. Routledge, 1991, pp. 82–98.

Jameson, Fredric. *Postmodernism; or, The Culture of Late Capitalism*. Duke UP, 1991.
Jameson, Fredric. *Raymond Chandler: The Detections of Totality*. Verso, 2022.
Kaplan, E. Ann. "Introduction to New Edition." *Women in Film Noir*, edited by E. Ann Kaplan, British Film Institute, 2005, pp. 5–14.
Kennedy, J. Gerald. "The Limits of Reason: Poe's Deluded Detectives." *American Literature*, vol. 47, no. 2, 1975, pp. 184–96.
Kent, Brian. "Stephen King and His Readers: A Dirty, Compelling Romance." *A Casebook on "The Stand,"* edited by Anthony Magistrale, Starmont House, 1992, pp. 37–68.
King, Stephen. *The Body*. *Different Seasons*, Viking, 1982.
King, Stephen. *The Colorado Kid*. Hard Case Crime, 2005.
King, Stephen. *Danse Macabre*. Everest House, 1981.
King, Stephen. *The Dark Half*. Viking, 1989.
King, Stephen. *The Dark Tower*, vols. I-VII. Various publishers, 1982–2004.
King, Stephen. *The Dead Zone*. 1979. Reissue ed, Gallery Books, 2016.
King, Stephen. *Dolores Claiborne*. Viking, 1993.
King, Stephen. *Duma Key*. Scribner, 2008.
King, Stephen. *11/22/63*. Simon & Schuster, 2012.
King, Stephen. "Five to One, One in Five: UMO in the '60s." *Hearts in Suspension*, edited by Jim Bishop, Maine UP, 2016, pp. 23–76.
King, Stephen. *Holly*. Scribner, 2023.
King, Stephen. "The Importance of Being Bachman." *Lilja's Library: The World of Stephen King*, 29 Jan. 2010, liljas-library.com/page.php?id=13.
King, Stephen. Interview with Michael Strahan. *Good Morning America*, 5 Sept. 2023, abcnews.go.com/GMA/Culture/video/stephen-king-talks-new-book-holly-102923408.
King, Stephen. *IT*. Viking, 1986.
King, Stephen. *Joyland*. Hard Case Crime, 2013.
King, Stephen. *Later*. Hard Case Crime, 2021.
King, Stephen. *Lisey's Story*. Scribner, 2006.
King, Stephen. "Morality." *The Bazaar of Bad Dreams*, Scribner, 2018, pp. 163–93.
King, Stephen. *Nightmares and Dreamscapes*. Viking, 1993.
King, Stephen. "On Becoming a Brand Name." *Fear Itself: The Horror Fiction of Stephen King*, edited by Tim Underwood and Chuck Miller, Underwood Books, 1982, pp. 15–42.
King, Stephen. *On Writing*. Simon & Schuster, 2000.
King, Stephen. *The Outsider*. Scribner, 2018.
King, Stephen. "Quick Question." Personal communication with Tony Magistrale. 8 Jan. 2024.
King, Stephen. "Review of *Hannibal* by Thomas Harris." *The New York Times*, 13 June 1999, archive.nytimes.com/www.nytimes.com/books/99/06/13/reviews/990613.13kingct.html?0208fl.
King, Stephen. *The Shining*. Doubleday, 1977.
King, Stephen. *The Stand*. 1978. Doubleday, 1990.
King, Stephen. "Steve's Take: Interview with Tony Magistrale." *The Films of Stephen King*, Palgrave, 2003, pp. 1–20.
King, Stephen. "The Wedding Gig." *Skeleton Crew*, Putnam, 1985.

King, Stephen. "Why I Was Richard Bachman." *The Bachman Books: Four Early Novels by Stephen King*, New American Library, 1985, pp. v–x.

King, Stephen [Richard Bachman]. *Roadwork. The Bachman Books*, New American Library, 1985, pp. 435–708.

King, Stephen, and Peter Straub. *The Talisman*. Viking and G. P. Putnam's Sons, 1987.

King, Stephen, interviewed by Andy Greene. "The *Rolling Stone* Interview." *Rolling Stone*, 31 Oct. 2014, www.rollingstone.com/culture/culture-features/stephen-king-the-rolling-stone-interview-191529/.

King, Stephen, interviewed by Anthony Breznican. "Where There's Smoke: Stephen King Revisits *Firestarter*." *Vanity Fair*, 13 May 2022, www.vanityfair.com/hollywood/2022/05/firestarter-stephen-king-movie-remake.

King, Stephen, interviewed by Nathaniel Rich and Christopher Lehmann-Haupt. "The Art of Fiction, No. 189." *The Paris Review*, no. 178, Fall 2006, www.theparisreview.org/interviews/5653/the-art-of-fiction-no-189-stephen-king.

Kinsman, Margaret. "Feminist Crime Fiction." *American Crime Fiction*, edited by Catherine Ross Nickerson, Cambridge UP, 2010, pp. 148–62.

Klute. Directed by Alan Pakula, Gus Productions, 1971.

Krutnick, Frank. In a Lonely Street: Film Noir, Genre, Masculinity. Routledge, 1991.

Lacan, Jacques. "Seminar on 'The Purloined Letter.'" *The Purloined Poe: Lacan, Derrida, and Psychoanalytic Reading*, edited by John Muller and William Richardson, Johns Hopkins UP, 1987, pp. 28–55.

Lehman, David. *The Mysterious Romance of Murder: Crime, Detection, and the Spirit of Noir*. Cornell UP, 2022.

Leifert, Don. "They Collide by Night: Film Noir Meets the Horror Genre." *Midnight Marquee*, vol. 48, Winter 1995, pp. 57–62.

The Long Goodbye. Directed by Robert Altman, Lion's Gate Films, 1973.

Magistrale, Tony. *Hollywood's Stephen King*. Palgrave-Macmillan-Springer, 2002.

Magistrale, Tony. *Landscape of Fear: Stephen King's American Gothic*. Popular Press, 1988.

Magistrale, Tony. *Stephen King: The Second Decade, "Danse Macabre" to "The Dark Half."* Twayne, 1991.

Magistrale, Tony, and Michael J. Blouin. *Stephen King and American History*. Routledge, 2021.

Magistrale, Tony, and Sidney Poger. *Poe's Children: Connections Between Tales of Terror and Detection*. Peter Lang, 1999.

Magistrale, Tony. "Toward Defining an American Gothic." *Critical Insights: Stephen King*, edited by Gary Hoppenstand, Salem Press, 2011, pp. 184–98.

Macdonald, Ross. *The Goodbye Look*. Reprint ed., Vintage Crime/Black Lizard, 2000.

Macdonald, Ross. *The Three Roads*. Reprint ed., Vintage Crime/Black Lizard, 2011.

Matheson, Neil. *Surrealism and the Gothic*. Routledge, 2020.

McBain, Ed. *Sadie When She Died*. Doubleday, 1972.

McCann, Sean. *Gumshoe America: Hard-Boiled Crime Fiction and the Rise and Fall of New Deal Liberalism*. Duke UP, 2000.

Merivale, Patricia, and Susan Sweeney. "The Game's Afoot: On the Trail of the Metaphysical Detective Story." *Detecting Texts: The Metaphysical Detective Story from Poe to*

Postmodernism, edited by Patricia Merivale and Susan Sweeney, UP of Pennsylvania, 1998, pp. 1–27.
Mulvey, Laura. *Visual and Other Pleasures*. Indiana UP, 1989.
Munt, Sally. *Murder by the Book? Feminism and the Crime Novel*. Routledge, 1994.
Mustazza, Leonard. "The Red Death's Sway: Setting and Character in Poe's 'Masque of the Red Death' and King's *The Shining*." *"The Shining" Reader*, edited by Anthony Magistrale, Starmont House, 1991, pp. 105–20.
Naremore, James. *Film Noir: A Very Short Introduction*. Oxford UP, 2019.
Out of the Past. Directed by Jacques Tourneur, RKO Pictures, 1947.
Pepper, Andrew. "The American Roman Noir." *American Crime Fiction*, edited by Catherine Ross Nickerson, Cambridge UP, 2010, pp. 58–71.
Perry, Dennis R., and Carl H. Sederholm, editors. *Adapting Poe: Re-Imaginings in Popular Culture*. Palgrave, 2012.
Pippin, Robert. *Fatalism in American Film Noir: Some Cinematic Philosophy*. UP of Virginia, 2012.
The Pit and the Pendulum. Directed by Roger Corman, American International Pictures, 1961.
Poe, Edgar Allan. "The Black Cat." Quinn, pp. 597–606.
Poe, Edgar Allan. "A Descent into the Maelstrom." Quinn, pp. 432–48.
Poe, Edgar Allan. "Elizabeth." Quinn, p. 61.
Poe, Edgar Allan. *Eureka*. Quinn, pp. 1261–359.
Poe, Edgar Allan. "The Fall of the House of Usher." Quinn, pp. 317–36.
Poe, Edgar Allan. "The Gold-Bug." Quinn, pp. 560–97.
Poe, Edgar Allan. "Ligeia." Quinn, pp. 262–77.
Poe, Edgar Allan. "The Man of the Crowd." Quinn, pp. 388–96.
Poe, Edgar Allan. "The Masque of the Red Death." Quinn, pp. 485–90.
Poe, Edgar Allan. "M.S. Found in a Bottle." Quinn, pp. 189–99.
Poe, Edgar Allan. "The Murders in the Rue Morgue." Quinn, pp. 397–432.
Poe, Edgar Allan. "The Pit and the Pendulum." Quinn, pp. 491–505.
Poe, Edgar Allan. "The Poetic Principle." Quinn, pp. 1431–54.
Poe, Edgar Allan. "The Purloined Letter." Quinn, pp. 680–99.
Poe, Edgar Allan. "The Raven." Quinn, pp. 81–86.
Poe, Edgar Allan. "'Thou Art the Man.'" Quinn, pp. 728–43.
Poe, Edgar Allan. "William Wilson." Quinn, pp. 337–57.
Psycho. Directed by Alfred Hitchcock, Shamley Productions, 1940.
Quinn, Patrick, editor. *Edgar Allan Poe: Poetry and Tales*. Library of America, 1984.
Rabinowitz, Peter. *Before Reading: Narrative Conventions and the Politics of Interpretation*. Ohio State University, 1998.
Reddy, Maureen. *Sisters in Crime: Feminism and the Crime Novel*. Continuum, 1988.
Scaggs, John. *Crime Fiction*. Routledge, 2005.
Schrader, Paul. "Notes on Film Noir." *Film Theory and Criticism*, 7th ed., edited by Leo Braudy and Marshall Cohen, Oxford UP, 2009, pp. 581–91.
Senf, Carol A. "*Gerald's Game* and *Dolores Claiborne*: Stephen King and the Evolution of an Authentic Female Narrative Voice." *Imagining the Worst: Stephen King and the Representation of Women*, Greenwood Press, 1998, pp. 91–107.
The Shining. Directed by Stanley Kubrick, Warner Bros., 1980.

Skenazy, Paul. "Bringing It All Back Home: Ross Macdonald's Lost Father." *The Threepenny Review*, vol. 12, 1983, pp. 9–11.
Somer, Eric. "The Noir-Horror of *Cat People*." *Film Noir Reader 4*, edited by Alain Silver and James Ursini, Limelight, 2004, pp. 191–207.
Sontag, Susan. *Illness as Metaphor*. Vintage, 1978.
Sophocles. "Oedipus the King." *Greek Tragedies 1*, 3rd ed., U of Chicago P, 2013, pp. 113–87.
Spillane, Mickey. *Kiss Me, Deadly*. Signet, 1952.
Stables, Kate. "The Postmodern Always Rings Twice: Constructing the *Femme Fatale* in 90s Cinema." *Women in Film Noir*, edited by E. Ann Kaplan, British Film Institute, 2005, pp. 151–64.
Stadler, Gustavus. "Poe and Queer Studies." *Poe Studies/Dark Romanticism*, vol. 33, 2000, pp. 19–22.
Stand by Me. Directed by Rob Reiner, Columbia Pictures, 1986.
Stephen King's The Shining. Directed by Mick Garris. Warner Bros. Television, ABC-TV, 1997.
Stevenson, Robert Louis. *The Strange Case of Dr. Jekyll and Mr. Hyde*. Signet, 1987.
Strengell, Heidi. *Dissecting Stephen King: From the Gothic to Literary Naturalism*. Popular Press, 2005.
Thoms, Peter. "Poe's Dupin and the Power of Detection." *Cambridge Companion to Edgar Allan Poe*, edited by Kevin J. Hayes, Cambridge UP, 2002, pp. 133–48.
Todorov, Tzvetan. *The Poetics of Prose*. Cornell UP, 2008.
Tresch, John. *The Reason for the Darkness of the Night: Edgar Allan Poe and the Forging of American Science*. Farrar, Straus and Giroux, 2021.
Twain, Mark. "A Double-Barreled Detective Story." *The Complete Short Stories of Mark Twain*, Random House, 2005, pp. 508–65.
Twain, Mark. *Tom Sawyer, Detective*. Wordsworth Editions, 2009.
Underwood, Tim, and Chuck Miller, editors. *Bare Bones: Conversations on Terror with Stephen King*. McGraw-Hill, 1998.
Underwood, Tim, and Chuck Miller, editors. *Feast of Fear: Conversations with Stephen King*. Carroll & Graf, 1992.
Van Leer, David. *Detecting Truth: The World of the Dupin Tales*. Cambridge UP, 1993.
Vonnegut, Kurt. *Wampeters, Foma & Granfalloons*. Random House, 1999.
Walsh, John. *Poe the Detective: The Curious Circumstances Behind "The Mystery of Marie Rogêt."* Rutgers UP, 1968.
Wiater, Stanley, Christopher Golden, and Hank Wagner. *The Complete Stephen King Universe: A Guide to the Worlds of Stephen King*. St. Martin's Griffin, 2006.
Wilson, Edmund. *Classics and Commercials: A Literary Chronicle of the Forties*. Farrar, Straus and Company, 1950. Internet Archive, archive.org/details/classicscommercioowils/page/n5/mode/2up.
Woods, Scott. "Stephen King Needs More Black Friends." *LEVEL*, 15 Jan. 2020, level.medium.com/stephen-king-needs-more-black-friends-5547f245d424.
Yarbro, Chelsea Quinn. "*Cinderella*'s Revenge: Twists of Fairy Tale and Mythic Themes in the Work of Stephen King." *Fear Itself: The Horror Fiction of Stephen King*, edited by Tim Underwood and Chuck Miller, Signet, 1985, pp. 61–74.
Ziff, Larzer. *Literary Democracy: The Declaration of Cultural Independence in America*. Viking, 1981.

INDEX

America, post-9/11, 6, 18, 79, 87, 104
American West, 15
Apt Pupil, 62, 66

Bachman, Richard persona, 10; King's reasons for, 65–78. *See also* King, Stephen; King, Stephen, works of
Bag of Bones, 108
Big Sleep, The, 170, 176
Body, The, 7, 14, 33, 68, 166–78, 180
Bogart, Humphrey, 6, 69
Braddon, Mary Elizabeth, 123
Burke, Edmund, 8, 35

Cain, James M., 5, 9, 11, 60, 68, 192, 208, 232n8; *Double Indemnity*, 5, 76–77; *The Postman Always Rings Twice*, 60, 209
capitalism, 60, 70, 188
Carrie, 12, 227n2
Chandler, Raymond, 4, 58, 68, 93, 160–90, 193, 226n11; *The Big Sleep*, 170, 176; *Farewell, My Lovely*, 160; *The Little Sister*, 12, 231n6 (chap. 8); *The Simple Art of Murder*, 23. *See also* Marlowe, Philip
Christie, Agatha, 17, 20–21, 24, 100
Colorado Kid, The, 6, 10, 15, 21, 22–27, 143, 156, 168–79, 180, 182, 185–87, 190, 193
commercialism, 7, 11, 16
Crime and Punishment, 9, 194–95, 232n2
crime fiction, genres of: classic detective, 17, 38; English, 8; film noir, 4, 9, 16–17, 58–60, 66–67, 75, 180, 226n10, 228n2; hard-boiled, 4–17, 21, 22–24, 33, 37, 39, 58–59, 61, 65–78, 79–90, 93, 97–101, 104–7, 108, 110, 117, 121, 143, 146, 160–80, 188, 193–95, 199–201, 215, 219, 222–23, 225nn4–5, 231n1, 232n8 (chap. 8), 232n1 (chap. 1); mystery tale, 17; pulp, 5, 6, 11, 17, 22–23, 27, 43, 101, 166–68, 194; *roman noir*, 9, 17, 57–60, 63, 67, 78; true crime, 7
criminality, 10, 14, 67–73, 79, 85, 119–21, 127, 160, 184, 191–96, 224, 227n4
Cujo, 62

Dark Half, The, 12–14, 61–67, 77, 113, 191, 197, 213–17, 233n7, 233n9
Dark Tower, The, 13, 33, 56–57, 102, 162, 179, 195, 217, 222–23
Dead Zone, The, 5, 16, 17, 33, 34, 44–46, 48, 66, 148
Derrida, Jacques, 48–51, 154, 203–4
"Descent into the Maelstrom, A," 8, 30
Doctor Sleep, 104, 200, 206–8
Dolores Claiborne, 7, 10, 12, 17, 33, 91, 108–9, 120–42, 172, 191, 193–94, 230n1
Dostoevsky, Fyodor, 9, 194–96, 204–5, 216, 232n2; *Crime and Punishment*, 9, 194–95, 232n2
Double Indemnity, 5, 76–77
Doyle, Arthur Conan, 43, 112, 125, 143–44, 213, 218, 225n7. *See also* Holmes, Sherlock

Duma Key, 47–54, 233n7
Dupin, C. Auguste, 14, 30, 32–35, 40–53, 83–85, 90–91, 111–12, 125–27, 133, 183–85, 195, 202–4, 213–17, 222–23. *See also* Poe, Edgar Allan

elitism, 11, 15, 103, 227n7
"Elizabeth," 51
Eureka, 31–32, 43

"Fall of the House of Usher, The," 29, 30, 48
Farewell, My Lovely, 160
femme fatale, 12, 39, 76, 82, 219–20, 222
Fincher, David, 7

generic hybridization, 8, 32, 39
Gerald's Game, 33, 108, 221, 230n1, 233n1
globalization, 6, 18, 79, 87
"Gold-Bug, The," 30, 42

Harris, Thomas, 7, 58, 85, 103, 145, 228n1; *Red Dragon*, 7, 14, 85; *The Silence of the Lambs*, 85, 103
Hawthorne, Nathaniel, 5
Holly, 5, 20–21, 100, 102–7
Holmes, Sherlock, 8, 15, 16, 65, 90, 98, 112, 125, 128, 130, 144–45, 154, 213–19, 222, 225n7. *See also* Doyle, Arthur Conan
Hopper, Edward: *Early Sunday Morning*, 4; *Nighthawks*, 4; *Room in New York*, 3, 4
Hugo, Victor, 9

intertextuality, 50–52, 154
Italian American caricatures, 11

James, Henry, 6, 225n6
Joyland, 6, 17, 20, 22–27, 156, 168–69, 180–90, 224, 232n9

Kaplan, E. Ann, 82, 220; *Women in Film Noir*, 82, 220
King, Stephen, 3, 19, 22; collaboration with Hard Case Crime, 25–28; crime themes in works, 6–18, 23–24, 33–34; influences on, 4–6, 10–17, 19–21, 24, 29–32, 34;
interview with *Playboy* magazine, 3, 221, 228n5, 229n1; metacommentary, 13, 52, 79, 122, 137, 146, 148, 154, 170, 192, 205; multiverse, 6, 13, 69, 80, 191, 217, 224; time spent at University of Maine, 5, 64
King, Stephen, works of: *Apt Pupil*, 62, 66; *Bag of Bones*, 108; *The Body*, 7, 14, 33, 68, 166–78, 180; *Carrie*, 12, 227n2; *The Colorado Kid*, 6, 10, 15, 21, 22–27, 143, 156, 168–79, 180, 182, 185–87, 190, 193; *Cujo*, 62; *The Dark Half*, 12–14, 61–67, 77, 113, 191, 197, 213–17, 233n7, 233n9; *The Dark Tower*, 13, 33, 56–57, 102, 162, 179, 195, 217, 222–23; *The Dead Zone*, 5, 16, 17, 33, 34, 44–46, 48, 66, 148; *Doctor Sleep*, 104, 200, 206–8; *Dolores Claiborne*, 7, 10, 12, 17, 33, 91, 108–9, 120–42, 172, 191, 193–94, 230n1; *Duma Key*, 47–54, 233n7; *Gerald's Game*, 33, 108, 221, 230n1, 233n1; *Holly*, 5, 20–21, 100, 102–7; *Later*, 6, 22–27, 143–59, 173, 231n5 (chap. 7); *Joyland*, 6, 17, 20, 22–27, 156, 168–69, 180–90, 224, 232n9; *Misery*, 10, 17, 33, 91, 108–20, 125, 139–41, 172, 191, 193, 214; *Mr. Mercedes*, 5, 6, 10, 11, 17, 21, 33, 65, 77, 79–101, 104–5, 107, 172, 191, 199, 214, 223, 224, 229nn5–6; *On Writing*, 29, 90–94, 154, 229n10; *The Outsider*, 6, 102, 105; *Pet Sematary*, 62; *Roadwork*, 11, 17, 61, 68–78, 96, 193, 199, 227n2; *Rose Madder*, 108, 179, 233n7; *The Shining*, 7, 10, 11, 17, 29, 34–40, 44, 50, 53, 77, 92, 101, 200–201, 206–10, 226n1, 231n5 (chap. 7), 233n10; *The Stand*, 12, 50, 66, 89, 217, 220, 222–23, 230n5, 234n2; *Thinner*, 11, 60, 66, 73, 227n2; *Umney's Last Case*, 12–14, 20, 148–50, 163, 170, 193, 197

Lacan, Jacques, 122, 132–35
Later, 6, 22–27, 143–59, 173, 231n5 (chap. 7)
Little Sister, The, 12, 231n6 (chap. 8)
Lynch, David, 7

Macdonald, Ross, 20, 24, 128, 151, 225n8, 231n1
Marlowe, Philip, 24, 70, 84–85, 97, 160–66, 170–78, 187–89, 204, 217, 222–24, 231n6 (chap. 8). *See also* Chandler, Raymond
masculinity, 9, 11, 59, 78, 108
"Masque of the Red Death, The," 29–30, 34
McBain, Ed, 5, 20, 62, 66, 161, 166, 225n4
mise-en-abyme, 13–15, 101, 123, 140, 170, 178, 210
mise-en-scéne, 9
Misery, 10, 17, 33, 91, 108–20, 125, 139–41, 172, 191, 193, 214
modernity, 5, 10, 68–77, 193, 201, 219, 224
Mr. Mercedes, 5, 6, 10, 11, 17, 21, 33, 65, 77, 79–101, 104–5, 107, 172, 191, 199, 214, 223, 224, 229nn5–6
"Murders in the Rue Morgue, The," 8, 30, 32, 42–43, 46, 91, 111, 185
"Mystery of Marie Rogêt, The," 8, 30, 185

New York Times, 8, 92, 227n7, 228n1

Oates, Joyce Carol, 7
On Writing, 29, 90–94, 154, 229n10
Out of the Past, 75, 166, 201
Outsider, The, 6, 102, 105

patriarchy, 17, 109, 132, 137
Pet Sematary, 62, 66, 210, 217
"Pit and the Pendulum, The," 30, 38–39
Poe, Edgar Allan, 8–9, 14–17, 29–55, 83, 85, 91, 99–100, 111–12, 120, 125–28, 132–34, 149, 154, 183–85, 191, 195, 202–6, 211, 213–15, 222, 226n2, 227n6, 233nn3–4, 234n3; "A Descent into the Maelström," 8, 30; "Elizabeth," 51; *Eureka*, 31–32, 43; "The Fall of the House of Usher," 29, 30, 48; "The Gold-Bug," 30, 42; "The Masque of the Red Death," 29–30, 34; "The Murders in the Rue Morgue," 8, 30, 32, 42–43, 46, 91, 111, 185; "The Mystery of Marie Rogêt," 8, 30, 185; "The Pit and the Pendulum," 30, 38–39;

"The Purloined Letter," 8, 30, 38, 43–44, 47, 99, 112, 132, 133, 135, 154, 183–85, 203–4. *See also* Dupin, C. Auguste
Postman Always Rings Twice, The, 60, 209
postmodernism, 12, 14, 73, 101, 149, 151–54, 159, 210
psychoanalysis, 9, 122–32, 230n5
"Purloined Letter, The," 8, 30, 38, 43–44, 47, 99, 112, 132, 133, 135, 154, 183–85, 203–4

ratiocination, 7–8, 13, 17, 30–55, 109, 114, 119, 143–44, 191–92, 218; the Constant Reader, 7, 144, 153, 157
Red Dragon, 7, 14, 85
Rice, Anne, 43
Roadwork, 11, 17, 61, 68–78, 96, 193, 199, 227n2
Rose Madder, 108, 179, 233n7; female sexuality, 11, 76, 82, 88, 152, 221–22, 226n1

Shining, The, 7, 10, 11, 17, 29, 34–40, 44, 50, 53, 77, 92, 101, 200–201, 206–10, 226n1, 231n5 (chap. 8), 233n10
Silence of the Lambs, The, 85, 103
Simple Art of Murder, The, 23
Stand, The, 12, 50, 66, 89, 217, 220, 222–23, 230n5, 234n2

Tempest, The, 50
Thinner, 11, 60, 66, 73, 227n2
Trump, Donald, 86, 104, 193–94, 205, 211
Twain, Mark, 14–16, 176

Umney's Last Case, 12–14, 20, 148–50, 163, 170, 193, 197

Vietnam War, 18, 62, 83, 228n4, 228n8

Women in Film Noir, 82, 220

ABOUT THE AUTHORS

Photo by Kathleen Marie

TONY MAGISTRALE is author of twenty-three books and over seventy book chapters and articles in professional books and journals. Most of his books and articles have centered on defining and tracing Anglo-American Gothicism, from its origins in nineteenth-century romanticism to its contemporary manifestations in popular culture, particularly in the work of Edgar Allan Poe and Stephen King. He has published three separate interviews with King; from 2005 to 2009, Magistrale and Blouin both served as research assistants to Mr. King.

Photo courtesy of the author

MICHAEL J. BLOUIN has published extensively on the American Gothic, especially on Stephen King's fiction. In addition to his monograph *Stephen King and American Politics*, Blouin coauthored *Stephen King and American History* (with Magistrale); one of the chapters of that book unanimously won the Carl Bode prize for the best essay published in the *Journal of American Culture* 2020. He is also author of *Democracy and the American Gothic* (2024).